T0360747

The European Corporation

The product of a long-standing collaboration and collective research effort by members of the CGEUI network, *The European Corporation* makes an important contribution to the ongoing debate over convergence to the Anglo-Saxon model of corporate governance versus the persistence in corporate governance and law in Europe. This book contributes to this debate by addressing the lack of country-specific evidence on the evolution of ownership and control, a lack which has proven to be a serious impediment to both legal and economic analysis and evidence-based policymaking. The book provides systematic and comparable accounts of structural changes in ownership and control (respectively persistence) in large firms across Europe over the decades following the "global corporate governance revolution" in the 1990s.

KLAUS GUGLER is Full Professor of Economics at the WU Vienna University of Economics and Business. He published in top refereed economics journals including the *Economic Journal* and *The Review of Economics and Statistics* and is the editor of *Corporate Governance and Economic Performance* (Oxford University Press, 2001).

EVGENI PEEV is a co-founder of the CGEUI network and Scientific Director of the European Research and Education Institute. He has initiated studies on novel corporate governance issues in Europe, transition countries, Southeast Europe, and Bulgaria. He has published in top academic journals and is the editor of *Separation of Ownership from Control in Southeast Europe: A Comparison of Bulgaria, Romania and Albania 1990–1996* (Kota, 1999).

The European Corporation

Ownership and Control after 25 Years of Corporate Governance Reforms

Edited by

KLAUS GUGLER
WU Vienna University of Economics and Business

EVGENI PEEV
European Research and Education Institute

CAMBRIDGE
UNIVERSITY PRESS

Shaftesbury Road, Cambridge CB2 8EA, United Kingdom

One Liberty Plaza, 20th Floor, New York, NY 10006, USA

477 Williamstown Road, Port Melbourne, VIC 3207, Australia

314–321, 3rd Floor, Plot 3, Splendor Forum, Jasola District Centre,
New Delhi – 110025, India

103 Penang Road, #05-06/07, Visioncrest Commercial, Singapore 238467

Cambridge University Press is part of Cambridge University Press & Assessment,
a department of the University of Cambridge.

We share the University's mission to contribute to society through the pursuit of
education, learning and research at the highest international levels of excellence.

www.cambridge.org
Information on this title: www.cambridge.org/9781009244633

DOI: 10.1017/9781009244640

First published 2023

A catalogue record for this publication is available from the British Library.

Library of Congress Cataloging-in-Publication Data
Names: Gugler, Klaus, editor.
Title: The European corporation : ownership and control after 25 years of corporate
governance reforms / edited by Klaus Gugler, WU Vienna University of Economics and
Business, Evgeni Peev, WU Vienna University of Economics and Business.
Description: New York, NY : Cambridge University Press, 2022. |
Includes bibliographical references and index.
Identifiers: LCCN 2022044745 (print) | LCCN 2022044746 (ebook) |
ISBN 9781009244633 (hardback) | ISBN 9781009244626 (paperback) |
ISBN 9781009244640 (epub)
Subjects: LCSH: Corporate governance–Europe. | Europe–Economic conditions.
Classification: LCC HD2741 .E898 2022 (print) | LCC HD2741 (ebook) |
DDC 658.40094–dc23/eng/20221125
LC record available at https://lccn.loc.gov/2022044745
LC ebook record available at https://lccn.loc.gov/2022044746

ISBN 978-1-009-24463-3 Hardback

Contents

List of Figures	*page* viii
List of Tables	x
Notes on Contributors	xiii
Preface	xxi
Acknowledgements	xxiv

1 Introduction
   Klaus Gugler and Evgeni Peev   1
   1.1 The Research Questions   1
   1.2 The Global Corporate Governance Revolution   4
   1.3 The Determinants of Corporate Ownership   7
   1.4 The Data   16
   1.5 Main Chapter Contents   18
   1.6 Conclusion   24

   Part I   Anglo-Saxon Countries   31

2 The United Kingdom   33
   Marc Goergen
   2.1 Introduction: Corporate Governance Legal and
       Institutional Reforms   33
   2.2 The Data   40
   2.3 The Ownership Structure   41
   2.4 The Determinants of Ownership Changes   48
   2.5 Conclusion   51

   Part II   Central European Countries   53

3 Austria   55
   Klaus Gugler, Evgeni Peev and Martin Winner
   3.1 Introduction   55
   3.2 Corporate Governance Legal and Institutional Reforms   56

3.3 The Data   63
3.4 The Ownership Structures   64
3.5 The Determinants of Ownership Change   75
3.6 Conclusion   82

4 Germany   84
  Evgeni Peev
  4.1 Introduction   84
  4.2 Corporate Governance Framework   85
  4.3 The Data   89
  4.4 The Ownership Structures   89
  4.5 The Determinants of change in Ownership Structure   97
  4.6 Conclusion   106

5 Switzerland   108
  Alexander F. Wagner and Christoph Wenk Bernasconi
  5.1 Introduction   108
  5.2 Corporate Governance Framework and Recent Legal and
      Institutional Reforms   109
  5.3 Broad Developments in Corporate Ownership from the
      1990s to the late 2010s   116
  5.4 Main Results: Shareholder Structure and Shareholder
      Behaviour in Swiss-Listed Companies 2008–2018   123
  5.5 Drivers of Change in Shareholder Structure   145
  5.6 Conclusion and Outlook: Active, Not Activist Shareholders 146

Part III   Scandinavian Countries   149

6 Sweden   151
  Johan Eklund and Evgeni Peev
  6.1 Introduction   151
  6.2 Corporate Governance Framework and Legal Reforms   152
  6.3 The Data   158
  6.4 The Ownership Structures   158
  6.5 The Determinants of Ownership Change   168
  6.6 Conclusion   171

Part IV   Mediterranean Countries   173

7 Italy   175
  Laura Abrardi and Laura Rondi
  7.1 Introduction: Corporate Governance, Legal and
      Institutional Framework   175

7.2 The Data	182
7.3 The Ownership Structures: Descriptive Analysis	182
7.4 The Determinants of Change in Corporate Ownership and Control	196
7.5 Family Firms: Evolution of Control Structures and Determinants of Family Ownership	200
7.6 Conclusions	203

Part V   European Transition Countries 207

8   Bulgaria 209
  Evgeni Peev and Todor Yalamov
8.1 Introduction	209
8.2 Privatization, Corporate Governance and Legal Reforms	210
8.3 The Data	217
8.4 The Ownership Structures	218
8.5 The Determinants of Ownership Change	230
8.6 Recent Developments and Conclusion	236

9   Slovenia 237
  Jože P. Damijan, Anamarija Cijan and Jakob Stemberger
9.1 Introduction	237
9.2 Privatization and Corporate Governance Reforms	239
9.3 Legal Framework of Corporate Governance in Slovenia	243
9.4 Regulation of State-Owned Enterprises	247
9.5 Main Patterns of Ownership Change since 1990	248
9.6 Political Economy of Corporate Governance and Ownership Changes in Slovenia	257

References	264
Index	281

Figures

2.1 Geographic distribution of ownership (%) by foreign
investors (on 31 December 2018), United Kingdom   *page* 40
5.1 Proportion of Swiss shareholders relative to company's
market capitalization among top 100 companies,
2008–2018   136
5.2 Development of BlackRock's shareholdings in
Swiss companies   139
5.3 Shareholder AGM average participation rate in the
largest 100 companies listed on the Swiss
Performance Index   141
5.4 Value of voting rights in Swiss companies, 2015   142
7.1 Ownership concentration of Italian listed companies in
1994–2017   189
7.2 Share of family firms over the total of Italian
private firms   201
7.3 Average controlling share of family and non-family
Italian private firms   201
7.4 Share of Italian family firms with a family CEO   202
9.1 Change in median ownership share in Slovenian
companies by largest shareholders, mid-1990s to
mid-2010s (%)   250
9.2 Change in composition of ownership shares among the
three largest shareholders in Slovenian companies,
mid-1990s to mid-2010s (%)   251
9.3 Percentage of firms with majority shareholders by
ownership type in the top 100 Slovenian firms in the
first and the last year of the sample   253
9.4 Percentage of firms with majority shareholders by
ownership type in the top 20 Slovenian firms in the first
and the last year of the sample   254

9.5 Ownership share of the largest shareholder by
ownership categories in the top 100 Slovenian firms in
the first and the last year of the sample (%)   255
9.6 Ownership share of the largest shareholder by
ownership categories in the top 20 Slovenian firms in
the first and the last year of the sample (%)   256
9.7 Ownership share of the largest shareholder by
ownership categories in listed Slovenian companies in
the first and the last year of the sample (%)   257

Tables

1.1 The determinants of corporate ownership *page* 8
2.1 Beneficial ownership of UK quoted shares in
     percentages, 1963–2018   37
2.2 Ownership concentration in the 1990s in the
     United Kingdom   42
2.3 Percentage of listed companies and 100%-owned
     subsidiaries in the top 20 and top 100 in the 1990s in
     the United Kingdom   43
2.4 Largest shareholders by ownership categories in the
     1990s in the United Kingdom   44
2.5 Ownership concentration in 2018–2019 in the
     United Kingdom   45
2.6 Percentage of listed companies and 100%-owned
     subsidiaries in the top 20 and top 100 in 2018–2019
     in the United Kingdom   46
2.7 Largest shareholders by ownership categories in
     2018–2019 in the United Kingdom   47
3.1 Austrian 600 largest companies: Ownership
     concentration by company size and ownership stake
     size class, 1996   64
3.2 Austrian listed companies: Ownership concentration by
     company size and ownership stake size class, 1996 65
3.3 Ownership concentration in the 1990s in Austria   66
3.4 Largest shareholders by ownership categories in the
     1990s in Austria   67
3.5 Ownership concentration in 2018–2019
     in Austria   69
3.6 Percentage of listed companies and 100%-owned
     subsidiaries in the top 20 and top 100 in Austria 70
3.7 Largest shareholders by ownership categories in
     2018–2019 in Austria   71

3.8 Austrian 600 largest corporations: Direct, ultimate
ownership and largest ultimate shareholder by
investors and size classes, 1990s 73
3.9 Austrian listed companies: Direct, ultimate
ownership and largest ultimate shareholder by
investors and size classes, 1996 74
3.10 Ultimate beneficial ownership of the twenty largest
companies in Austria in 2015 75
4.1 Ownership concentration in 1990 in Germany 91
4.2 Largest shareholders by ownership categories in 1990
in Germany 92
4.3 Ownership concentration in 2018–2019
in Germany 94
4.4 Largest shareholders by ownership categories in
2018–2019 in Germany 95
5.1 Ownership concentration in the 1990s
in Switzerland 118
5.2 Largest shareholders by ownership categories in the
1990s in Switzerland 119
5.3 Ownership concentration in
2018 in Switzerland 120
5.4 Largest shareholders by ownership categories in
2018 in Switzerland 121
5.5 Sector overview, Switzerland 124
5.6 Sample coverage SWIPRA surveys 2013–2019
in Switzerland 125
5.7 Shareholdings in the full sample, Switzerland 126
5.8 Shareholdings in the full-period
sample, Switzerland 130
5.9 Developments in different company groups by
size, Switzerland 135
5.10 Passive investors development, Switzerland 139
5.11 Swiss companies' AGM voting outcomes on
compensation report items, 2008–2019 143
6.1 Ownership concentration in the 1990s in Sweden 160
6.2 Largest shareholders by ownership categories in the
1990s in Sweden 161
6.3 Largest shareholders by ownership categories in the
1990s (10% cut-off) in Sweden 162

6.4 Ownership concentration in 2018–2019
      in Sweden   164
6.5 Largest shareholders by ownership categories in
      2018–2019 in Sweden   165
6.6 Largest shareholders by ownership categories in
      2018–2019 (10% cut-off) in Sweden   166
6.7 Ultimate ownership of the largest shareholders in
      2018–2019 (10% cut-off) in Sweden   167
7.1 Top 20 Italian non-financial firms in 1990 by sales   183
7.2 Top 20 Italian non-financial firms in 2018 by sales   184
7.3 Ownership concentration of Italian non-listed
      companies in 1993, 2005 and 2016   186
7.4 Type of ownership in Italian non-listed companies in
      1993, 2005 and 2016   187
7.5 Ownership concentration in Italian listed companies
      in 1990–2017 (weighted averages by market value;
      percentages on total capitalization by year)   191
7.6 Control models of Italian listed companies
      (1996–2017)   192
7.7 Type of ownership in Italian listed companies in
      1996–2002   194
7.8 Type of ownership in Italian listed companies in
      2012–2017   195
8.1 Ownership concentration in the 1990s
      in Bulgaria   219
8.2 Largest shareholders by ownership categories in the
      1990s in Bulgaria   221
8.3 Ownership concentration in 2018–2019
      in Bulgaria   223
8.4 Largest shareholders by ownership categories in
      2018–2019 in Bulgaria   225
8.5 Matrix of ownership change of the top 100 firms
      (type of the largest shareholder) in Bulgaria   227
9.1 Changes in concentration of ownership in Slovenia by
      largest shareholders, mid-1990s to mid-2010s (%)   250
9.2 Changes in composition of companies in the top
      20 and top 100 group in Slovenia between the
      mid-1990s and mid-2010s   252

Contributors

Laura Abrardi is Assistant Professor of Applied Economics at the Polytechnic University of Turin (Department of Management), where she teaches Economics and Firm Theory. Her research interests are in the field of industrial organization and corporate governance, with a focus on applications of contract theory to managerial incentives, the ownership structure of the firm, regulation, platform economics and digital technologies. Abrardi's work includes publications in the *Journal of Economic Surveys, Journal of Economic Behavior and Organization, Economic Inquiry, Small Business Economics, Journal of Industrial and Business Economics* and in volumes published by Elsevier Academic Press. She received her PhD in Economics from the Università Cattolica del Sacro Cuore, Milan (Italy) and is currently a member of the Scientific Committee of the Italian Society of Industrial and Business Economics.

Christoph Wenk Bernasconi is a lecturer and researcher at the Department of Banking and Finance at the University of Zurich and founding partner of SWIPRA Services, an advisory firm and think tank for corporate governance and sustainability in Switzerland. He is co-author of the 'SWIPRA Considerations for Corporate Governance' and of the SFI White Paper on corporate governance and is responsible for the annual SWIPRA AGM analysis and corporate governance survey. Since 2021, he has served on the ICGN Committee on Natural Capital. Bernasconi completed the PhD programme in Economics of the Swiss National Bank in Gerzensee and wrote his thesis in the field of empirical corporate finance at the Department of Banking and Finance at the University of Zurich.

Anamarija Cijan is a teaching assistant and a PhD student at the University of Ljubljana, School of Economics and Business. Her research interests cover granularity, more specifically if and how idiosyncratic shocks affect the macroeconomic performance of a country or region, international trade and trade policy, digitalization and foreign direct investment. Cijan has contributed to three academic papers in the last five years. She also worked at EY for almost two years in financial accounting advisory and in audit. She completed her undergraduate degree at the University of Ljubljana, School of Economics and her master's degree at University of Birmingham, Birmingham Business School.

Jože P. Damijan is a full professor at the University of Ljubljana, School of Economics and Business, and Visiting Professor at the University of Leuven, Belgium. His research interests and teaching cover international economics and trade policy, globalization, foreign direct investment, innovation, corporate governance, firm performance, labour markets, corruption and development. In the last ten years, he has published more than thirty peer-reviewed academic papers. Recent publications include papers in *The World Economy, Review of World Economics, World Development, Oxford Bulletin of Economics and Statistics, Journal of Comparative Economics, Economics of Transition, Economic Letters* and *Economic Systems.* Chapters in monographs were published by Edward Elgar, Palgrave MacMillan, the World Bank and the like. He has partnered more than two dozen international research projects funded by the European Commission, the World Bank's Global Development Network (GDN), the United Nations, the European Bank for Reconstruction and Development (EBRD) and the Organisation for Economic Cooperation and Development (OECD). He served as Minister for Growth in the Slovenian government, Vice-President of the Council of Economic Advisors to the Prime Minister of Slovenia and President of a Board of Reforms. Since 2008, he has been a special economic advisor to various ministries of the Slovenian government and to the parliament on various economic policy issues. He has also led several dozen consultancy projects for key domestic and foreign companies, government ministries and agencies.

Johan Eklund is the Managing Director of the Swedish Entrepreneurship Forum and Professor at Blekinge Institute of Technology (BTH) and Jönköping International Business School (JIBS), where he received his doctorate in economics in 2008. He is also affiliated to Indiana

University, School of Policy and Environmental Affairs and Institute for Development Studies, USA. Eklund has more than 100 publications to his name, of which approximately 25% are peer-reviewed articles. He is a Fellow of the Royal Swedish Academy of Engineering Sciences (IVA). Eklund's main research interests concern the relationship between institutions – in particular regulations – and their long-term effects on economic development and growth. He has broad interests in industrial economics, institutional economics and law and economics. Eklund conducts research in regulatory economics and economics of education/ human capital as well. More recent research interests include entrepreneurship and how institutions and the regulatory environment affect entrepreneurship. Eklund's research is naturally positioned towards both academic and policy audiences. Previously, Eklund was a researcher at Ratio Institute, and was a guest researcher at George Mason University. He has served as Associate Dean at Jönköping International Business School.

Marc Goergen holds a DPhil in Economics from Oxford University, a master's degree from Solvay Business School and a bachelor's degree in economics from the Université Libre de Bruxelles. He is a full professor of finance at IE Business School, IE University, in Madrid. Previous appointments include the University of Manchester Institute of Science and Technology (UMIST) and the Universities of Cardiff, Manchester, Reading and Sheffield. Goergen is an honorary professor at Cardiff Business School, a research member of the European Corporate Governance Institute (ECGI) and a board member of the International Corporate Governance Society (ICGS). He is the joint editor-in-chief of *Annals of Corporate Governance* and an associate editor of the *British Accounting Review*, the *British Journal of Management*, *European Financial Management* and the *European Journal of Finance*. Goergen's research interests are corporate finance and corporate governance. His research papers have appeared in top academic journals, such as *Entrepreneurship Theory and Practice*, the *Journal of Finance*, the *Journal of Financial Intermediation* and the *Journal of Corporate Finance*. Goergen has also authored or co-authored three monographs on corporate governance. He has contributed chapters to numerous edited books. The second version of his successful textbook on corporate governance, entitled *Corporate Governance. A Global Perspective*, was published by Cengage in 2018.

Klaus Gugler's research interests are in empirical industrial organization, especially corporate governance, and competition and regulatory policy. Before the appointment to Full Professor of Economics at the WU Vienna University of Economics and Business, he was Associate Professor of Economics at the University of Vienna, where he earned his PhD in 1997. He gained valuable scientific experience during research stays at the Wissenschaftszentrum Berlin, London Business School and Harvard Law School. Gugler published in top-refereed economics journals including the *Economic Journal*, *The Review of Economics and Statistics* and the *European Economic Review*. He is a member of the 'Industrieökonomischer Ausschuss' and of the 'Verein für Socialpolitik', and head of the Research Institute for Regulatory Economics at WU. Gugler has been a member of the Austrian Competition Commission as well as a witness in numerous antitrust cases such as mergers and abuse of dominance cases for the Austrian Cartel Court. He is the editor of the book *Corporate Governance and Economic Performance* published by Oxford University Press in 2001.

Evgeni Peev's research interests are in corporate governance and country institutions. He is a co-founder of Corporate Governance and European Integration (CGEUI) network and Scientific Director of the European Research and Education Institute. He has been CGEUI Principal Investigator at the Institute for Quantitative Economics WU, Marie Curie Senior Research Fellow at the University of Vienna and Associate Professor at the Economic Research Institute, Bulgarian Academy of Sciences. He has been Visiting Professor at the Hitotsubashi University, Tokyo, Visiting Fellow at the University of Zurich, the Technical University Freiberg, Copenhagen Business School and Heriot-Watt University, UK. He is involved in consultancy work for the European Commission and has been an initiator of studies on novel corporate governance issues in Europe, transition countries, Southeast Europe and Bulgaria, funded by the European Commission, the Research Support Scheme (RSS), Deutscher Akademischer Austauschdienst (DAAD), Austrian Institute for Eastern and Southeastern Europe, CERGE-EI, World Bank (GDN), Austrian National Bank, Austrian Scientific Fund, the European Education and Culture Executive Agency (EACEA) and the Bulgarian National Fund for Scientific Studies. Peev has published in top academic journals, including the *Journal of Corporate Finance*, *Journal of Institutional and Theoretical*

Economics, *International Review of Law and Economics* and *Journal of Comparative Economics*. He is the editor of *Separation of Ownership from Control in Southeast Europe: A Comparison of Bulgaria, Romania and Albania 1990–1996*, Sofia, Kota, 1999.

Laura Rondi is Full Professor of Applied Economics at the Polytechnic University of Turin (Department of Management), where she teaches Firm Theory and Corporate Governance. She is a member of the Corporate Governance and European Union Integration (CGEUI) network. Her research interests are in the area of industrial organization and corporate finance, with a strong focus on the application of panel econometric techniques to firm-level data. Rondi has contributed to the literature on financing constraints to firm growth; corporate governance and managerial incentives; ownership and capital structure of regulated firms; and industrial organization in the EU. On these issues she has published in leading journals (*Journal of Public Economics, Journal of Comparative Economics, Journal of Economics and Management Strategy, Economic Inquiry, Corporate Governance: An International Review, European Journal of Political Economy, Review of Industrial Organization, International Journal of Industrial Organization* and *Journal of Regulatory Economics*) and in volumes published by Elsevier Academic Press, Edward Elgar, Clarendon Press (Oxford), Palgrave Macmillan and Cambridge University Press. She serves on the editorial boards of the *Review of Industrial Organization* and *Journal of Industrial and Business Economics*.

Jakob Stemberger is a Young Researcher and a PhD student at the University of Ljubljana, School of Economics and Business. His research interests include global value chains and how inclusion in them affects firms' performance, and international trade and foreign direct investment. He has contributed to three academic papers in the last five years. Prior to starting his PhD he worked as an advisor in the financial industry. He completed his undergraduate degree at the University of Ljubljana, School of Economics and his master's degree at University of Birmingham, Birmingham Business School.

Alexander F. Wagner is a professor of Finance at the University of Zurich (UZH) and a Senior Chair at the Swiss Finance Institute. He leads the Executive Education of UZH's Faculty of Business, Economics, and Informatics, and he is Co-head of the UZH Center for Crisis Competence. Wagner earned his PhD in Political Economy and Government from Harvard University. Prior to that, he completed studies in economics and law in his hometown of Linz, Austria. Wagner's prior practical experience derives from his work as an independent counsel for PwC and from serving as the chairman of a proxy advisor. His research focuses on corporate finance and governance, sustainable finance, and behavioural economics and finance. His talk on 'What really motivates people to be honest in business' is available on TED.com.

Martin Winner is Full Professor of Business Law at WU Vienna University of Business and Economics. He specializes in company law, capital markets law and intellectual property law, with a strong comparative focus. Winner has published numerous textbooks, articles and commentaries, both in German and in English, for example recently an English-language volume on the Market Abuse Regulation, edited together with Susanne Kalss, Martin Oppitz and Ulrich Torggler. He is a member of the Informal Company Law Expert Group (ICLEG), the standing advisory group for company law of the European Commission; on a national level, he has been involved in the drafting of many acts on company law over the last twenty-five years. From 2009 until 2021, Winner was Chairman of the Austrian Takeover Commission, the regulator for public mergers and acquisitions.

Todor Yalamov is an associate professor in Management and Vice-Dean for Research, Innovation and Projects at the Faculty of Economics and Business Administration, Sofia University St. Kliment Ohridski. His teaching portfolio includes diverse courses such as e-business, innovation management, gamification, economic security, learning organization and not-for-profit management. He has an educational background in mathematics, philosophy and economics and management (master's degrees) and a PhD in Management. Yalamov has extensive experience over more than twenty years of working as senior analyst for the Center for the Study of Democracy, doing research and advocacy in the fields of anticorruption, informal economy and good governance, and as a consultant for the World Bank in Eastern Europe and Central Asia assisting incubation, entrepreneurial and innovation ecosystems. He is Director of an international MBA programme with a focus on strategic management, attracting students from more than twenty countries. Yalamov has been a Fulbright Scholar at the Center for International Private Enterprise in Washington DC, an independent non-profit affiliate of the US Chamber of Commerce (2013–2014) and a Fellow of the International Visitor Leadership Program of the US Department of State (2010). He delivered a summer school course on the business of games and gamification at the University of Cologne in 2019.

Preface

It falls to me to write this preface because I was the leader of a project on the Corporate Governance and European Integration (CGEUI) network aiming at teaching and researching recent trends in corporate development (www.cgeui.eu). The project was financed by the Jean Monnet Network Action of the Erasmus + Programme of the European Union.

Shortly after the completion of the final draft of this book, the *British Medical Journal* published an article about integrity issues in a pivotal COVID-19 vaccine trial by a major global pharmaceutical corporation. Public debates in Europe during the global COVID-19 crisis have frequently discussed the crucial role of corporations and the motivation of their shareholders. Yet very little is known about the structure of shareholders in European corporations, the evolution of their largest shareholders over the past few decades and the major forces determining their past and eventually their future.

We hope that this book will contribute to a more comprehensive understanding of the forces shaping the European corporate landscape. The book presents a long-term view of corporate ownership and control structure of major businesses in European countries. Documenting those businesses that have had the largest long-time shareholders may also guide public debates about their role in society during the recent pandemics and further inevitable crises in the future.

Klaus Gugler and I launched our corporate governance journey at the beginning of the 1990s, when one of us (Klaus Gugler) first examined Austria. He then moved on to examine international comparative corporate governance issues. The other (Evgeni Peev) first studied corporate governance in Bulgaria. He then expanded his studies into corporate governance in European transition countries and the EU. What has been most striking to both of us, as we recall our quite different research experience at that time, is the common feeling of having witnessed an era of great change. These were the years of the 'global corporate governance revolution', with the prediction by law professors Hansmann and Kraakman that 'the ideology of shareholder primacy is likely to press all major jurisdictions toward similar rules of corporate law and practice' and Francis Fukuyama's augury about 'the universalization of Western liberal democracy as the final form of human government'. Going back to the 1990s, there was a common consensus about the type of corporate governance to which Europe would have to converge. While in the 1980s, studies stressed the advantages of the German or Japanese 'insider system' of corporate governance, this changed in the 1990s and the early 2000s when most studies documented the primacy of the Anglo-Saxon 'outsider system'. Mainstream corporate governance research (e.g. law and finance literature) and policy papers (e.g. the OECD Principles of Corporate Governance of 1999 and also 2004, 2014–2015) have been promoting the corporate ideology of shareholder primacy. Corporate governance reforms in Europe have been navigated according to this ideology. In both Western Europe and Eastern Europe the existing corporate governance structures have been under pressure to converge with the Anglo-Saxon corporate governance model. However, since the US corporate scandals in 2000–2002 and especially since the global financial crisis of 2008–2009, more critical views on US shareholders' capitalism have again emerged. Studies have documented a number of problems. Examples of these problems are the contradictory purpose of 'footloose' companies with diffused ownership and their negative impact on society, the substantial rise of corporate political power, the rise of inequality and 'supermanagers', the rise of corporate tax evasion and the fall in public wealth, and so on.

   In this context, the CGEUI network launched a study of European corporations. This book is the product of a long-standing collaboration and collective research effort by members of the CGEUI network. The participants in the CGEUI seminars and summer schools have revealed a major demand for more systematic knowledge about the ownership and control evolution of large companies in Europe in the past few decades and how important the Anglo-American corporate governance model has become since the start of the 'global corporate governance revolution' in the 1990s. The gap in the literature was mainly due to data limitations. In the course of the CGEUI network debates, we have decided to write a book using both unique databases provided by CGEUI members and newly prepared datasets. We have retrieved, collected, augmented and connected the project partners' datasets and produced unique datasets used for writing the book.

The book is related to the early seminal contributions on ownership and control in Europe edited by Fabrizio Barca and Marco Becht (*The Control of Corporate Europe*, 2001, Oxford University Press) and by Gugler Klaus (*Corporate Governance and Economic Performance*, 2001, Oxford University Press), studying a cross section of large European companies in the mid-1990s. This volume examines ownership structure change (and conversely stability) in large firms across Europe in the following decades. The book is also related to recent key publications on convergence and persistence edited by Jeffrey N. Gordon and Mark J. Roe (*Convergence and Persistence in Corporate Governance*, 2004, Cambridge University Press) and by Jeffrey N. Gordon and Wolf-Georg Ringe ('Convergence and Persistence in Corporate Law and Governance', in *The Oxford Handbook of Corporate Law and Governance*, 2018, Oxford University Press). Both publications are written mostly by legal scholars and are mainly focused on the legal aspects of convergence to the Anglo-Saxon model of corporate governance. This book should be viewed as supplementary to this literature and will hopefully be used in the ongoing debate on corporate governance development in Europe. The book presents ample evidence of the evolution of ownership and control of large firms and its determinants in Europe in the decades following the 'global corporate governance revolution' in the 1990s.

Evgeni Peev
Vienna
February 2022

Acknowledgements

This research benefited from the support of the Jean Monnet Network Action of the Erasmus + Programme of the European Union 'Corporate Governance and European Union Integration'. We have had helpful discussions and received comments on the book from numerous people. Our particular thanks are due to the participants in the CGEUI workshops and seminars in Stockholm in 2017, Cardiff in 2018 and Barcelona in 2019, and the CGEUI summer schools in Ljubljana in 2017 and in Vienna in 2018, involving experienced researchers, PhD students and early career researchers. The discussions with PhD students and early career researchers have been especially motivating in the development of this book. We are indebted to Dennis Mueller for some very fruitful discussions. We are grateful to Wolfgang Bessler and Bruno Schönfelder for their very helpful suggestions. We would like to thank Alistair Johnson who made many valuable suggestions for improvements in the text. Our particular thanks are due to Edith Genser at the European Education and Culture Executive Agency (EACEA), who provided us with excellent methodological help in the course of the CGEUI project. Last but not least, we would like to give our thanks to the anonymous referees and Philip Good, the editors and others involved in this publication.

1 Introduction

KLAUS GUGLER AND EVGENI PEEV

1.1 The Research Questions

From the 1990s onwards, the corporate governance and ownership structures in Europe have been under pressure from globalized markets (Hansmann and Kraakman, 2001), supranational organizations such as the OECD, IMF, World Bank, G-20 (Gordon, 2018), the European Commission (Hopt, 2015a), the US government (Gordon, 2003), institutional investors (Gelter, 2017) and other special interest groups. Two major institutional changes in Europe might be outlined. The first is the creation of a single capital market in the European Union (EU) since 1993, and the struggles for launching a market for corporate control in the EU. The second is the post-communist privatization and financial liberalization in Central and Eastern Europe since 1989. Scholars have noticed this global pressure for corporate governance change and dubbed it the 'global corporate governance revolution' (Cheffins, 2001) or 'corporate governance movement' (Gelter, 2017).

Surprisingly, the bulk of the corporate governance literature on European countries presents a static view of ownership and control structures (see e.g. the most-cited research in the law and finance literature such as La Porta et al. 1997, 1998, 1999; see also Barca and Becht, 2001). A few studies have discussed ownership changes. Ringe (2015) documented the erosion of 'Deutschland AG'. Franks and Mayer (2017) presented evidence on the decrease in individual ownership and the increase in internationalization of public firms in the United Kingdom. Nachemson-Ekwall (2017) described the increase in the role of institutional investors in Sweden. Gugler et al. (2013) observed a rise in foreign control of large firms after privatization in European transition countries. Yet to date, no study has presented systematic evidence of long-term developments in ownership and control across European countries following the corporate governance changes in the 1990s.[1] The first contribution of the book is to fill this gap in the empirical corporate governance literature.

One of the main objectives of this book is to make available systematic and comparable accounts of ownership structure change (respectively persistence) in large firms across Europe over the last few decades. The book focuses on countries in the four major European regions: Western Europe, Eastern Europe, Southern Europe and Northern Europe. It examines countries from all legal origin families: Anglo-Saxon (the United Kingdom), Germanic (Austria, Germany, Switzerland), Scandinavian (Sweden) and French legal origin (Italy) as well as two transition countries (Bulgaria, Slovenia). While the book provides in-depth analyses of the corporate governance systems in the respective countries examining changes in ownership and control structure in the last few decades, it also asks the following basic questions for all countries:

(1) To what extent has the role of corporate insiders (e.g. families, banks) and the state decreased in the ownership structure of large firms?
(2) Is there an increase in widely held companies and institutional investors?
(3) Is there an increase in foreign ownership?

The second main objective of this book is to examine the likely determinants of ownership structure change in each country. The ongoing debate on determinants of ownership structure in large firms started with Mark Roe's political determinants hypothesis in the early 1990s (Roe, 1991, 1994) and was further developed by the law and finance literature, which launched the legal origin hypothesis in the mid-1990s (La Porta et al. 1997). Other important inputs to this debate have been the path-dependence hypothesis (Bebchuk and Roe, 1999) and the corporate law and corporate governance convergence hypothesis (Hansmann and Kraakman, 2001; Gordon and Roe, 2004;

---

[1] For example, La Porta et al. (1999) examine ultimate ownership in a few countries in Western Europe in 1996; Faccio and Lang (2002) present a cross-sectional study of ultimate ownership in thirteen countries in Western Europe between 1996 and 1999; De La Cruz et al. (2019) examine listed companies in 2017; Barca and Becht (2001) and Gugler (2001) report cross-sectional studies of large European companies in the mid-1990s. Recently, Aminadav and Papaioannou (2020) examine listed firms from 2004 to 2012.

Gordon, 2018). The starting points of the debate were the Berle–Means corporation of diffuse ownership, and the questions of why it has diffuse ownership, why there exist deviations from its ownership structure around the world and why there will be eventual convergence to this structure in other countries. This book contributes to this debate, documenting country context variables and explaining the observed ownership patterns in eight European countries over the last twenty-five to thirty years. It asks the following basic questions:

(1) Which have been the likely determinants of the (eventual) decreasing role of corporate insiders and the state in European countries since the 1990s?
(2) Which are the likely determinants of the observed patterns of ownership change (e.g. the rise of foreign and institutional investors)?
(3) Or, equally important in the European context, which are the likely determinants of observed ownership persistence?

The third objective of this book is to apply an international comparative approach to ownership structure changes to shed some light on the questions of whether similar forces impact ownership change or persistence in each country, whether particular institutional factors influence ownership change/persistence and whether the eventual decline of corporate insiders and the state and the rise of foreign and institutional investors are influenced by similar forces in each country.[2] The starting point of the analysis is the specific context in each of the countries in our study.

In this introductory chapter, we proceed as follows. Section 1.2 provides an overview of the corporate governance revolution in the 1990s as well as its countervailing forces. Section 1.3 discusses the

---

[2] Our research is also related to a few corporate governance studies stressing the importance of a country-specific context. See e.g. Aguilera and Jackson (2010) on case based, historical and actor-centred forms of institutional explanations; Franks and Mayer (2017) on historical country studies of ownership evolution in the United States, the United Kingdom, Germany and Japan; Vatiero (2017) on the Swiss corporate governance exception. For early studies critically discussing the convergence and unification of company law and corporate governance across countries, see e.g. Enrique (2006) on European company law harmonization; Thomson (2006) on corporate governance codes unification and its agenda-setters; Bebchuk and Hamdani (2009) on the elusive quest for global corporate governance standards. For a critical view of 'one-size-fits-all' and 'best practice' approaches in general, see e.g. Rodrik (2006).

theoretical assumptions about the determinants of corporate ownership. Section 1.4 describes the data used in the country chapters.
Section 1.5 gives an overview of the chapter contents. Section 1.6
presents cross-country conclusions, implications for the theory of the
firm and policy implications.

1.2 The Global Corporate Governance Revolution

About three decades ago, there were great expectations about 'universalization' and 'convergence'. At the beginning of the globalization-
centred 1990s, in *The End of History and the Last Man?* Francis
Fukuyama wrote:

What we may be witnessing is not just the end of the Cold War, or the
passing of a particular period of post-war history, but the end of history as
such: that is, the end point of mankind's ideological evolution and the
universalization of Western liberal democracy as the final form of human
government. (Fukuyama, 1989)

In the mid-1990s in 'The End of History for Corporate Law', Hansmann
and Kraakman (2001) convincingly claimed:

Despite the apparent divergence in institutions of governance, share ownership, capital markets, and business culture across developed economies, the
basic law of the corporate form has already achieved a high degree of uniformity, and continued convergence is likely. A principal reason for convergence is a
widespread normative consensus that corporate managers should act exclusively in the economic interests of shareholders, including noncontrolling
shareholders. This consensus on a shareholder-oriented model of the corporation results in part from the failure of alternative models of the corporation,
including the manager-oriented model that evolved in the U.S. in the 1950's
and 60's, the labour-oriented model that reached its apogee in German code-
termination, and the state-oriented model that until recently was dominant in
France and much of Asia ... Since the dominant corporate ideology of shareholder primacy is unlikely to be undone, its success represents the end of
history for corporate law. The ideology of shareholder primacy is likely to
press all major jurisdictions toward similar rules of corporate law and practice.

In this book, we will show that countervailing forces to the 'convergence to the shareholder-oriented model of the corporation' are at least
as forceful as the forces of convergence. In this context, it is useful to
ask, how important is ownership change for legal convergence? First,
globalization and European integration may include market forces for

ownership change in Europe. Ringe (2015) argued that one of the important messages that the story of Germany can teach us is the centrality of ownership structure in shaping legal rules. While Hansmann and Kraakman (2001) focus on the direct link between global markets' pressure and the shape of corporate laws, Ringe (2015) outlines a two-step process: (1) global competition can drive ownership changes and (2) ownership changes, in turn, can translate into legal reform. He claimed that ownership-driven change may be more effective than a direct attempt to modify legal rules. Where market forces succeed in modifying the ownership structure in a jurisdiction, the change will be more persistent, and the case for law reform will be more urgent.

Second, Gordon (2003) argued that the pace of convergence in corporate governance depends crucially on the commitment of countries to the project of European integration. This transnational project may be best advanced by the spread of widely held companies as in the Anglo-American model, because such ownership structures facilitate the contestability of control, which helps to curb economic nationalism. The author coined the term 'strong form' convergence on the shareholder capitalism model for the process of the spread of public firms with diffuse ownership in European countries. He claimed that the evolving international share ownership of widely held public companies would make economic nationalism seem more anachronistic. Thus, the European integration objective generates a case for diffused ownership that does not necessarily follow from efficiency-based arguments for convergence. Gordon (2003) wrote: 'Diffusely-owned firms may not be more efficient (indeed, to the contrary) but the contestability of control may more effectively restrain economic nationalism' (p. 3). In the 1990s, thus, both economic and political forces appeared to drive the move towards widely held companies in European countries.[3]

---

[3] Consistently, the Report of the High-Level Group of Company Law Experts on Issues Related to Takeover Bids (10 January 2002) recommended the further development of a market for corporate control in Europe, arguing that markets must be integrated on a European level to enable the restructuring of European industry and the integration of European securities markets must proceed with reasonable efficiency and speed. While the prospects for a proposal and adoption of a revised 13th Directive along the lines of the Experts Report were uncertain, Gordon (2003) noted: 'In substantially increasing the control contestability of corporations in the EU it would work a revolution in EU corporate governance and a revolution in much else besides.'

However, corporate scandals in US companies such as Enron and WorldCom in 2000–2002 revealed crucial weaknesses in the Anglo-Saxon corporate governance model. The global financial crisis in 2008–2009 delivered the next blow to the mainstream argument for the superiority of the Anglo-Saxon corporate governance model.[4] Political pressure against globalization and towards economic protectionism gradually developed in both Europe and the United States.[5] Nationalism understood as 'the political resolve to favour territorial insiders over outsiders through protectionist policies' influences the most important features of the governance landscape, ranging from ownership structures and takeover defences to laws on investor protection (Pargendler, 2019).

Not only might the convergence to the Berle–Means corporation have stalled in Europe, the ultimate target of convergence might have been changing, too. Recent studies review a key change in corporate control in large contemporary corporations in the United States. Gilson and Gordon (2013) documented a rising importance of institutional investors and the emergence of 'agency capitalism'. They observed a 're-concentration' of ownership in the hands of institutional investment intermediaries. It appears that the Berle–Means corporation has been gradually decreasing its dominant role in the corporate landscape of the United States, and its future has been debatable (Cheffins, 2018). The rise of giant US tech companies such as Facebook, Google and Amazon under concentrated control, sometimes utilizing dual or even multiple voting shares, underpins this change of sentiment. Moreover, Franks and Mayer (2017) documented a recent decline in the number of public companies in the United States and the United Kingdom. This development seems puzzling,

---

[4] After the crisis critics argued that the strong form of global convergence in corporate governance is now a historical relict, but perhaps one worth remembering (Branson, 2012). Nevertheless, the European Commission appeared to preserve its positive stance for further legal harmonization aiming at the European capital market union development (for a critical review of the EU initiatives in 2012–2015, see e.g. Hopt, 2015a). The debate about the shareholder-oriented corporate governance model even entered the US presidential elections contest in 2020. See e.g. the agenda on corporate governance reform against the harmful corporate obsession with maximizing shareholder returns at all costs in the United States presented by US Senator Elizabeth Warren (www.warren.senate.gov/newsroom/press-releases/warren-introduces-accountable-capitalism-act, consulted on 1 March 2022).

[5] For example, in 2014 a new French law, the 'Law to Recapture the Real Economy' (Loi Florange), shields French corporations from foreign public takeovers.

keeping in mind that both countries were 'exceptional' with respect to their large public securities markets and the great pressure for developing local stock exchanges in Europe in the 1990s and the 2000s.

What are the net effects then of the forces of the 'global corporate governance revolution' on the one hand and of countervailing conservative/protectionist/path-dependent forces on the other hand in Europe? The book provides empirical evidence of the described trends in the specific context of eight European countries: the United Kingdom, Austria, Germany, Switzerland, Sweden, Italy, Bulgaria and Slovenia.

1.3 The Determinants of Corporate Ownership

All country studies in this book report (at least) three kinds of result: (1) ownership structures (concentration and types) in the initial period (the mid-1990s) and the end period (2018–2019), (2) patterns of ownership change (or stability) in large companies over the past decades and (3) an analysis of the likely determinants of ownership and ownership change. In this section, we discuss the determinants of corporate ownership derived from a mixed bag of literatures and theories including (1) law and finance, (2) politics, (3) global competition and convergence, (4) privatization, (5) path dependence, (6) varieties of capitalism, (7) economic entrenchment and (8) interest groups and financial development (Table 1.1). Any literature presented in Table 1.1 concerns somewhat both ownership change and stability, some stressing more on ownership change, others focusing more on ownership stability. For the sake of clarity of our further discussion, we separate the determinants of corporate ownership into two broad groups: determinants of corporate ownership change and determinants of corporate ownership stability. The discussed determinants of corporate ownership as well as country-specific factors are examined in the context of the eight European countries mentioned earlier.

1.3.1 Law and Finance

La Porta et al. (1997, 1998) argued that widely held companies (Berle–Means corporations) should be more common in countries with good legal protection of minority shareholders. In countries with weak investor protection, widely held companies are subject to severe agency

Table 1.1 *The determinants of corporate ownership*

Literature	The determinants of corporate ownership
	1. Ownership change
Law and finance	Shareholders' protection
Politics	Left-wing politics
Global competition and convergence	Global market forces
Privatization	Failings of state ownership
	2. Ownership stability
Path dependency	Initial conditions
Varieties of capitalism	Complementary institutions
Economic entrenchment	Economic entrenchment
Interest groups theory of financial development	Incumbents opposing financial development

problems between managers and shareholders, which large blockholders can overcome because of their greater incentives to monitor managers. Thus, concentrated family ownership emerges as a solution to agency problems in countries with weak investor protection. The law and finance view therefore predicts that family firms will be more represented in countries with weak investor protection, and widely held companies will be more prevalent in countries with strong investor protection. The law and finance literature also reveals the primacy of common law and Anglo-Saxon legal origin over the legal traditions in Europe. Djankov et al. (2008) summarized the evidence about the positive effects of the Anglo-Saxon model on investor legal protection, the development of widely held companies, financial development (proxied by stock exchange market capitalization or turnover), investment and economic growth. This literature predicts that legal and corporate governance reforms leading to stronger legal protection of shareholders will increase companies with diffused ownership in Europe and around the world.

1.3.2 Politics

Mark Roe (2000, 2003) offers an alternative explanation for the differences in ownership structures between Europe and the United

States to that of La Porta et al. (1998). Roe questions the legal origin explanation and argues that the differences lay in their politics and not in their legal systems. Where labour, through politics, has stronger protection, capital must concentrate to respond effectively. Those people who own equity in social democracies prefer large blocks, which offer them some protection against corporate insiders' opportunistic behaviour. Mark Roe identified social democratic politics as the driving force towards ownership concentration.[6]

1.3.3 Global Competition and Convergence

This literature presents theoretical arguments about global market-driven ownership changes. The choice of the most efficient business model of corporate governance by companies (banks) is the key factor. In a country study, Ringe (2015) argues that the recent ownership change in Germany can partly be explained by direct market forces. German banks came under strong pressure to divest their ownership stakes due to increased internationalization of banking during the 1990s. In a general discussion, Gordon and Roe (2004) claim that (1) if corporate governance is an element of comparative advantage in global product markets, the corporate governance norms that tend towards efficient production would disseminate widely; and (2) if corporate governance is an element of comparative advantage in global capital markets, because institutional investors would push for a standardized corporate governance model, this source of comparative advantage would suggest a convergence towards an international standard of corporate governance with a lower cost of equity capital. Thus, global market forces are responsible for the changing business models of companies and banks to adjust their corporate governance and ownership structures. According to the convergence hypothesis,

---

[6] For the social democratic political influence in Sweden since 1932, see e.g. Hogfeldt (2005); for the recent role of the German Social Democratic Party on corporate governance reform in Germany, see e.g. Höpner (2007); for the recent shift of the centre of political gravity to the right, see Roe and Coan (2017); for the effect of political change (stability) on corporate ownership structure in nine East Asian countries from 1996 to 2008, see Carney and Child (2013).

globalized markets induce countries to converge to 'the best' Anglo-Saxon corporate governance model of diffused ownership.[7]

1.3.4 Privatization of State-Owned Enterprises

Megginson and Netter (2001) surveyed the literature on privatization in developed, developing and transition countries. They showed that privatization was observed in both Western and Eastern Europe. In Western Europe, privatization was part of the broader process of liberalization of European markets and the deepening of EU integration in the 1980s and 1990s. After the collapse of communism in Eastern Europe, privatization was a key pillar of the Washington Consensus policy in European transition countries (the other key pillars were financial stabilization and liberalization of markets).[8] Corporate insiders (directors of the state-owned enterprises) and the state were seen as major impediments to post-communist reforms (Frydman and Rapaczynski, 1993).

The privatization literature is closely linked to the narrative on the detrimental role of corporate insiders discussed in Subsections 1.3.6 and 1.3.7. In the case of privatization, the main culprit has been seen in state bureaucracy and managers of state-owned firms. In the 1990s and 2000s, studies discussed the triple agency problems of state-owned firms and presented consistent evidence on the negative effects of state-owned companies on economic performance (see e.g. Mueller, 2003). Thus, privatization has been a response to the failings of state ownership (Megginson and Netter, 2001).

1.3.5 Path Dependence

According to path-dependence theory, the choice of the 'the best' Anglo-Saxon corporate governance model of diffused ownership is

---

[7] For the role of the European economic integration, see e.g. Hansman and Kraakman (2001); for the impact of a single capital market on the increase in widely held companies and for the impact of global competition on the decrease in bank ownership in Germany, see e.g. Ringe (2015); for the effect of liberalization of the capital market and the abolishing of capital control, see e.g. Rydqvist, Spizman and Strebulaev (2014).

[8] For a cross-country comparison of the effects of liberalization of markets on economic performance in Eastern Europe, see e.g. Peev and Mueller (2012) and Peev (2015).

constrained by the forces of path dependence because corporate governance is embedded in national legal and institutional systems. From an efficiency perspective, a particular national system is linked to a set of complementary institutions, so that a governance change to conform to the 'international' model might reduce the value of the firm and, indeed, its global competitiveness. Thus, corporate governance and ownership changes without regard for these complementary institutions would result in inefficient companies. As a response, corporate insiders may defend the domestic corporate governance and ownership structures.[9] According to the law and finance literature, the existence of good law gives rise to widely held and efficient controlling shareholder systems. According to the path-dependence theory, the direction of causation is reversed, initial conditions giving rise to a shareholding pattern that then demands good law.

The role of institutional complementarities is also discussed in the literature on the varieties of capitalism (Hall and Soskice, 2001). This literature has identified two types of political economy: liberal market economies (e.g. the United Kingdom, the United States) and coordinated market economies (e.g. Germany, Austria, Sweden). These two types can be distinguished by the way in which firms coordinate with each other and other actors. In liberal market economies, firms coordinate their activities primarily by hierarchies and market mechanisms. In coordinated market economies, firms depend more on non-market relationships in the coordination of their relationships with other actors (Hall and Soskice, 2001). According to the literature on the varieties of capitalism, ownership change to widely held companies may be feasible only in the broader context of political economy reforms.

1.3.6 Economic Entrenchment

Morck et al. (2000) examined the role of family owners in Canada and coined the term 'Canadian disease'. They showed that liberalization of markets in Canada in 1988 led to important corporate control changes – a decrease in heir-family-controlled firms and an increase of widely held companies over the period 1988–1994. Morck et al. (2005) presented a survey of the literature on corporate governance and economic entrenchment. The authors claimed that outside the

---

[9] See Bebchuk and Roe (1999) and Gordon and Roe (2004).

United States and the United Kingdom, large corporations usually have controlling owners, who are very wealthy families. Pyramidal control structures, cross shareholding and super-voting rights let such families control corporations without making a commensurate capital investment. In many countries, a few such families end up controlling considerable proportions of their countries' economies and have greatly amplified political influence relative to their actual wealth. This influence has distorted public policy regarding property rights protection, capital markets development and other institutions. The authors denoted this phenomenon as '*economic entrenchment*', and posited a relationship between the distribution of corporate control and institutional development that generates and preserves economic entrenchment as one possible equilibrium.

The roots of the literature on economic entrenchment can be partly found in the influential research by Mancur Olson. Olson (1982) presented a theory of interest groups focusing on their long-term stability and redistribution policies. Olson described the stability of interest groups in the United Kingdom as the 'British disease' or 'English disease'. In seminal contributions, he argued that 'institutional sclerosis' and the long-term persistence of groups of special interests involved in redistribution are key factors for economic performance (Olson, 1982; Mueller, 1983). Olson identified labour unions, professional associations and the like as the most important interest groups in the United States. He never focused on corporate insiders such as corporate CEOs and members of the board of directors.

Interestingly, the main concern of literature on economic entrenchment has been corporate insiders in East Asian countries, Canada and Germany but not their counterparts in the United Kingdom despite the 'British disease' problems identified by Olson. According to Olson's analysis, the war, invasion and totalitarian regimes led to the destruction of domestic interest groups with special interest and the emergence of new firms and business configurations for higher economic growth. According to the literature on economic entrenchment, this creative destruction role can be played by liberalization of markets.

1.3.7 *Interest Groups and Financial Development*

Studies on the impact of financial development on ownership structure show that greater financial development leads to higher liquidity of financial markets and an increase in the incentives of controlling families to sell equity, thus increasing the share of widely held companies. For example, Helwege, Pirinsky and Stulz (2007) reported that firms with more liquid stocks tend to become widely held more quickly in the United States. However, financial development is endogenous and varies among countries. Rajan and Zingales (2003) proposed that incumbents oppose financial development because it breeds competition. They predict that incumbents' opposition will be weaker when an economy allows both cross-border trade and capital flows. According to their theory, incumbent interests are least able to coordinate to obstruct or reverse financial development when a country is open to both trade and capital flows. When a country is open to neither, incumbents coordinate to keep finance under their heel. The authors claim that direct measures of the political power of interest groups and their ability to influence outcomes are controversial at best illustrating the problems with an example from the French financial liberalization in 1983 by a socialist government. At that time, socialists did not seem to be an interest group that would push for liberalization. However, there was a liberalizing faction in the French Socialist Party, led by Prime Minister Pierre Mauroy and Finance Minister Jacques Delors, whose hand was strengthened by France's increased trade integration into the European Community. This faction argued that liberalization was necessary to preserve trade and won the day (for a thorough study of financial liberalization in Europe see e.g. Abdelal, 2009).

Both economic entrenchment literature (Morck et al., 2005) and interest groups and financial development literature (Rajan and Zingales, 2003) predict that trade and financial liberalization decrease the role of corporate insiders in the ownership structure of large companies.

1.3.8 Challenges

The theoretical divide between the Anglo-American model of diffused ownership (in e.g. the United Kingdom and the United States) and the ownership model of concentrated ownership in Continental Europe (in e.g. Germany) has been challenged by a number of studies. For example, Gilson (2005) provided a more nuanced taxonomy of corporate insiders. In particular, he distinguished between efficient and inefficient controlling shareholders, and between pecuniary and non-pecuniary private benefits of control. He argued that the appropriate dichotomy is between countries with functionally good law, which support companies with both widely held and controlling shareholder distributions, and countries with functionally bad law, which support only controlling shareholder distributions. Gilson has argued that both the United States and Sweden belong to a corporate family with essentially common features such as 'good' law. The policy implications that flow from his taxonomy support diverse shareholder distributions.

Recent studies also challenged the major pillar of law and finance literature about the key role of investor protection for the development of widely held companies, financial development and economic prosperity. For example, Franck and Mayer (2017) argue that the historical evidence from the United Kingdom, Germany, Japan and the United States illustrates that it was not investor protection that allowed stock markets to develop at the beginning of the twentieth century. In all four cases, stock markets flourished and ownership was dispersed in the absence of strong investor protection. Instead, other institutions and individuals were important in upholding relations of trust between investors and firms. Franks and Mayer (2017) also argued that equity markets may be important for economic development but dispersed ownership and control by outside shareholders may not be. They claimed that providing corporations with access to external sources of equity finance from stock markets is not the same as conferring control on those outside investors. The authors showed that the experience of the United Kingdom, Germany, Japan and the United States in the first half of the twentieth century and that of China, Japan and Korea in the second half of the century are illustrative of that. Ownership was dispersed in the first four countries in the absence of strong investor protection and the last three countries displayed remarkable growth in the presence of dominant insider owners and the absence of external shareholder control.

The view about the primacy of common law and Anglo-Saxon legal origin was also challenged by the historical evidence on the 'British disease' presented by Olson (1982) or on 'personal capitalism' in the United Kingdom discussed by Alfred Chandler (1990). In a seminal contribution, Alfred Chandler examined the key difference between the United Kingdom, on the one hand, and Germany and the United States (both having professional managers), on the other. In the United

Kingdom, before World War II (around 1938) companies were managed by family owners. He coined the term 'personal capitalism' to separate the British model from the 'managerial capitalism' in both Germany and the United States. (For critical evidence on personal capitalism in the United Kingdom, see e.g. Lloyd-Jones and Lewis, 1994.)

1.3.9 Summary

Which of the literatures and theories discussed previously would best explain ownership *change* or eventual *stability* in large companies in European countries over the past decades? This appears an open empirical question. The links between legal rules, politics, global competition, national institutions and ownership structures appear especially complex, and it is not always easy to disentangle the effects of one group of factors from another. For example, following Ringe (2015) we may outline at least six key interactions partly explaining recent ownership change in large German companies: (1) the impact of global competition on the changing business models of German banks and insurance companies (the link between global markets and financial firms), (2) the need for German banks and insurance companies to offload their equity blocks, driving their possible lobbying for changes to the tax regime governing the sale of their holdings (the link between financial firms and politicians), (3) global market pressure driving legal change (global markets – legal rules), (4) legal rules also creating competition (legal rules – global markets), (5) the German left-wing government initiating legal and tax reforms largely motivated by intrinsic political and strategic considerations (politicians – legal rules) and (6) the German company ownership network eroding even before the legal reforms in the late 1990s and both network participants and politicians questioning the rationale for its existence (the links between path dependence, firms and politicians). This kind of complexity has created a number of research and policy problems such as model uncertainty in econometric studies or an ignorance of the country context and a 'one-size-fits-all' policy approach to corporate governance reforms. In this volume, we carry out an in-depth empirical analysis of ownership and control developments in the context of each country in our sample. First, we construct unique datasets of ownership and control (see Section 1.4) in order to identify the patterns of ownership change or persistence in the past few decades. Second, in each country we have examined both unique country factors and the specific country expression of the determinants of corporate ownership shown in Table 1.1. The new evidence thus presented in the country studies has important theoretical and policy implications, which are discussed in Section 1.6 of this introductory chapter.

1.4 The Data

We have collected data on both private and listed large non-financial companies for each of the eight countries in our study.[10] The empirical analysis in the book is based on unique datasets derived from the Amadeus/Orbis databases of Bureau van Dijk (BvD) and a number of sources such as the London Share Price Database (LSPD), the Standard & Poor's Capital IQ, the Companies House (United Kingdom); the Wirtschafts-Trend Zeitschriftenverlagsgesellschaft m.b.H (Austria); the Thomson Reuters Datastream, the SIX Swiss Exchange, SWIPRA Services (Switzerland); the Swedish Companies Registration Office (Sweden); Consob and Bank of Italy (Italy); APIS and the Commercial Register (Bulgaria); AJPES (Slovenia); plus company annual reports, stock exchanges and numerous other online sources.

We have constructed four unique datasets (partly drawn from the Amadeus and Orbis databases provided by BvD) on the ownership of the top 100 domestic non-financial firms (measured by average total assets) and all the domestic listed non-financial firms for the initial period T0 (i.e. mid-1990s) and the most recent data point T1 (i.e. 2018–2019): sample '*Top 100 in T0*', sample '*Listed in T0*', sample '*Top 100 in T1*' and sample '*Listed in T1*'. We assemble the top 100 companies based on total assets in each country, and all listed companies with all data points available with information on ownership of at least the largest shareholder and its identity. We use a cut-off point of 20% of the shares to class a company as having a large shareholder or having dispersed ownership. This cut-off point is chosen to guarantee comparability with prior research on ultimate

---

[10] Most studies examine listed firms in Europe. However, Franks et al. (2012) have shown that listed firms are less economically important than private firms in Europe. Ringe (2015) reviews studies on ownership structures in Germany and shows that they are limited to listed firms and no study has examined a broader sample that would include non-listed firms in Germany. Recent research reveals a process of delisting of public companies (Franks and Mayer, 2017).

control in Europe (e.g. La Porta et al. (1999) and Faccio and Lang (2002) for Western Europe, and Gugler et al. (2013) for Central and Eastern Europe). If present, the large shareholder (if there is more than one shareholder owning at least 20% of the equity, this would be the largest of them) is classed as a family or individual, the state, a non-financial or financial company, a holding company, others or a foreign shareholder. The state category includes three levels of government, that is central (directly owned by the central government), regional and local (e.g. directly owned by a local authority). We rely on the pre-defined ownership types in the Amadeus/Orbis databases in order to identify financial institutions such as banks and institutional investors (including mutual funds, pension funds, nominees, trusts, private equity firms and venture capital companies). The institutional invest-ors' category also includes financial holding companies and other financial companies. Holding companies include non-financial holding companies as per BvD. Companies with their largest shareholder being the employees, the company managers or directors, a cooperative or a foundation or a research institute are classed as others. Additional data cleaning was required as sometimes the largest shareholder could not be identified within the Amadeus database (including name, nationality and exact shareholding) or its type was wrong or other issues applied.

For constructing sample '*Top 100 in T0*' and sample '*Listed in T0*', we first created a ranked list of entries of non-financial companies (identified by economic sector information in the database) based on total assets. Each company enters the list with each data point (year) available in the dataset. The procedure for company selection is as follows: (1) we take the top 100 companies based on total assets and all listed companies with all data points available. (2) We double-check for financial companies (quite often there are financial holding and other financial companies with wrong codes) and replace them with the next entry if needed. (3) We match the available data on company assets with ownership data using the following algorithm: if there is an exact year match we add ownership data to the asset data; if there is no exact year match we take the closest year available to the data point with assets data and if there are two points (x years after and x years before the assets data point) we take the earliest data point available. Then we take the data points with the smallest difference of years between company assets and ownership, and the earliest data point with company assets. We end up with a list of companies, which include top 100 companies by assets plus all listed companies with information on ownership of at least the largest shareholder and its identity. The procedure is done individually for each country. We use this complicated procedure to construct the 'sample T0' as if we limit our sample only to a given year or even exact year match (yet allowing different years in the dataset) we will be missing important large companies. This approach allows us to have the largest companies from the 1990s in the dataset with the best proxies available for company assets and ownership. In a few cases the algorithm led to inclusion of data from 1987, 1988 and 1989 (Switzerland, Germany and Sweden).

For constructing sample '*Top 100 in T1*' and sample '*Listed in T1*', we follow a similar approach to that for the initial period T0. We use Orbis data and extract data for the top 250 companies by total assets in 2018–2019 for non-financial companies and all listed (quoted) companies. Additional cleaning was performed, as there were various financial holdings that were codified as holdings and not as financial enterprises. We take all available owners with information about their ownership share and type. Ownership data is for 31 December 2018 and in some cases where data were not available, we used as a proxy 'latest available data', up to November 2019. In cases of missing ownership data for listed companies, information was collected from online aggregators in November 2019. Additional data cleaning was applied as the sum of ownership was sometimes higher than 100% or there was no information about the nationality of the owner, but it had more than 20%.

1.5 Main Chapter Contents

In this section we briefly summarize the contents of the book's subsequent chapters.

In **Chapter 2**, Marc Goergen presents evidence of ownership and control change in the United Kingdom, which was the first country to develop a code of best practice of corporate governance. This chapter gives a brief overview of the UK corporate governance regulation, including recent reforms, followed by a discussion of the listing and disclosure rules. It then performs an empirical study of the control and ownership of the top 20, top 100 and the listed UK companies for two distinct points in time, that is the 1990s and 2018–2019. The following patterns emerge. Over the period ranging from the late 1990s to 2018–2019, the percentage of listed companies in the top 20 and top 100 suffered a substantial decrease. In contrast, the percentage of fully owned subsidiaries among the top UK companies shot up from virtually nil to more than half of such companies. Still, the average listed UK company remains widely held in 2018–2019 (Goergen and Renneboog, 2001). The chapter then proceeds by identifying potential determinants explaining the observed ownership changes. The chapter concludes with a number of reflections on how UK corporate ownership and control may change during the post-Brexit period.

In **Chapter 3**, Klaus Gugler, Evgeni Peev and Martin Winner use several datasets to trace the ownership and control structures in Austria around twenty-five years ago and compare them to the situation in 2018–2019. Like many other European countries, Austria experienced a shake-up in securities law, mainly induced by EU Directives (such as those on shareholder rights, takeovers and transparency). Despite investor-favourable changes in securities law, ownership concentration remains very high in Austria in listed and unlisted companies alike. Thus, large shareholders have preserved their role of the predominant corporate governance model in Austria. The identities of the controlling shareholders remained very much the same during the past decades with one important exception, banks. Pyramidal ownership structures have remained prevalent as of 2018–2019 in Austria, since non-financial firms and holding companies together controlled nearly half of the top 100 Austrian firms. Thus, families and individuals who stand behind those companies remained the most important ultimate controlling owners. There was a remarkable decline in state control of listed companies after privatization, but the state retained an important role as a large and controlling shareholder in many of the largest (listed and unlisted) Austrian companies. While around twenty-five years ago foreign owners already controlled around 20% of the largest Austrian companies, this percentage continued to increase. Thus, in Austria one does not see the kind of convergence to Anglo-American corporate governance and ownership structures predicted by, for example, Hansmann and Kraakman (2001) or Franks and Mayer (2001). In speculating why this might be the case, 'complementary institutions' that hinder this convergence may be the preferences of both controlling owners as well as prospective buyers, and a missing political will to embrace a more shareholder-oriented model.

In **Chapter 4**, Evgeni Peev presents evidence on ownership and control change in Germany. Ownership concentration dropped in the large German companies over the past few decades. Yet it remained relatively higher than its counterparts in the Anglo-American world. There was an increase in the number of companies with dispersed ownership. Yet the widely held companies accounted for only 20% of the top 20 firms, 17% of the top 100 and 21% of listed companies in 2018–2019. The share of other German companies (non-financial and holding companies), domestic banks and insurance companies, and the state as largest shareholders in the large German companies has declined, and there has been a rise in foreign investors. The role of families as key largest shareholders has varied by company size. The chapter also discusses the determinants of corporate ownership persistence and why the forces of path dependence stemming from the German national system of 'coordinated market economy' appear to be more powerful than the pressure coming from global markets and legal reforms in the 1990s. The chapter has partly answered the question, posed by Hellwig (2000) about whether the internationalization of German large corporations and their shareholders will limit the power of corporate insiders. German individuals, families and other German companies still appear to be the dominant shareholders in the top 20, top 100 and listed German companies. Nevertheless, the share of non-traditional owners for 'Deutschland AG' such as foreign blockholders and widely held companies has significantly increased in the past few decades. The emergence of a hybrid ownership landscape may challenge future corporate law and governance developments in Germany.

Chapter 5, by Alexander F. Wagner and Christoph Wenk Bernasconi, analyses ownership and control changes in Swiss corporations. A major finding is that in listed companies, there has been a substantial decrease in the ownership percentage by the top three shareholders. For example, for the listed companies ranked 21 to 100, the median stake of the three largest shareholders dropped from 42.5% in 2008 to 36.6% in 2018. More generally, the concentration of the disclosed shareholders has decreased. Non-domestic investors hold large stakes in companies listed in Switzerland and have become more important in the largest, most mature companies – not only has their share ownership significantly increased, they are also more active in exercising their voting rights and in engaging with companies. The chapter also provides some evidence, drawing on a series of surveys of market participants, that these developments, especially the presence and increasing activity of non-domestic investors, have direct implications for the governance practice of companies listed in Switzerland. While it is difficult to pinpoint specific drivers for the ownership and control developments of Swiss corporations, overall the pattern is consistent with the life-cycle hypothesis of Franks et al. (2012), who postulate a life-cycle theory for family firms. Moreover, the openness of Switzerland has limited the potential for insiders to coordinate to keep companies tightly under their control (Rajan and Zingales 2003). The increase in non-domestic investors leads to a significant spill-over of regulation enacted in the United Kingdom, the EU or the United States to companies listed in Switzerland. This is generally aligned with the theory of converging corporate governance due to institutional investors striving for a global model as suggested by Gordon and Roe (2004).

Chapter 6 by Johan Eklund and Evgeni Peev is on ownership and control changes of Swedish companies. While Sweden witnessed a significant increase in ownership concentration in the top 20 and top 100 firms in the past few decades, equity ownership concentration remained virtually the same in listed companies. The large shareholders remained the dominant corporate governance model in Sweden. The largest domestic shareholders, such as families and holding companies (closed-end investment funds) have persisted in the past few decades. There was an increase in the share of foreign owners as the largest shareholders in both the top 100 and listed companies. There was also an emergence of new entrepreneurs as the largest shareholders in large Swedish companies. The presented evidence cannot confirm the expectations about the abolishment of the pivotal pyramidal holding companies in Sweden (see e.g. Agnblad et al., 2001). The chapter has documented both the persistence of corporate insiders and ownership changes (e.g. an increase in foreign ownership and the establishment of new domestic largest individual shareholders) in the past few decades. It also shows the importance of domestic institutional investors. The chapter discusses a few reasons why the ownership structure remains persistent despite the substantial influence of global market forces, liberalization of domestic markets and corporate governance and legal reforms in Sweden.

Chapter 7, by Laura Abrardi and Laura Rondi, presents evidence on ownership and control developments in Italy. The chapter portrays the evolution of the ownership and control structure of Italian firms from the early 1990s to date, in which period institutional changes, external shocks and reforms affected the economy, the financial system and the legal protection of shareholders. Specifically, the chapter provides a detailed account of the organization forms of Italian companies, the control models of listed and unlisted firms, the identity of the largest shareholders, the role of institutional investors and the control-enhancing mechanisms of family listed firms, which still represent the largest share in the private companies' segment of the stock exchange. It finds that many features of the ownership structure and the control models are still in place. The Italian economy remains characterized by a predominance of small and medium-sized enterprises (SMEs) that rely on banks for external finance, family firms reluctant to go public and to release control, and a high ownership concentration even among listed firms. And yet institutional reforms did change the corporate governance system, ownership transparency and the attitude towards minority investors because pressures from the regulatory authorities led pyramidal groups to shorten the control chains and to dismantle cross-shareholdings, which eventually sparked a growing interest by foreign institutional investors in recent years. The chapter discusses the effects of legal and institutional changes, institutional investors and the changes in the use of control-enhancing mechanisms on corporate ownership and control.

Chapter 8, by Evgeni Peev and Todor Yalamov, draws a picture of ownership and control change of large Bulgarian companies after the collapse of communism in 1989. Post-communist privatization has fundamentally changed the ownership landscape in Bulgaria. In 2018–2019 the state was the largest shareholder in only 9% of the top 100 companies (down from 42% in the mid-1990s). The state has virtually disappeared as a direct largest shareholder of listed companies. Nevertheless, the state has still remained among the key ultimate owners among the top 20 companies. Foreign investors have become the largest shareholders in 46% of the top 100 companies (up from 31% in the mid-1990s) and in 11.7% of listed companies (up from 6.25% in the mid-1990s). There was a remarkable increase in ownership concentration in listed companies and the percentage of listed companies with dispersed ownership has declined. The destruction of large Bulgarian firms, proxied by their exit rate, was not coupled with an entry of newly established private firms into the cohort of the top 100 companies. There was no sustainable development of domestic largest shareholders. The chapter discusses a few factors explaining the observed ownership patterns.

In **Chapter 9**, Jože P. Damijan, Anamarija Cijan and Jakob Stemberger study the ownership and control transformation of large Slovenian enterprises after 1991. Although the Slovenian ownership structure was not formally dominated by the state initially (due to so-called social ownership), it became so due to the distribution formula applied in the course of privatization. Until 2008, Slovenia was perceived as the new EU member state with the largest state holdings and the lowest share of foreign ownership. However, due to numerous management buyouts and ownership consolidations within and across industries before 2009, the landscape of Slovenian corporate ownership changed dramatically in the decade following the financial crisis. The main reason was that companies involved in management buyouts, mergers and acquisitions became insolvent after refinancing conditions tightened with the onset of the financial crisis. This led to radical changes in ownership through a series of foreign takeovers of troubled companies, the privatization of fifteen state-owned enterprises and all the banks receiving state aid in the course of bank restructuring. This explains the radical increase in ownership concentration in the top 100 Slovenian companies over the three decades and the rise of holding companies and foreign strategic investors as the main owners of the large Slovenian companies in the late 2010s. The chapter discusses the political economy of corporate governance and ownership changes in the past three decades.

1.6 Conclusion

This book contributes to the debate about the convergence and persistence of corporate governance and law (see e.g. Hansmann and Kraakman, 2001; Gordon and Roe, 2004; and Gordon and Ringe, 2018). It presents evidence about the evolution of ownership and control of large firms in Europe in the decades following the global corporate governance revolution in the 1990s. The book consists of eight country studies carrying out in-depth analysis of patterns of ownership change or stability in each country. The countries studied are the United Kingdom, Austria, Germany, Switzerland, Sweden, Italy, Bulgaria and Slovenia. A few important findings deserve mentioning: First, the data show two types of country. On the one hand, there are countries with very low or decreasing ownership concentration of large firms (the United Kingdom, Germany and Switzerland). On the other hand, there are countries preserving a high or even increasing ownership concentration (Austria, Italy, Sweden, Bulgaria and Slovenia). Consistently, in the past decades in the United Kingdom, Austria and Bulgaria, the percentage of listed companies has seen a significant drop while the percentage of fully owned subsidiaries has increased. On the other hand, the opposite trend of an increase in the role of listed companies has been observed in Switzerland.

Second, the documented stability of ownership and control structures is largely inconsistent with widespread convergence to the Anglo-Saxon corporate governance and ownership model. The global corporate governance revolution in the 1990s appears to have stalled. While in Germany and Switzerland ownership concentration indeed decreased, even in these countries average ownership concentration remained high. If at all, only the largest companies in these countries display the shift to dispersed ownership expected by the convergence hypothesis. Ownership concentration of large companies in all other countries except the United Kingdom has remained high and even increased over the past decades. Large shareholders have remained the dominant corporate governance model in Austria, Germany, Sweden, Switzerland and Italy. Moreover, this model was also established in Bulgaria and Slovenia, which began their post-communist transition to private ownership structure from scratch.

Third, we have asked to what extent the role of corporate insiders (e.g. families, banks) and the state has decreased in large firms in European countries over the past decades. Our answer is: to a *small extent*. State-controlled firms were and still are important players in, for example Austria and Italy but also Bulgaria and Slovenia. However, there are signs that while state control has remained important, the role and behaviour of the state has changed, for example the state owns only partial ownership stakes in listed firms and has exerted only partial control. Families have preserved their role as the largest shareholders in large companies in all the non-transition countries in Continental Europe studied in this volume (Austria, Germany, Switzerland, Sweden and Italy). The only major change has been observed with banks, which were among the most important largest shareholders in Austria and Germany, but their role in non-financial companies declined over the past few decades.

Fourth, the book presents evidence about an increase in foreign ownership in large firms in all the countries examined in this volume. While there is significant country variation in the presence of foreign large owners, the forces of globalization and EU integration appear to be strong. There is also evidence that foreign institutional investors have become more pronounced in the largest listed companies.

Which have been the likely determinants of observed ownership change or persistence? There are complex driving forces playing *pro* and *contra* the global corporate governance revolution in each country. However, a striking common observation appears to be that despite the bulk of corporate governance and law reforms in all the countries in the last decades, the data show a great deal of *stability* of ownership structures in large firms. First, path dependence matters. Complementary country institutions of coordinated market economies appear to be the major driving forces behind the persistence of corporate insiders in Austria or Germany. Pre-existing country economic structures (e.g. efficient family-owned multinational companies competitive in the global markets) seem to play a decisive role in the persistence of corporate insiders' ownership in Sweden. The persistence of the family ownership structure of Italian listed companies reflects structural and cultural factors and ultimately can be linked to the owner's reluctance to release the firm's controlling stake.

Second, a general pattern of both relative ownership *stability and change* has been observed in Germany, Sweden and Switzerland. The emerging ownership patterns of the large German companies present a dichotomous structure of traditional blockholders (a dominant part) and new structures such as foreign and dispersed ownership stemming from globalization forces. Swedish companies have demonstrated both the persistence of corporate insiders (e.g. families, closed-end investment funds) and ownership changes, such as an increase in foreign ownership and the emergence of new domestic largest individual shareholders. A similar trend has been observed in the Swiss top listed companies where there is an increase in the role of foreign institutional investors only in the largest (top 20) listed companies, but in the rest of the top 100 companies, ownership stability has been documented. In Switzerland, the openness of the economy has been associated with a decrease in family ownership and a rise in dispersed and foreign ownership in the past decades. The emergence of a hybrid ownership landscape in Germany and Sweden, and perhaps in other countries with a large domestic capital market (e.g. Switzerland) may challenge the future corporate law and governance developments in Europe.

Third, politics matters for ownership *change*. Besides forces of globalization and European integration, a driving force for the ownership transformation in Germany was the change of government in 1998, and the politics of the new centre–left government against corporate insiders. The substantial ownership change in Bulgaria and Slovenia was preceded by a radical political transformation leading to a post-communist transition to a market economy. Thus, the book findings show that potentially large corporate governance and ownership changes are mostly possible after a change in the politics. This corroborates a few previous studies on the role of politics (see e.g. Ringe, 2015 on Schroeder's government in Germany since 1998; Kandel et al., 2019 on Roosevelt's government in the United States in 1934 on tax policy for dismantling corporate pyramids; and Carney and Child, 2013 on the government changes in a few East Asian countries since 1996). Among the variety of policy tools, tax policy change appears to be one of the factors behind ownership changes in Germany and the United Kingdom in the past decades. This confirms the results of other studies documenting the impact of tax policy on ownership structure (see e.g. Gilson and Gordon, 2013 and Kandel et al., 2019 on the United States; Rydqvist et al. 2014 on eight developed countries). The book's findings also reveal the importance of capital control abolishment as a decisive driving force for the increase in foreign ownership in Sweden. This corroborates the results of other studies on the impact of capital control on company ownership (see e.g. Carney and Child, 2013 on East Asian corporations).

What are the implications of our findings for the theory of the firm? In Section 1.3, we set up theoretical arguments about a number of determinants of corporate structure (see Table 1.1). We can assess these arguments in light of the results which we have gathered from the country studies. First, it is difficult to reconcile the bulk of the evidence presented in the country studies with the predictions of the *law and finance* literature about the impact of stronger investors' protection on the rise of dispersed ownership. The substantial institutional and legal reforms, driven by EU integration or international institutional investors, or both, have led to better protection of shareholders in all of the countries studied in this volume. Yet this did not straightforwardly materialize into a decrease in ownership concentration or a rise in the share of companies with diffused ownership. The legal reforms appeared not deep enough to touch fundamental institutions of the pre-existing corporate governance models, such as co-determination in Germany or the hierarchical governance structure consisting of the shareholders' meeting, the board of directors and the chief executive officer (CEO) in Sweden. The impact of the improvement of shareholders' protection appears only moderate and by no means led to a convergence to the Anglo-Saxon ownership structure.

Second, the assumptions of the theory on the *political determinants* of corporate ownership structure are partly corroborated by the evidence on Germany, Sweden, Bulgaria and Slovenia. Political change appears as an important prerequisite for ownership change.

Third, the arguments of the *convergence* literature about ownership changes driven by economic efficiency considerations stemming from global market pressure are highly convincing, but they were only mildly supported by the evidence presented in country studies. The pre-existing globally competitive multinational companies in Sweden and Switzerland belonged to the status quo protecting corporate insiders, and it appeared that they did not need to adjust substantially their business models and ownership structures as a response to the global markets pressure since the beginning of the 1990s.

Fourth, the *path-dependence* theory predictions about the decisive role of initial conditions and the country complementary institutions were very much confirmed by the evidence presented on the coordinated market economies in Austria and Germany, the Swedish social and corporate governance model and in Italy and Bulgaria. The stability of the ownership structures of Italian listed companies reflected structural and cultural factors. In Bulgaria, the driving force for transition was the former communist regime circles, which created a strong path-dependence impact and an ambivalence for corporate ownership transformation.

The reader can also find a number of *specific country events*, such as corporate scandals (the United Kingdom), financial crises (Slovenia, Sweden) or political regime collapse (Bulgaria, Slovenia), which cannot be classified as belonging to any major determinants of corporate ownership described in the literature but actually triggered the most significant corporate governance and ownership reforms in the particular countries.

In sum, none of the determinants shown in Table 1.1 received consistent confirmation across the eight countries. A key conclusion one might draw from the results is that since no single assumption explains corporate ownership changes or stability, a variety of assumptions must govern, and it seems that an 'eclectic' theory of corporate ownership holds. We leave the development of such an eclectic theory of corporate ownership as an important task for future research. In our study, we have asked only a few basic questions about ownership and control change in Europe in the past few decades. We hope this study will stimulate an interest in further cross-country research on the (r)evolution of corporate ownership and control in Europe.

What are the key policy implications of our study? In contrast to a number of legal studies of corporate law and governance, which examined only 'ideal types' of ownership at a very high level of generality and which were reasonable for the purposes of these studies (see e.g. Kraakman et al., 2017), we have documented granular differences in ownership structures both across and within the eight European countries. Thus, our results may comprehensively serve legal practitioners in their evidence-based policy making. We have presented the ownership and control 'in motion' over the past decades. This would be especially valuable for practitioners working on recent corporate law reforms, aiming at increasing the protection available to shareholders. The evidence presented in this volume (e.g. the emergence of a hybrid ownership landscape) would establish the institutional background of the evolution of agency problems to be investigated. More generally, the facts documented in our study on the heterogeneity of the largest shareholders presenting both traditional European corporate governance models and non-domestic institutional and strategic investors show the necessity for the development of a different 'optimal' corporate law because the interests of shareholders are heterogeneous (see also Kraakman et al., 2017).

Finally, the book's results may serve as a basis for a more general discussion about institutional change and its ideological underpinnings. Francis Fukuyama predicted 'the universalization of Western liberal democracy as the final form of human government' (Fukuyama, 1989), and Hansmann and Kraakman (2001) predicted that '[t]he ideology of shareholder primacy is likely to press all major jurisdictions toward similar rules of corporate law and practice.' We have documented that the global corporate governance revolution against corporate insiders and state ownership was only partly successful in Europe. It appears that market forces and legal changes alone (e.g. globalization, the global financial crisis, the introduction of the EU single capital market, corporate law and corporate governance reforms) were not capable of overcoming the path-dependence factors in Western European countries preserving coordinated market economies and domestic economic structures.

In the end, a lack of political will supporting shareholder capitalism in Western Europe, partly due to the growing doubts about the actual efficiency of the Anglo-Saxon corporate ownership structure, partly due to the rent-seeking of European corporate insiders, has been one of the decisive forces opposing the pressure by globalized markets for convergence to the Anglo-Saxon corporate governance and ownership model.

Anglo-Saxon Countries

2 | *The United Kingdom*

MARC GOERGEN

2.1 Introduction: Corporate Governance Legal and Institutional Reforms

This chapter presents evidence on ownership and control change in the United Kingdom in the past decades. In this introductory section, I provide an overview of the types of company and corporate governance reform in the United Kingdom. Section 2.2 describes the data used in the ownership analysis. Section 2.3 presents the ownership structures of large companies in the United Kingdom and their evolution over the period ranging from the late 1990s to 2018–2019. The determinants of the changes in this structure are discussed in Section 2.4. Section 2.5 concludes.

2.1.1 Types of Company

Part 1 of the Companies Act 2006 (previously, the Companies Act 1985) distinguishes between the following types of company:

(1) limited and unlimited companies;
(2) private and public companies;
(3) companies limited by guarantee and having share capital; and
(4) community interest companies.

In what follows, we focus on the listed firms as well as unlisted firms that are among the top 20 or top 100 largest companies in the United Kingdom as measured by their total assets. As these companies are all in the form of public limited companies and private limited companies, we do not review the remaining types of company. Further, companies limited by guarantee and having a share capital are limited to a few legacy companies predating 1982 and can no longer be formed. The reader interested in community interest companies is referred to the Companies Act 2006.

Importantly, as not all of these types of company have shareholders, UK company law uses the broader term 'member' to refer to the associates. Similar to other jurisdictions, the liability of a member of a limited company is limited. If the company has shares, then the member's liability is limited to the shares held by the member. A public company is a company limited by shares (or limited by guarantee and having a share capital) and whose certificate of incorporation states that it is a public company. All other companies are private companies. Only public limited companies can be admitted to the London Stock Exchange (LSE).

2.1.2 Corporate Governance Reforms

The United Kingdom was the first country to develop a code of best practice in corporate governance. The impetus for the first code of best practice, the 1992 Cadbury Report, was a series of cases of corporate financial fraud. The two most prolific cases were Polly Peck International (PPI) and Coloroll. From relatively humble beginnings, PPI grew to becoming a constituent of the FTSE 100 index, with its CEO Asil Nadir at the helm, who took over in 1980 (Bates, 2010). However, in 1990 the Serious Fraud Office (SFO) launched an investigation into PPI, which eventually collapsed with debts totalling £1.3 billion. Nadir managed to flee to Northern Cyprus before a hearing at the Old Bailey, and it was only in 2010 that he voluntarily returned to the United Kingdom to face a court of law. He was finally put on trial two years later (BBC, 2012). Coloroll underwent a similar demise (Bowen, 1993). Under John Ashcroft, who became CEO of the group in 1982, it went on a shopping spree, buying up a series of businesses during the 1980s. Its downfall started in 1988 when it bought the John Crowther group. Both Coloroll and John Growther had been cooking the books to conceal losses. Coloroll eventually collapsed in 1990 when it filed for bankruptcy.

As a reaction to these scandals, the Financial Reporting Council (FRC), the accountancy profession and the LSE set up the Committee on the Financial Aspects of Corporate Governance in May 1991. Given that the Committee was chaired by Sir Adrian Cadbury, a former director of the Bank of England and the former chairman of Cadbury Schweppes, it is commonly known as the Cadbury Committee. Following the Bank of Credit and Commerce International (BCCI) and the Robert Maxwell scandals of 1991, the remit of the Cadbury Committee was then extended beyond financial fraud.

What all of these scandals had in common was a powerful CEO as well as a weak board of directors dominated by executives (Goergen, 2018). More generally, when comparing the UK boards of directors with their US counterparts around the time of these scandals, a clear pattern emerges. Almost all of the FTSE 500 companies (i.e. 479 companies) had a board dominated by executives in 1988. In contrast, among the US Fortune 500 companies, only 113 companies had a board with a majority of executives (Dahya, McConnell and Travlos, 2002). It is then no surprise that the 1992 Cadbury Report – as well as consecutive UK codes of best practice in corporate governance – focused on strengthening corporate boards of directors by recommending gradual increases in the number and percentage of non-executive directors on corporate boards. Nevertheless, the Cadbury Report's recommendation about board composition refrained from prescribing a minimum of non-executive directors: 'The board should include non-executive directors of sufficient calibre and number for their views to carry significant weight in the board's decisions' (Cadbury Committee, 1992, para. 1.3).

It was the 2003 Higgs Report that made a precise recommendation by expecting companies to have a majority of (independent) non-executives on their board. This would exclude the chair. Although successive UK codes of best practice, starting with the Cadbury Report, have adopted the 'comply-or-explain' approach, the uptake of the recommendations on board composition was nevertheless surprisingly rapid. For example, Mira, Goergen and O'Sullivan (2019) report that the mean percentage of non-executives in their sample reached 44% in 1994, while exceeding 68% by the end of 2010.

Another aspect of board composition on which successive UK codes of best practice focused was a recommendation against CEO duality, that is the practice of combining the roles of the CEO and chair of the board. Conversely, in the United States minds are still split about whether CEO duality should be discouraged or not. While the percentages of firms with CEO duality in the UK FTSE 500 (66%) and the US Fortune 500 (70%) were very similar in 1988 (Dahya et al., 2002), only a few UK companies now have CEO duality. Indeed, Mira et al. (2019) report CEO duality for only 15% of their sample for 1997–2014. In contrast, Duru, Wang and Zhao (2013) and Chhaochharia and

Grindstein (2007) report CEO–chair duality in 64% and 75% of their US samples. This suggests that successive codes of best practice have been successful in reducing CEO duality in the United Kingdom.

Apart from the aforementioned two aspects of board composition, successive UK codes of best practice have also focused on the important role of institutional investors. Institutional investors have been the most important type of shareholder since the late 1960s when the beneficial ownership by individuals of UK quoted shares dropped below 50% (Table 2.1; see also Table 4.1 of Goergen, 2018). Hence, starting with the Cadbury Report, successive codes have highlighted the importance of voting for institutional shareholders. Specifically, the Myners Report (its official name being *Institutional Investment in the UK: A Review*) was to focus exclusively on the role of institutional shareholders. While the Cadbury Report had encouraged institutional shareholders to exercise their votes at the shareholder meetings of their investee companies, nine years later the Myners Report still lamented the passiveness of UK institutional investors. Nevertheless, the United Kingdom decided not to go down the road taken by the United States, which with the 1974 Employee Retirement Income Security Act (ERISA) had effectively made voting compulsory for US private health and retirement funds (Goergen, 2018). Rather, the United Kingdom preferred to encourage institutional investors to improve their engagement with their investee firms. For example, the FRC published the first UK Stewardship Code in 2010, a code of best practice aimed at institutional investors. The Code recommended that institutional investors should have a clear policy on voting as well as disclosing their voting activity (FRC, 2010).

Another important feature of the UK corporate governance system has been – as mentioned earlier – the 'comply-or-explain' approach. Both the Cadbury Report and the 1995 Greenbury Report, which issued a set of recommendations about executive pay, had adopted this approach. This approach was also embraced by the first Combined Code, which combined the two previous reports and was published in the summer of 1998. Nevertheless, the 2008 financial crisis called for revisiting this approach. The Walker Review was led by Sir David Walker, a former banker, and its remit was to look into the governance of banks and other financial institutions. It concluded that the comply-or-explain approach was still valid and that there was no strong case for a move to a more prescriptive system, such as the US system. In

Table 2.1 *Beneficial ownership of UK quoted shares in percentages, 1963–2018*

	1963	1975	1981	1990	1991	1992	1993	1994	1997	1998	1999	2000	2001	2002	2003	2004	2006	2008	2010	2012	2014	2016	2018
Rest of the world	7.0	5.6	3.6	11.8	12.8	13.1	16.3	16.3	28.0	30.7	33.0	35.7	35.7	35.9	36.1	36.3	40.0	41.5	43.1	53.3	53.7	53.9	54.9
Insurance companies	10.0	15.9	20.5	20.4	20.8	19.5	20.0	21.9	23.6	21.6	21.6	21.0	20.0	19.9	17.3	17.2	14.7	13.4	8.8	6.2	5.9	4.9	4.0
Pension funds	6.4	16.8	26.7	31.7	31.3	32.4	31.7	27.8	22.1	21.7	19.6	17.7	16.1	15.6	16.0	15.7	12.7	12.8	5.6	4.7	3.0	3.0	2.4
Individuals	54.0	37.5	28.2	20.3	19.9	20.4	17.7	20.3	16.5	16.7	15.3	16.0	14.8	14.3	14.9	14.1	12.8	10.2	10.6	10.6	12.4	12.3	13.5
Unit trusts	1.3	4.1	3.6	6.1	5.7	6.2	6.6	6.8	4.2	2.0	1.6	1.1	1.3	1.2	1.5	1.4	1.6	1.8	8.8	9.5	9.1	9.5	9.6
Investment trusts				1.6	1.5	2.1	2.5	2.0	1.2	1.3	1.2	1.3	1.6	1.3	1.7	2.5	2.4	1.9	2.1	1.7	1.8	2.1	1.4
Other financial institutions	11.3	10.5	6.8	0.7	0.8	0.4	0.4	0.6	1.3	2.7	3.1	2.8	7.2	7.7	8.3	8.2	9.6	10.0	12.3	6.6	7.1	8.1	8.1
Charities	2.1	2.3	2.2	1.9	2.4	1.8	1.6	1.3	1.9	1.4	1.3	1.4	1.0	1.1	1.2	1.1	0.9	0.8	0.9	0.6	1.1	1.0	0.5
Private non-financial companies	5.1	3.0	5.1	2.8	3.3	1.8	1.5	1.1	1.2	1.4	2.2	1.5	1.0	0.8	0.7	0.6	1.8	3.0	2.2	2.3	2.0	2.2	2.6
Public sector	1.5	3.6	3.0	2.0	1.3	1.8	1.3	0.8	0.1	0.1	0.1	–	–	0.1	0.1	0.1	0.1	1.1	3.0	2.5	2.6	1.1	0.9
Banks	1.3	0.7	0.3	0.7	0.2	0.5	0.6	0.4	0.1	0.6	1.0	1.4	1.3	2.1	2.2	2.7	3.4	3.5	2.5	1.9	1.4	1.8	2.1
Total	100.0	100.0	100.0	100.0	100.0	100.0	100.0	100.0	100.0	100.0	100.0	100.0	100.0	100.0	100.0	100.0	100.0	100.0	100.0	100.0	100.0	100.0	100.0

Note: The percentages may not total 100 due to rounding errors.

Source: Office for National Statistics (www.ons.gov.uk/economy/investmentpensionsandtrusts/datasets/ownershipofukshares).

contrast, the US response to various crises has been highly prescriptive legislation such as the 2002 Sarbanes–Oxley Act, the response to the Enron scandal, and the 2010 Dodd–Frank Act, the response to the 2008 financial crisis (Goergen, 2018).

2.1.3 Listing and Disclosure Rules

Goergen and Renneboog (2001) reviewed the recent history on ownership disclosure in the United Kingdom. It was in 1945 that the Cohen committee recommended that beneficial ownership of shares should be disclosed. A holding is beneficial if the holder receives the cash flows (typically the dividends) generated by the holding. Otherwise, the holding would be a non-beneficial holding. This distinction is typically made for tax purposes: a company director may hold non-beneficial holdings for the benefit of their spouse or infant children, but the dividends are earned by the actual owners of these holdings.

Again, it is important to note that UK company law tends to use the all-encompassing term *member* to refer to both the shareholders of a public limited company and the associates of companies without shares. In particular, Section 113 of the Companies Act 2006 (which was preceded by the Companies Act 1985) requires every company to hold a register of members. This register has to include information about each member, including their name and address, the number of shares (assuming the company has shares) they hold (of each class, if the company has more than one class of shares) and the date when they became a member. When they cease to become a member, the relevant date also has to be entered into the register.

For both listed and unlisted companies with shares, the disclosure threshold was 5% from 1985 to 1989, when it was reduced to 3%. The members of the board of directors have to disclose their interests and changes in their stakes regardless of the number of shares they hold. Finally, the Financial Conduct Authority (FCA) is the body in charge of the rules governing the disclosure of share ownership in UK listed firms. It doubles up as the UK Listing Authority (UKLA).[1] The

---

[1] The FCA has gradually phased out the term 'UKLA' starting in 2017 as it claimed that the term confused its stakeholders who often mistakenly concluded that the UKLA was a separate body from the FCA. However, the UKLA was merely a term used to designate the FCA's primary market functions. See www.fca.org.uk/markets/primary-markets (consulted on 17 June 2020).

rules reflect the EU Transparency Directive (2013/50/EU). A person[2] must notify the company if the percentage of his *voting rights* exceeds or falls below 3%, 4%, 5%, 6%, 7%, 8%, 9%, 10% and each 1% threshold thereafter up to 100%.[3]

Turning to a detailed discussion of the evolution of ownership and control in UK listed companies, Table 2.1 suggests the following trends. First, while the majority of quoted shares was held by individuals in the early 1960s (see Goergen, 2018), ownership by individuals has experienced a steady decrease until 2012. However, recent years have seen a slight increase in this percentage from a low of 10.6% in 2012 to a high of 13.5% in 2018. Second, the percentage of shares held by foreign investors has been steadily rising with an almost fivefold increase experienced from 1990 (11.8%) to 2018 (54.9%) (see also Ivanova 2017). Figure 2.1 shows the geographic distribution of foreign investors. The vast majority are from North America (51.3%) followed by Europe, a distant second (with 24.1%). Third, the percentage of quoted shares held by UK insurers was on the increase until 1997 when it reached its peak of 23.6%. However, since then it has suffered from a steady decrease, resulting in a low of only 4.0% in 2018. The decrease since 1997 can be explained by a gradual shift by insurers from UK shares to foreign shares and mutual funds (ONS 2020). Fourth, the percentage of quoted shares held by UK pension funds has been gradually falling from a high of 31.7% in 1990 to a low of 2.4% in 2018. Finally, other patterns worth mentioning include the following. The percentage of shares held by the public sector increased from 0.1% in 2006 to a high of 3.0% in 2010, as a result of the government rescuing a number of financial institutions. However, since 2012 this percentage has been declining. Moreover, while the

---

[2] In UK Company Law and various legal and regulatory documents, the term 'person' as well as the pronouns 'he' and 'him' may refer to both 'individuals' and 'bodies corporate' (companies). See Mayson, French and Ryan (1996), section 0.1.9 'A note on terminology' for more detail. The term 'individual' is used if corporations are to be excluded. See also Goergen and Renneboog (2001).

[3] See *FCA Handbook*, DTR 5.3 'Notification of voting rights arising from the holding of certain financial instruments' as well as DTR 5.1 'Notification of the acquisition or disposal of major shareholdings' (in particular, DTR 5.1.2) (www .handbook.fca.org.uk/handbook/DTR/, consulted on 17 June 2020). Again, from 1985 to 1989, the threshold was 5% (Goergen and Renneboog, 2001).

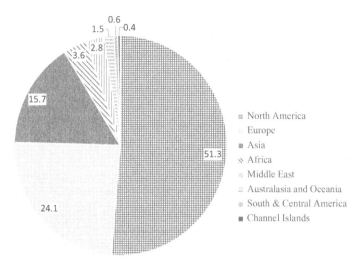

Figure 2.1 Geographic distribution of ownership (%) by foreign investors (on 31 December 2018), United Kingdom.

Note: The Channel Islands include Jersey, Guernsey and the Isle of Man. Asia excludes the Middle East. The Middle East includes Bahrain, Israel, Jordan, Kuwait, Lebanon, Oman, Qatar, Saudi Arabia and the United Arab Emirates.

Source: Office for National Statistics (2018, section 9).

percentage of shares held by non-financial institutions has been modest over 1990–2018, in recent years this percentage has recovered and is now just below 3%.

2.2 The Data

Similar to other chapters in this book, this chapter is based on four unique datasets – partly drawn from the Amadeus and Orbis databases provided by Bureau van Dijk (BvD) – on the ownership of the hundred largest domestic non-financial firms (measured by average total assets) and all the domestic listed non-financial firms in the United Kingdom for the 1990s (typically 1995–1997) and the 2010s (typically 2018–2019). The collection and construction of the datasets are described in the introductory chapter of this volume. All companies are cross-checked with the help of the London Share Price Database (LSPD) and Standard & Poor's Capital IQ. All companies must have the United Kingdom as their country of incorporation. Listed companies also must have an International Securities Identification Number (ISIN) starting with the country code 'GB',[4] and have their primary listing on the LSE, including the Official List, the Unlisted Securities Market (USM) and the Alternative Investment Market (AIM), as evidenced by their ticker symbol. Finally, additional checks are performed with the help of LSPD and the Companies House website for companies with missing information.

2.3 The Ownership Structure

Table 2.2 reports descriptive statistics on the ownership concentration of the top 100, the top 20 and the listed companies for the United Kingdom in the 1990s. For all three types of company, the average (median) shareholding of the largest shareholder falls well below the cut-off point of 20%, ranging from 13.95% for the top 20 companies to 16.04% for the top 100 companies. This implies that the average (median) UK company is widely held. In contrast, in the rest of Europe most companies tend to have a large shareholder. Also, in direct contrast to the rest of Europe, the second- and third-largest shareholders tend to be relatively large, when compared to the largest shareholder, with an average shareholding ranging from 7.36% to 8.89% and from 4.26% to 6.03%, respectively. These patterns confirm those observed by Goergen and Renneboog (2001) for the United Kingdom for the period 1988–1992.

Table 2.3 shows the percentages of listed companies and 100%-owned subsidiaries among the top 20 and top 100 companies for the 1990s. Sixty percent and 68% of the top 20 and top 100 companies, respectively, are listed on the LSE. Conversely, for both the top 20 and top 100 companies, the percentage of 100%-owned subsidiaries is negligible. In subsequent discussions, we shall see how both the percentage of listed companies and the percentage of fully owned subsidiaries changed significantly over time.

Table 2.4 focuses on the category of the largest shareholder. The table confirms that the vast majority, that is just above three-quarters, of the top 100 companies are widely held. The percentage of widely held listed companies is similar at 79%, whereas the percentage of

---

[4] Both criteria eliminate a number of companies incorporated in the Channel Islands as well as some overseas territories of the United Kingdom, including the Falklands and the Turks and Caicos Islands.

Table 2.2 Ownership concentration in the 1990s in the United Kingdom

	Number of firms	Largest shareholder (C1)[a]				Second-largest shareholder (C2)[a]				Third-largest shareholder (C3)[a]				All largest shareholders (largest SH)[b]			
		Min.	Med.	Mean	Max.	Min.	Med.	Mean	Max.	Min.	Med.	Mean	Max.	Min.	Med.	Mean	Max.
Top 100[c]	100	3.01	8.86	16.04	100.00	3.00	5.05	7.36	35.80	2.10	4.04	5.05	13.40	10.03	24.60	34.53	100.00
Top 20[d]	20	3.01	6.65	13.95	99.60	3.10	4.50	8.89	27.70	2.10	3.85	4.26	7.00	10.06	24.02	35.34	99.60
Listed[e]	537	1.10	11.41	15.79	74.20	1.70	7.50	8.66	55.89	1.40	5.30	6.03	16.50	10.00	23.90	28.71	81.10

Notes:

[a] The table shows results for the first year with available ownership data in the 1990s. C1, C2 and C3 are the shareholding in % of the largest, second- and third-largest shareholder in a company, respectively.

[b] Largest SH is the total share stake of all shareholders holding 10% or more of the shares outstanding of a company.

[c] Top 100 are the largest 100 firms (both listed and unlisted) in the United Kingdom.

[d] Top 20 are the largest 20 firms (both listed and unlisted) in the United Kingdom.

[e] Listed are listed firms in the United Kingdom.

Source: Bureau van Dijk (1999), Amadeus database, own calculations.

Table 2.3 *Percentage of listed companies and 100%-owned subsidiaries in the top 20 and top 100 in the 1990s in the United Kingdom*

	Listed	Subsidiaries (100% owned)
Top 20	60%	0%
Top 100	68%	1%

Source: Bureau van Dijk (1999), Amadeus database, own calculations.

widely held companies in the top 20 is higher – as one would expect – at 85%. Given the small number of companies with a large shareholder in the top 100, it is difficult to identify any clear patterns in the importance of specific categories of shareholders. The same point can be made about the listed companies.

Moving onto the descriptive statistics for UK corporate ownership in 2018–2019, Table 2.5 suggests that the patterns revealed for the 1990s for listed firms still hold. Importantly, although there is a slight increase in ownership concentration, the average listed UK firm is still widely held. Also similar to the 1990s, the second- and third-largest shareholders are relatively large when compared to the largest shareholder.

In contrast, there has been a significant increase in ownership concentration for the top 20 and top 100 companies. The average equity stake of the largest shareholder in the top 20 companies is now 67.58% compared to only 13.95% in the 1990s. A similar increase for the top 100 companies can be observed with the average stake of the largest shareholder now being 77.58% compared to 16.04% in the earlier period.

Why do we observe such a large increase in ownership concentration for the United Kingdom over time? Table 2.6 provides an answer to this question. First, the percentage of listed firms in the top 20 (top 100) has decreased substantially from 60% (68%) to 35% (19%). Second, while the average listed firm is still widely held as was the case during the 1990s, its free float has also fallen from 79% (see Table 2.4) to 67% in 2018–2019 (see Table 2.7). Third, the percentage of fully owned subsidiaries has also increased substantially from zero (near zero) to 50% (58%) for the top 20 (top 100) companies. A visual inspection of these fifty-eight fully owned subsidiaries among the top 100 companies reveals the following patterns. A few of these fully owned subsidiaries used to be independent, listed companies such as Grandmetropolitan

Table 2.4 *Largest shareholders by ownership categories in the 1990s in the United Kingdom*

Ownership categories[a]	Top 100 (percentage of firms)[b]	Min.[c]	Med.	Mean	Max.	Top 20 (percentage of firms)[b]	Min.[c]	Med.	Mean	Max.	Listed (percentage of firms)[b]	Min.[c]	Med.	Mean	Max.
Families/ individuals	2	39.00	44.50	44.50	50.00						5.96	20.38	31.80	37.22	74.20
State	1	99.60	99.60	56.33	99.60	5	99.60	99.60	99.60	99.60	0.19	28.52	28.52	28.52	28.52
Non-financial	3	26.80	42.20	56.33	100.00						2.79	20.00	29.10	36.67	59.20
Financial	6	20.97	29.66	36.38	61.80	5	33.50	33.50	33.50	33.50	5.59	20.33	28.96	34.65	72.25
Holdings											2.98	21.00	32.34	37.39	68.20
Others	4	24.60	30.30	31.23	39.70	5	27.10	27.10	27.10	27.10	2.42	20.00	29.40	32.76	57.30
Foreign	6	30.61	59.50	49.23	69.73						1.49	21.36	38.02	40.22	63.00
Dispersed	78	3.01	6.62	7.79	19.80	85	3.01	5.90	6.99	18.00	78.58	1.10	10.13	10.24	19.90
Total	*100*					*100*					*100*				
Number of firms	100					20					537				

Notes:

[a] The table shows results for the first year with available ownership data in the 1990s. We identify the company's direct controlling owner as the largest shareholder holding 20% or more of the shares outstanding. When no single entity owns at least 20%, a company is categorized as having dispersed ownership. Ownership categories: Families/individuals, state, non-financial firms, financial (banks, other financial institutions) and holdings are domestic shareholders. Foreign are all foreign shareholders (physical and legal persons).

[b] Percentage of firms is the percentage of firms controlled by each ownership category or with dispersed ownership.

[c] The descriptive statistics (min., med., mean and max.) are based on the percentage stake of the ownership category in firms controlled by this ownership category.

Source: Bureau van Dijk (1999), Amadeus database, own calculations.

Table 2.5 *Ownership concentration in 2018–2019 in the United Kingdom*

	Number of firms	Largest shareholder (C1)[a]				Second-largest shareholder (C2)[a]				Third-largest shareholder (C3)[a]				All largest shareholders (largest SH)[b]			
		Min.	Med.	Mean	Max.	Min.	Med.	Mean	Max.	Min.	Med.	Mean	Max.	Min.	Med.	Mean	Max.
Top 100[c]	100	0.48	100.00	77.58	100.00	0.01	3.98	9.08	38.88	0.01	2.13	3.04	13.67	10.78	100.00	91.46	100.00
Top 20[d]	20	2.12	100.00	67.58	100.00	0.02	2.24	2.82	9.46	0.01	0.10	1.54	3.92	10.78	100.00	83.58	100.00
Listed[e]	924	0.18	14.92	18.85	92.34	0.01	9.44	10.06	35.16	0.01	6.42	6.78	24.52	10.00	30.27	35.05	98.83

Notes:
[a] C1, C2 and C3 are the shareholdings in % of the largest, second- and third-largest shareholder in a company, respectively.
[b] Largest SH is the total share stake of all shareholders holding 10% or more of the shares outstanding of a company.
[c] Top 100 are the largest 100 firms (both listed and unlisted) in the United Kingdom.
[d] Top 20 are the largest 20 firms (both listed and unlisted) in the United Kingdom.
[e] Listed are listed firms in the United Kingdom.
Source: Bureau van Dijk (2020), Orbis database, own calculations.

Table 2.6 *Percentage of listed companies and 100%-owned subsidiaries in the top 20 and top 100 in 2018–2019 in the United Kingdom*

	Listed	Subsidiaries (100% owned)
Top 20	35%	50%
Top 100	19%	58%

Source: Bureau van Dijk (2020), Orbis database, own calculations.

Plc, which was acquired by Diageo Plc in 1997. Most are subsidiaries of UK listed companies – such as BT Group Investments Limited, which operates as a subsidiary of BT Group Plc, and B.A.T. Industries Plc, which is a subsidiary of British American Tobacco Plc – or subsidiaries of foreign companies – such as Dell International Holdings Limited. Such subsidiaries might be set up for regulatory reasons and/or for tax reasons. For example, as BT Group Plc is engaged in the regulated telecommunications industry, it might ring-fence its regulated companies from companies operating in unregulated industries. Finally, five of these fully owned subsidiaries[5] have links with the former Hanson Plc. Hanson Trust, the precursor of Hanson Plc, was founded in 1964 by James Hanson, who later became Lord Hanson. James Hanson acquired a number of underperforming companies and then turned them back into profitable businesses. As Hanson frequently split up businesses, getting rid of what he considered to be deadweight, he was repeatedly accused of being an asset stripper (The Independent, 2004). After Lord Hanson retired in 1997, Hanson Plc focused on building materials. In 2007, the German company Heidelberg Cement AG then took over Hanson Plc.

Table 2.7 suggests that the percentage of listed companies with a foreign shareholder as their largest shareholder has increased substantially from only 1.49% to 16.13%. This confirms the pattern observed in Table 2.1. Table 2.7 also confirms that most of the fully owned subsidiaries in Table 2.6 are owned by non-financial companies as well as by holding companies. Nevertheless, and similar to the 1990s, the

---

[5] These include Hanson Quarry Products Europe Limited, Hanson Holdings (1) Limited, Hanson Overseas Holdings Limited, Hanson Limited (the former Hanson Plc) and Hanson Building Materials Limited.

Table 2.7 *Largest shareholders by ownership categories in 2018–2019 in the United Kingdom*

Ownership categories[a]	Top 100 (percentage of firms)[b]	Min.[c]	Med.	Mean	Max.	Top 20 (percentage of firms)[b]	Min.[c]	Med.	Mean	Max.	Listed (percentage of firms)[b]	Min.[c]	Med.	Mean	Max.
Families/individuals	2	24.35	62.18	62.18	100.00	5	100.00	100.00	100.00	100.00	6.17	20.27	32.85	35.17	68.60
State	1	100.00	100.00	100.00	100.00	5	100.00	100.00	100.00	100.00	0.10	86.40	86.40	86.40	86.40
Non-financial	38	44.31	100.00	95.51	100.00	35	86.21	100.00	98.03	100.00	2.71	20.60	27.24	35.26	71.54
Financial	7	97.88	100.00	99.69	100.00	5	99.99	99.99	99.99	99.99	6.17	20.00	26.00	29.65	72.65
Holdings	21	61.66	100.00	94.93	100.00	10	100.00	100.00	100.00	100.00	1.84	20.00	26.32	32.05	65.11
Others															
Foreign	14	21.99	100.00	78.47	100.00	10	27.31	63.66	63.66	100.00	16.13	20.17	28.92	34.52	92.34
Dispersed	17	0.48	5.00	6.72	13.02	30	2.12	4.62	6.36	13.02	66.88	0.18	11.06	11.43	19.99
Total	*100*					*100*					*100*				
Number of firms	100					20					924				

Notes:

[a] We identify the company's direct controlling owner as the largest shareholder holding 20% or more of the shares outstanding. When no single entity owns at least 20%, a company is categorized as having dispersed ownership. Ownership categories: Families/individuals, state, non-financial firms, financial (banks, other financial institutions) and holdings are domestic shareholders. Foreign are all foreign shareholders. Foreign are all foreign shareholders (physical and legal persons).

[b] Percentage of firms is the percentage of firms controlled by each ownership category or with dispersed ownership.

[c] The descriptive statistics (min., med., mean and max.) are based on the percentage stake of the ownership category in firms controlled by this ownership category.

Source: Bureau van Dijk (2020), Orbis database, own calculations.

vast majority of listed UK companies are widely held, and it is difficult to identify any clear patterns in the relative frequency of the various categories of large shareholders given the small number of companies that are not widely held.

To sum up, over the period ranging from the late 1990s to 2018–2019, the percentage of listed companies in the top 20 and top 100 has seen a marked drop while the percentage of fully owned subsidiaries among the top UK companies has increased from near zero to the majority of such companies. The average listed UK company is still widely held in 2018–2019 (see Goergen and Renneboog, 2001).

2.4 The Determinants of Ownership Changes

We observed an increase in ownership concentration from the 1990s to the late 2010s across the board, that is, for the top 20, top 100 and to a lesser extent all listed firms. Nevertheless, one needs to be careful when drawing inferences and one needs to avoid concluding hastily that the average UK firm is moving away from being a widely held company. For example, some of the firms that appear in the 2018–2019 top 100 list are relatively newly created subsidiaries of some of the largest listed UK firms. For example, in 2005 GlaxoSmithKline Plc created GlaxoSmithKline Holdings Limited, the latter being in the top 20 firms for 2018–2019. Similarly, British Telecommunications Plc, as a result of a 2001 reorganization, is now a 100%-owned subsidiary of BT Group Plc.[6] Section 2.3 mentions other similar examples of firms that were created via mergers and demergers. Concerning listed companies, a possible reason for the slight increase in ownership concentration might be due to the success of the Alternative Investment Market (AIM), which was created in 1995 as a second-tier segment of the LSE (Espenlaub and Khurshed, 2012). In contrast to the Official List, the first-tier segment of the LSE, which required a minimum of 25% of the equity shares to be dispersed with small shareholders immediately after the initial public offering (IPO), the AIM did not have a requirement about a minimum free float.

---

[6] BT Group plc was founded in 2001 when the mmO2 business (BT's mobile activities in the United Kingdom, the Netherlands, Germany and the Republic of Ireland) was spun off (BT Group, 2002).

We also observed that individual ownership of corporations in the United Kingdom was gradually replaced by institutional ownership. Armour and Skeel (2007) suggest at least two reasons why this is the case. First, taxation discriminated in favour of institutional shareholders and against individuals. In detail, pension funds were exempt from tax on dividends while insurance companies benefited from more limited tax relief. In contrast, the tax rate applied to investment income earned by individuals was 90% from the end of World War II until 1974 when it rose to 98% and stayed at that level until 1979. The increase in corporate ownership by institutional investors carried on until the early 1990s but then dropped thereafter (see Table 2.1; see also subsequent discussions). Although the Thatcher government started a privatization process of state-owned businesses in 1979–1983, which carried on until the 2000s, with the explicit aim of increasing individual ownership (including employee ownership), it failed to achieve this aim (Goergen, 2018; see also Table 2.1).

Second, frequently the heirs of the company founder, given the high tax on dividend income, would prefer to sell their shares rather than hold onto them after the founder had passed away (Bank and Cheffins, 2008). Typically, the buyers of such shares were institutional shareholders. Given their increasing ownership, institutional investors were also the main drivers behind corporate governance regulation and best practice (Armour and Skeel, 2007): They[7] gradually pressured UK companies to get rid of any devices counter to the one-share, one-vote rule (Grossman and Hart, 1988), such as non-voting shares and anti-takeover mechanisms. This resulted in an active market for corporate control in the United Kingdom compared to the rest of Europe where this market remained underdeveloped.

In 1997, UK pension funds lost their favourable tax status (Trapp, 1997; Bond, Devereux and Klemm, 2007), which explains at least in part the downward trend in their share of UK corporate ownership (see Table 2.1) over 1998–2018. In addition (see also Section 2.2), 1997 witnessed the start of a decrease in corporate ownership held by UK insurance companies. As highlighted in Section 2.2, this trend was not

---

[7] UK institutional investors are typically represented by the Association of British Insurers (ABI) and the National Association of Pension Funds (NAPF). For example, the Committee on Corporate Governance, which was set up in 1995, was chaired by Sir Ronald Hampel and in 1998 published its final report, had input from the ABI and the NAPF.

only due to insurers moving from UK shares to foreign shares but also due to mutual funds given a shift from an active investing strategy to a passive one (ONS, 2020). Why did this shift happen? According to Warburton (2012), the 1997 change in regulation that permitted corporations to enter the fund management industry (previously, only trusts could operate in the industry) resulted in a significant and sudden increase in competition.[8] As a result, many actively managed funds moved to passive management given that in the past they had not performed sufficiently well for their risk-adjusted returns to cover their management fees. Finally, Bond et al. (2007) argue that the 1997 tax reform would also have negatively affected the equity holdings of those insurance companies that provided pension plans. This explains the decline in the ownership held by insurance companies, including the smaller magnitude of this decline when compared to pension funds.

In turn, the steady increase in corporate ownership by foreign investors was mainly due to the greater internationalization of the LSE, which made it increasingly easy for foreign investors, especially foreign individuals, to acquire shares in UK companies, for example via electronic trading platforms (ONS, 2020). Further, Bond et al. (2007) argue that the increase in ownership by foreign investors can at least be partly explained by the reduced attractiveness for UK equity securities for UK pension funds given the 1997 tax reform.

Finally, the UK government had to rescue a number of banks because of the 2008 financial crisis. This resulted in an increase in corporate ownership held by the UK government over 2008–2010. For example, in 2009 Her Majesty's (HM) Treasury took a 43.4% stake in the Lloyds Banking Group and a 70.3% stake in the Royal Bank of Scotland. It then reduced its stake in Lloyds in 2013 and finally sold the remaining shares in 2016. However, at the end of 2019, the UK government still owned 62.1% of the Royal Bank of Scotland's equity (Royal Bank of Scotland, 2019). This would explain why UK government ownership of corporations was still higher in 2018 (see Table 2.1) than in the pre-crisis year 2006.

---

[8] As highlighted by Warburton (2012), the main difference between trusts and corporations is that the latter offer greater limited liability protection for managers. Hence, allowing corporations to operate in this industry significantly decreased the originally high costs of entry.

2.5 Conclusion

Although the United Kingdom has experienced marked changes in the importance of different categories of shareholders over the last three decades, UK corporate ownership is still widely held in contrast to the rest of Europe where ownership and/or control tend to be concentrated and lie with one or a small number of shareholders. In addition, the second- and third-largest shareholders in the average UK company tend to be relatively large compared to the largest shareholder, whereas this is not the case in the average company from Continental Europe.

Nevertheless, it needs to be seen how Brexit will affect corporate ownership in the United Kingdom over the next decades. For example, Brexit may cause an increase in the number of UK companies being owned by US investors, possibly caused by an opening up of the UK National Health Service (NHS), followed by its gradual privatization.[9] Moreover, Tielmann and Schiereck (2017) provide preliminary evidence that post-Brexit UK companies might be relatively cheap takeover targets compared to companies elsewhere in Europe (see also Bloom et al., 2019). This could lead to further increases in foreign ownership of UK companies over the next few decades. In turn, ownership of companies based in the remaining twenty-seven EU member states held by UK companies may increase as the latter establish subsidiaries within the EU to guarantee their access to the Single Market post-Brexit (Breinlich et al., 2019). Likewise, companies from the twenty-seven EU member states may want to set up subsidiaries in the United Kingdom to ensure access to the British market post-Brexit.

---

[9] At the time of writing this chapter, it was as yet not entirely clear whether opening up the NHS to private health providers from the United States would be part of the conditions for a US–UK trade agreement (see e.g. Williams, 2020). Nevertheless, the UK government already seemed to be in a process to covertly privatize the NHS via outsourcing large chunks of its services to the private sector (see e.g. *The Guardian*, 2020).

PART II

Central European Countries

3 | Austria

KLAUS GUGLER, EVGENI PEEV AND
MARTIN WINNER

3.1 Introduction

In this chapter, we use several datasets to trace the ownership and
control structures in Austria a few decades ago and compare them to
the situation today. In particular, we first take a look at samples of the
600 largest non-financial corporations in Austria in 1996 (covering
about 30% of GDP at that time), of the top 20 and top 100 non-
financial firms and of listed non-financial companies in Austria in the
mid-1990s. We compare these samples to samples of Austrian firms in
the years 2018–2019. Moreover, we compare a sample of ultimate
ownership from the mid-1990s to a sample of ultimate ownership
in 2015.

We find that first, and most importantly, ownership concentration
was and is very high in Austria. Listed firms' samples in the mid-1990s
display majority control, on average, as do listed firm samples today.
Thus, the large shareholder control model was and is the predominant
corporate governance feature even in Austrian listed firms. The large
shareholder model was and is even more important in non-listed firms,
and if anything, ownership concentration has increased in the past
decades. The largest shareholder held around 60% of the shares in
the top 100 firms in the mid-1990s, while holding around 75% now.
Second, the identities of these controlling shareholders remained very
much the same during this time period with one important exception,
banks. Thus, while the state, ultimately family-controlled firms, and
foreign investors remained important ownership and control categories in top Austrian corporations, banks lost their significance in holding the equity of the largest companies. Finally, the widely held
corporation does not appear to become anywhere near a role model
for the Austrian corporation. While we witnessed an increase in the
number of widely held firms in the past decades in Austria, their
economic significance remains minor.

Prominent researchers have predicted convergence to Anglo-American corporate governance and ownership structures, that is widely held firms. For example, Hansmann and Kraakman (2001) claimed that the basic law of the corporate form has already achieved a high degree of uniformity and the ideology of shareholder primacy is likely to press all major jurisdictions towards similar rules of corporate law and practice. Franks and Mayer (2001) argued that competition between stock exchanges, the dismantling of control-enhancing mechanisms and the development of a market for corporate control might gradually produce a convergence of the ownership structures of German and Anglo-American stock markets. We cannot confirm these predictions for Austria. We identify a few 'complementary institutions' (see Deakin, Sarkar and Siems, 2018) that hinder this convergence. Among them are (1) the preferences of shareholders for establishing and preserving corporate control, (2) the risk aversion of Austrian people impeding equity investment, (3) the missing political will to embrace a more shareholder-oriented model and (4) the unwillingness to privatize the remaining state-controlled companies. Moreover, viable substitutes to the widely held company appear to exist, that is the 'Hausbank system', which is still an important provider of debt and the internal capital markets of foreign multinationals.

This chapter is structured as follows. Section 3.2 presents an overview of the main organizational forms and corporate governance reforms in Austria. Section 3.3 describes the data. Section 3.4 analyses the ownership structure of large firms and its development over the past decades. Section 3.5 discusses the determinants of ownership change. Conclusions are drawn in Section 3.6.

3.2 Corporate Governance Legal and Institutional Reforms

3.2.1 Organizational Forms

We provide an overview of the main forms of business organization in Austria for large companies.

3.2.1.1 Joint-Stock Company

A joint-stock company (*Aktiengesellschaft* (AG)) can be established by one or more shareholders. The required minimum share capital is

EUR 70,000. Shareholders do not become liable for the company's debts, but can only forfeit the equity capital subscribed. The shares of a joint-stock company may be listed on a stock exchange. The structure of joint-stock companies consists of an executive board (*Vorstand*), which is appointed by a supervisory board (*Aufsichtsrat*), whose role is to appoint and supervise the members of the executive board and to participate in key management decisions. The supervisory board is elected by the general meeting of shareholders (*Hauptversammlung*). The employees have co-determination rights to nominate representatives to the supervisory board (a third of the supervisory board's members).

3.2.1.2 Societas Europaea

A Societas Europaea (SE) or European Company is a type of joint-stock company regulated by EU law. The minimum capital of an SE is EUR 120,000. The shares of an SE may be listed on a stock exchange. An SE is incorporated in one EU member state and may have branches in other member states. An SE can facilitate cross-border transactions and move the company headquarters among the EU member states. The organizational structure is more flexible than the structure of the Austrian joint-stock company because the board of directors may be organized following a single-tier or a two-tier system.

3.2.1.3 Limited Liability Company (GmbH)

A limited liability company – *Gesellschaft mit beschränkter Haftung* (GmbH) – is the prevailing legal form of business organizations in Austria. As with the joint-stock company, members do not become liable for the company's debts, but can only forfeit the equity capital subscribed. The minimum share capital of a limited liability company is EUR 35,000. The managing directors are appointed by the members. Establishing a supervisory board consisting of at least three board members is voluntary, but under specific conditions (especially if the average number of employees exceeds 300) will become mandatory.

3.2.2 *Legal Rules for Listed Companies*

Austrian listed companies are incorporated in the form of a joint-stock company and less frequently in the form of an SE. The most relevant sources of law for listed companies are as follows:

(1) the Stock Exchange Act, which regulates disclosure rules and contains supplementary rules on insider trading, market manipulation and directors' dealings;
(2) the Joint Stock Companies Act, the Societas Europaea Act and the SE Regulation, which regulate the organizational framework for the company;
(3) the Takeover Act, which regulates public takeover bids;
(4) the Commercial Code, which – together with additional legislation – specifies the accounting rules;
(5) the Accounting Control Act, which stipulates mechanisms to ensure that financial and other information presented by listed companies complies with national and international accounting standards;
(6) regulations by the Austrian Financial Market Authority;
(7) the Austrian Corporate Governance Code, which contains best practice rules for listed companies.

The Corporate Governance Code is non-binding and only applies to listed companies that have committed themselves to complying with it. However, such a commitment is one of the requirements for companies to be listed on the prime market segment of the Vienna Stock Exchange. Listed companies have to publish a corporate governance report together with the annual financial statements. This report has to include, in a corporate governance statement, information about the company's commitment to the Corporate Governance Code (e.g. whether and for what reasons the company deviates from comply-or-explain rules of the Code).

3.2.3 Ownership Disclosure of Unlisted Companies

All companies must be registered in the Austrian Commercial Register (*Firmenbuch*), which is open to the public. Owners' identity and ownership information of GmbHs and the identity of any subsequent members pursuant to a transfer of shares must be registered in the *Firmenbuch*.

Unlisted joint-stock companies and SEs must keep an updated share register. The members of the executive board are responsible for keeping the company's share register in line with the legal requirements. In any case, the share register kept by the company is not open to inspection by the general public, but only by fellow shareholders. If a person (e.g. a shareholder) is of the opinion that the share register is kept inadequately, this person can inform the court, which then may review the situation and impose a fine if appropriate. All companies are obliged to keep records for seven years.

There is no corresponding obligation for listed companies, which instead of registered shares have to issue bearer shares and have to make use of the services of a central securities depository. Hence, any transaction in the shares takes place via deposit bookings, making use of the banking system.

3.2.4 Ownership Disclosure of Listed Companies

Shareholders of listed companies are under a statutory obligation to notify the company, the Stock Exchange and the Financial Market Authority if their shareholding (whether direct or indirect) reaches, exceeds or falls below one of the following thresholds: 4%, 5%, 10%, 15%, 20%, 25%, 30%, 35%, 40%, 45%, 50%, 75% and 90% of the voting rights. Companies can additionally set 3% as a further relevant threshold in their articles. These notifications are subsequently published by the listed company, typically within four trading days. Quite clearly, the ownership disclosure is concerned with influence on the company and not financial returns, as only the acquisition of voting shares triggers the notification obligation.

A major issue in practice concerns the aggregation of individual holdings, for example those held by shareholders who are part of a shareholders' agreement; here, notifications tend to be confusing and may in individual cases not properly reflect reality. Similarly, the disclosure obligation does not only cover the acquisition of shares themselves, but also of options or other rights to these shares; hence, the notification does not only purport to inform about current shareholdings, but also about likely future changes in these holdings.

This already shows that while the idea of disclosure of major shareholdings is conceptually simple, the details tend to be vexingly complicated, as the issue of cash-settled derivatives shows. In theory, such derivatives do not result in the rightholder receiving shares, but a cash settlement reflecting the difference between the market value and, for example, the option's strike price. In practice, however, the writer of the option has to hedge its position by acquiring the shares and, upon settlement of the option, has a strong incentive to offer these shares in lieu of the cash payment originally agreed upon. As a result, such cash-settled instruments have been employed in order to avoid disclosure, which originally only covered derivatives giving a right to the shares.[1] This example shows that recent developments strive to improve the system by covering all comparable instances. However, this comes at the price of increasing complexity.[2] Additionally, listed companies and their directors are subject to various disclosure requirements under the Stock Exchange Act – which are based on the EU's Market Abuse Regulation (MAR) – such as the publication of directors' dealings and ad hoc disclosure. Ad hoc disclosure is aimed at preventing insider trading, and requires listed companies to publish without undue delay any non-public information relating to the issuer that could have a material impact on the market price of the securities of the company.

The Beneficial Owners Register Act, which entered into force on 15 January 2018, requires listed and non-listed companies to maintain a register of its ultimate beneficial owners, and report the identity of its ultimate beneficial owners electronically to a newly established corporate service portal overseen by the Federal Ministry of Finance. First, according to the act as initially passed, this register was accessible for (1) public authorities; (2) credit and financial institutions, attorneys, auditors, tax advisers, as well as certain other professionals for the purpose of performing know-your-customer checks; and (3) any other person or entity that can prove a legitimate interest in connection with the prevention of money laundering or terrorist financing.

Second, recent amendments to the Beneficial Owners Register Act, which entered into force on 10 January 2020, led to far-reaching changes of the register, implementing the EU 5th Anti-Money Laundering Directive, on the one hand, and resulting in improvements in user-friendliness, on the other. According to these new rules, anyone is able to obtain an extract from the register of any legal entity. This extract contains the first name, last name, date of birth, nationality and country

---

[1] The legislators, both on the European and the national level, reacted by introducing rules covering cash-settled derivatives. However, they made disclosure obligatory not in the nominal amount of the contract, but on a delta-adjusted basis, which takes into account the amount of shares the writer of the option typically acquires for hedging purposes.

[2] Additionally, recent legislative activity increasingly concerns sanctions. On the one hand, administrative fines have been raised considerably, up to 5% of the perpetrator's annual turnover. On the other hand, non-disclosure results in disenfranchisement of voting rights, that is the perpetrator will lose his influence on the company, albeit ultimately only if other shareholders are aware of the violation and instigate proceedings to set aside a shareholder resolution.

of residence of the beneficial owner(s). However, a decision by the European Court of Justice from November 2022 has limited access to the data according to the 2018 model again.

Third, the reporting entity must register any changes identified or confirm that no changes have occurred at least annually. To ensure the accuracy and completeness of the registrations, the Austrian Ministry of Finance will compare the data entered in the register with other publicly available data sources (e.g. Commercial Register, Register of Associations, Central Register of Residents) and review registrations received on a random basis. The Ministry may at any time ask legal entities and their legal and beneficial owner(s) to provide information on the facts required for the assessment of the beneficial ownership and to submit corresponding documents.

Fourth, the penal provisions have been clarified and extended. Anyone who (1) makes an incorrect or incomplete notification and thereby fails to disclose beneficial owners, (2) fails to comply with the notification obligation despite two requests or (3) fails to register a change in the data of beneficial owners within four weeks of becoming aware of the change commits a financial offence with a fine of up to EUR 200,000 in the case of intent and of up to EUR 100,000 in the case of gross negligence. Equally, failure to keep copies of the documents and information necessary for compliance with the requirements to identify the beneficial owner(s) for at least five years after the end of the respective beneficial owner's ownership is also a financial offence (with a fine of up to EUR 75,000 in the case of intent and of up to EUR 25,000 in the case of gross negligence).

Under the Public Takeover Act, bidders must disclose their considerations, intentions or decisions regarding a mandatory or voluntary public takeover. The bidder shall immediately make public that its management and supervisory board have decided to make a bid or that circumstances have arisen triggering its obligation to make a bid. Additionally, the bidder has to make public that it is considering making a bid if rumours and speculations concerning the bid arise and there are reasonable grounds for assuming that these originate in the preparation of the bid by the bidder. After any such disclosure, the bidder has forty trading days to launch the bid; otherwise it is barred for one year ('put up or shut up'). These rules are designed to prevent the creation of false markets via rumours and to ensure that the offeree company is not hindered in the conduct of its affairs for longer than is reasonably necessary. To a certain extent they are similar to the disclosure of derivative positions within the major holdings regime as they try to give market participants insights into likely future changes in the ownership structure; additionally, takeover transparency strives to protect shareholders against selling their shares cheaply when a better offer is imminent.

3.2.5 Current Issues and Developments

Recently, the amendment to the Shareholders' Rights Directive (EU) 2017/828 of 17 May 2017 (EU Official Journal L-132/1) ('SRD II') aiming at the encouragement of long-term shareholder engagement led to a major development in corporate governance in Austria. This directive essentially comprises measures in the following four areas:

(1) special requirements for the identification of shareholders enabling direct communication between the company and its shareholders;
(2) increased transparency obligations for institutional investors, asset managers and proxy advisers to enable informed investor decisions;
(3) right to vote at the annual general meeting on the remuneration of members (via a remuneration policy and remuneration report) of the company management (management board and supervisory board) (say-on-pay);
(4) transparency and approval of transactions with related companies or individuals (related-party transactions).

On 23 July 2019, amendments to the Joint Stock Companies Act and the Stock Exchange Act implementing SRD II entered into force. When implementing the rules on the identification of shareholders, the Austrian legislator utilized the leeway provided by the Directive, giving listed companies the right to obtain information from intermediaries (banks) only on such shareholders with a holding of more than 0.5%. If financial institutions pass such shareholder information to companies upon their request, this will not qualify as a violation of banking secrecy. The information is designed to help the listed company to communicate with its shareholders ('know your shareholder'); due to the system of bearer shares, in the absence of such provisions the company is not able to identify its shareholders outside the general meeting and does not have to make the information public.

Additionally, institutional investors and asset managers are required to provide more transparency. They will need to publish how they will integrate shareholder involvement in their investment strategy and how the shareholder input has been implemented. Proxy advisers need to disclose which code of conduct they will apply and report on compliance with this code. Moreover, they will have to annually report on information gathering and processing and on potential conflicts of interests.

Quite clearly, over recent years Austria has tried to improve its corporate governance system, albeit often only after prodding by the European Union. This has positively affected the transparency on financial markets, which has been the focus of the above discussion. However, Austria has also introduced a number of rules to improve the investor's lot in substance, such as the mandatory bid rule once control over a listed company changes. Even if not all reforms have been focusing on minority shareholder – and hence investor – protection (see the recent regulation on related-party transactions, which is skewered towards management and dominant shareholders), in general the legal position of the investor has improved considerably. We turn to the issue of whether these improvements have brought forward deeper capital markets in Subsection 3.5.2.

3.3 The Data

In this country study, we use a few datasets. First, we examine a sample of the largest 600 non-financial corporations in Austria in 1996. Data about the 600 largest non-financial corporations in Austria (as measured by turnover) are provided by the Wirtschafts-Trend Zeitschriftenverlagsgesellschaft m.b.H[3] and are based on information collected by a credit-rating agency, the Österreichischer Kreditschutzverband von 1870, as well as information supplied by the corporations themselves. Ownership data are available for the year 1996. The sample includes companies employing about 25% of the Austrian workforce. The aggregate turnover of these companies accounts for about 30% of GDP. Second, we study samples of the top 20 and the top 100 non-financial firms (listed and non-listed), and a sample of listed non-financial companies in Austria at the two points

---

[3] The name of the CD-Rom is: trend TOP 500 CD-ROM.

in time: the mid-1990s and the years 2018–2019. The data collection and construction of samples are described in Chapter 1 of this volume. Third, we examine also a sample of ultimate ownership of the top 20 non-financial firms in Austria in 2015 (for data collection and construction of this sample, see Peev and Yalamov, 2020).

3.4 The Ownership Structures

3.4.1 Ownership Structures in the Mid-1990s

3.4.1.1 Ownership Concentration

Table 3.1 reports ownership concentration by company size of the 600 largest Austrian corporations in 1996. Direct ownership concentration is very high and prevalent in all size classes. Even in the largest 5% of the companies, the largest shareholder holds 67% of the equity on average. This percentage rises (though not monotonically) as companies become smaller, and the average largest stake in the 600 largest Austrian non-financial corporations is 82.2% (median 99.9%). In 297 companies, the largest stake is 100%. Only ninety-seven firms, have more than three owners.

Table 3.2 reports ownership concentration by company size of Austrian listed companies in 1996. Even for listed firms, ownership

Table 3.1 *Austrian 600 largest companies: Ownership concentration by company size and ownership stake size class, 1996*

Size classes by sales		Ownership distribution			
Class	Companies	Largest stake	2nd stake	3rd stake	Rest
95–100%	30	67.0	10.6	2.9	19.5
90–95%	30	84.1	4.1	1.0	10.8
75–90%	91	80.1	10.7	2.4	6.8
50–75%	149	83.4	9.8	1.3	5.5
25–50%	149	83.5	9.3	1.4	5.7
10–5%	91	83.9	9.2	2.1	4.8
5–10%	30	86.9	8.1	2.0	3.0
0–5%	30	78.3	11.6	3.9	6.2
All	600	82.2	9.5	1.9	6.5

Source: Trend, (www.trend.at), own calculations.

Table 3.2 *Austrian listed companies: Ownership concentration by company size and ownership stake size class, 1996*

Size classes by sales		Ownership distribution			
Class	Companies	Largest stake	2nd stake	3rd stake	Rest
75–100%	16	48.3	8.2	1.9	41.6
50–75%	15	59.6	15.5	3.1	21.8
25–50%	15	48.6	9.4	2.5	39.5
0–25%	16	53.3	9.6	3.9	33.2
All	62	52.4	10.6	2.9	34.1

Source: Trend, (www.trend.at), own calculations.

concentration remains very high. The largest shareholder owns on average 52.4% (median 53%).

Table 3.3 presents ownership concentration of the top 20 firms, top 100 firms and listed companies in Austria in the mid-1990s. In all samples, on average the largest shareholder owns a majority controlling stake. The second- and third-largest shareholders also own relatively large ownership stakes. The average stakes held by the second-largest shareholder range between 20% and 23%, and the third-largest shareholder on average owns a stake of around 15%. These results confirm that ownership concentration was indeed very high in the largest Austrian firms. Moreover, there are also large stakes held by the second- and third-largest shareholders.

3.4.1.2 Ownership Identities

Table 3.4 reports the direct largest shareholders by ownership categories of the top 20 firms, top 100 firms and the listed companies in Austria in the mid-1990s. In the top 20 sample, the state is the largest owner in 30% of firms. In the top 100 sample, other Austrian corporations (holdings, non-financial firms and financial companies) are the largest shareholders of 50% of firms, while foreign investors own about 21% and the state 10% of firms, respectively. Within these shareholder categories, majority control is the dominant corporate governance mechanism. In the listed companies, the most important largest shareholders are the state (22% of companies), foreign investors (22%) and Austrian financial institutions and holdings (each owning 17% of companies).

Table 3.3 *Ownership concentration in the 1990s in Austria*

	Number of firms	Largest shareholder (C1)[a]				Second-largest shareholder (C2)[a]				Third-largest shareholder (C3)[a]				All largest shareholders (Largest SH)[b]			
		Min.	Med.	Mean	Max.	Min.	Med.	Mean	Max.	Min.	Med.	Mean	Max.	Min.	Med.	Mean	Max.
Top 100[c]	58	10	52.2	59.48	100	1	21.3	21.94	49	5	15	15.55	24	10	71.71	73.15	100
Top 20[d]	20	10.8	51	52.8	100	5.5	19.35	19.99	37	5	17.38	15.46	24	10.8	59.45	64.59	100
Listed[e]	23	17.38	51	53.55	96.4	8.2	23.35	23.04	40.1	7.3	14	13.81	20	26	71	72.93	100

Notes:

[a] The table shows results for the first year with available ownership data in the 1990s. C1, C2 and C3 are the shareholdings in % of the largest, second- and third-largest shareholders in a company.

[b] Largest SH is the total share of all shareholders having 10% or more of outstanding shares in a company.

[c] Top 100 are the largest 100 firms (both listed and unlisted) in Austria.

[d] Top 20 are the largest 20 firms (both listed and unlisted) in Austria.

[e] Listed are listed firms in Austria.

Source: Bureau van Dijk (1999), Amadeus database, own calculations.

Table 3.4 *Largest shareholders by ownership categories in the 1990s in Austria*

Ownership categories[a]	Top 100					Top 20					Listed				
	(percentage of firms)[b]	Min.[c]	Med.	Mean	Max.	(percentage of firms)[b]	Min.[c]	Med.	Mean	Max.	(percentage of firms)[b]	Min.[c]	Med.	Mean	Max.
Families/individuals	8.62	31	48.6	55.72	100	10	48	49.5	49.5	51	4.35	51	51	51	51
State	10.34	26	51	58.87	96.4	30	26	51	58.87	96.4	21.74	26	51	62.88	96.4
Non-financial	17.24	35.9	80.7	78.91	100	15	60.2	100	86.73	100	8.7	35.9	58.75	58.75	81.6
Financial	12.07	35	52.1	56.04	72.41	5	66.36	66.36	66.36	66.36	17.39	35	50.2	50.44	66.36
Holdings	20.69	24	51	55.11	100	15	24	37.5	36.67	51	17.39	24	50.15	45.83	59
Others	5.17	45	56	54.67	63	5	63	63	63	63	4.35	56	56	56	56
Foreign	20.69	33.4	57.7	64.42	96.9	10	33.4	38	38	42.6	21.74	35.1	52.6	58.04	95
Dispersed	5.18	10	10.8	12.73	17.38	10	10.8	14.09	14.09	17.38	4.34	17.38	17.38	17.38	17.38
Total	100					100					100				
Number of firms	58					20					23				

Notes:

[a] The table shows results for the first year with available ownership data in the 1990s. We identify the company's direct controlling owner as the largest shareholder holding 20% or more of outstanding shares. When no single entity owned at least 20%, a company was categorized as having dispersed ownership. Ownership categories: Families/individuals, state, non-financial firms, financial (banks, other financial institutions) and holdings are domestic shareholders. Foreign are all foreign shareholders (physical and legal persons).

[b] Percentage of firms: percentage of firms controlled by each ownership category or with dispersed ownership.

[c] Descriptive statistics (min., med., mean and max.) are the percentage of ownership stake of the ownership category in firms controlled by this ownership category.

Source: Bureau van Dijk (1999), Amadeus database, own calculations.

3.4.2 Ownership Change and Persistence

How have Austrian ownership and control structures changed over the past decades? Table 3.5 shows ownership concentration of the top 20, top 100 and the listed companies in Austria in 2018–2019. In the top 20 and top 100 firms, we witness a significant increase in ownership concentration. This may be explained by the increase in the number of wholly owned subsidiaries among large Austrian firms from 10% to 50% of the top 20 and from 12% to 47% of the top 100 (Table 3.6). Moreover, there is a corresponding decrease in the number of listed firms from 45% of the top 20 (40% of the top 100) in the mid-1990s to 35% of the top 20 (21% of the top 100) in 2018–2019. Thus, it appears that large multinational companies increase their shareholdings, while the stock exchange does not serve as a source of external equity capital. This is the mirror image to countries such as Germany and Switzerland, where ownership concentration has decreased during the period analysed. These countries domicile many of the multinational corporations that increase corporate shareholdings or set up greenfield subsidiaries abroad. While they see decreasing ownership concentration, capital receiving countries such as Austria witness increasing ownership concentration.

Table 3.7 reports the direct largest shareholders by ownership categories of the top 20, the top 100 and the listed companies in Austria in 2018–2019. The table documents the persistence of Austrian non-financial firms and holding companies as the most important owners in the three samples of firms over nearly a quarter of century.

There are also ownership changes. Three major patterns of ownership change may be outlined. First, the rise of listed companies with dispersed ownership (widely held companies). The number of companies without a controlling (i.e. 20% or larger) shareholder has increased from 4% to 20%.[4] Yet, about 80% of the largest listed Austrian companies have a shareholder who owns more than 20% of the total shares outstanding in 2018–2019.

---

[4] Our data does not reflect shareholders agreement as a controlling device. Thus, the actual number of companies without a controlling shareholder is even lower than reported in Table 3.6. Nevertheless, this does not change our main findings and arguments for the low importance of widely held companies in Austria over the past decades.

Table 3.5 *Ownership concentration in 2018–2019 in Austria*

	Number of firms	Largest shareholder (C1)[a]				Second-largest shareholder (C2)[a]				Third-largest shareholder (C3)[a]				All largest shareholders (Largest SH)[b]			
		Min.	Med.	Mean	Max.	Min.	Med.	Mean	Max.	Min.	Med.	Mean	Max.	Min.	Med.	Mean	Max.
Top 100[c]	100	5	99.97	75.75	100	0.02	16.5	18.48	100	0.05	10	11.52	100	16.21	100	89.07	100
Top 20[d]	20	14.94	80.33	69.18	100	5.71	25.4	22.38	32.66	1.05	6.32	9.06	29.31	25.01	96.78	83.46	100
Listed[e]	54	5	47.7	44.33	100	1.17	11.01	15.93	52.9	0.07	5.4	6.62	20	11	64.88	61.48	100

Notes:

[a] C1, C2 and C3 are the shareholdings in % of the largest, second- and third-largest shareholders in a company.

[b] Largest SH is the total share of all shareholders having 10% or more of outstanding shares in a company.

[c] Top 100 are the largest 100 firms (both listed and unlisted) in Austria.

[d] Top 20 are the largest 20 firms (both listed and unlisted) in Austria.

[e] Listed are listed firms in Austria.

Source: Bureau van Dijk (2020), Orbis database, own calculations.

Table 3.6 *Percentage of listed companies and 100%-owned subsidiaries in the top 20 and top 100 in Austria*

	Listed	Subsidiaries (100% owned)
Mid-1990s		
Top 20	45%	10%
Top 100	40%	12%
2018–2019		
Top 20	35%	50%
Top 100	21%	47%

Source: Bureau van Dijk (1999), Amadeus database, own calculations; Bureau van Dijk (2020), Orbis database, own calculations.

Second, banks and financial firms were among the most important largest shareholders in Austria, but their role in non-financial companies remarkably declined over the past decades. Banks and financial firms virtually disappeared as the largest shareholders in the three samples of firms in Austria in 2018–2019.

Third, there was a decline in the number of listed companies with a *direct* majority state owner. The main factor for this was privatization. The state appears to preserve its important role as a *direct* largest shareholder in the top 20 firms, and also as an *ultimate* owner in the top 20 firms (see discussion in Subsection 3.4.3).

3.4.3 Ultimate Ownership

3.4.3.1 Ultimate Ownership in the 1990s

To account for the specific ownership structure in Austria in the 1990s, we have identified in the sample of the 600 largest Austrian firms the following ownership categories: bank, domestic firm, foreign firm, state, individual or family, and public ownership. In addition, corporate control in conjunction with the ownership structure is measured in three different ways: (1) direct ownership; (2) ultimate ownership, where ultimate owners of firms owned by other domestic firms are traced back (or better 'up' the pyramid) to the owner at the top of the pyramid[5]; and

---

[5] Ultimate foreign owners of Austrian firms cannot be traced back due to data limitations.

Table 3.7 Largest shareholders by ownership categories in 2018–2019 in Austria

Ownership categories[a]	Top 100 (percentage of firms)[b]	Min.[c]	Med.	Mean	Max.	Top 20 (percentage of firms)[b]	Min.[c]	Med.	Mean	Max.	Listed (percentage of firms)[b]	Min.[c]	Med.	Mean	Max.
Families/individuals	3	25	25	36.33	59	25				59	1.85	59	59	59	59
State	13	42.56	100	87.69	100	25	51	100	90.2	100	1.85	51	51	51	51
Non-financial	26	25.01	100	82.83	100	30	25.01	42.47	56.91	100	12.96	25.01	62.3	61.91	100
Financial	2	89.95	94.98	94.98	100										
Holdings	21	28.79	99.97	81.85	100	20	60.66	100	90.17	100	24.08	23.27	52.84	54.57	88
Others	7	21.86	55.08	57.32	100	5	26.4	26.4	26.4	26.4	14.81	21.86	43.19	43.72	83.33
Foreign	22	26.15	100	81.53	100	15	38.16	51	63.05	100	24.08	25.65	50.5	51.3	80.47
Dispersed	6	5	13.67	12.34	17.79	5	14.94	14.94	14.94	14.94	20.37	5	11.33	11.94	17.79
Total	100					100					100				
Number of firms	100					20					54				

Notes:

[a] We identify the company's direct controlling owner as the largest shareholder holding 20% or more of outstanding shares. When no single entity owned at least 20%, a company was categorized as having dispersed ownership. Ownership categories: Families/individuals, state, non-financial firms, financial (banks, other financial institutions) and holdings are domestic shareholders. Foreign are all foreign shareholders (physical and legal persons).

[b] Percentage of firms: percentage of firms controlled by each ownership category or with dispersed ownership.

[c] Descriptive statistics (min., med., mean and max.) are the percentage of ownership stake of the ownership category in firms controlled by this ownership category.

Source: Bureau van Dijk (2020), Orbis database, own calculations.

(3) largest ultimate shareholder, where a dummy of one is assigned to the largest shareholding class among bank, foreign firm, state, and individual or family. Franks and Mayer (2001) conjecture that control lies with the ownership category that constitutes ultimate control (i.e. on the 'top' of the pyramid).

Table 3.8 shows direct and ultimate ownership and largest ultimate shareholders by ownership categories and eight size classes as measured by total sales. The most important direct shareholders in Austria are domestic and foreign firms directly holding together nearly 64% of total equity. This underlines the importance of pyramiding as a means of extending control in the Austrian corporate governance model. At first sight, banks and the state play only a minor role in influencing companies by direct ownership claims. However, several factors increase the importance of the state and the (at that time mostly state-controlled) banks. First, the state more than doubles its shareholdings via indirect equity ownership (from 5.2% to 11.7%). Second, the state and the banks are the largest ultimate shareholders in 21.2% of the 600 largest companies. State and bank holdings concentrate in the largest size classes. More than half of the largest thirty companies were under state or bank control in the mid-1990s.

Table 3.9 focuses on listed companies. In the sample of Austrian listed companies in 1996, banks, in particular, are very active stakeholders in these listed firms where dispersed shareholdings are largest. This enables them to effectively control a company with a comparatively lower equity stake. Presumably, proxy votes also contribute to their rising voting power in general meetings. Together, the state and banks ultimately control twenty-two of the sixty-two listed companies in the sample (35.6% of firms). Families control 41.7% of companies and foreign firms control 19.4 %, respectively. Again, state and bank holdings have invested in the largest size classes in listed companies. Thus, predominantly the state controlled the largest Austrian corporations as of mid-1990s (43.8% in the largest size quartile).

3.4.3.2 Ultimate Ownership in 2015

What has been the development of ultimate ownership in large Austrian firms since the mid-1990s? Table 3.10 presents the ultimate ownership of the twenty largest listed and unlisted Austrian firms in 2015. Interestingly, the state remained the prevailing largest ultimate shareholder (40% of firms) but banks have become less important.

Table 3.8 Austrian 600 largest corporations: Direct, ultimate ownership, and largest ultimate shareholder by investors and size classes, 1990s

Size class	Banks			Domestic firms			Foreign firms			State			Family			Public		
	Dᵃ	Uᵇ	Lᶜ	D	U	L	D	U	L	D	U	L	D	U	L	D	U	L
95–100%	3.4	6.5	16.7	29.6	0.0	0.0	31.6	35.3	33.3	13.4	26.8	40.0	7.2	7.4	10.0	14.8	21.5	0.0
90–95%	8.9	9.6	10.0	32.6	0.0	0.0	32.3	29.7	30.0	8.4	18.1	23.3	8.4	19.1	36.7	9.4	23.6	0.0
75–90%	3.5	7.8	10.0	44.2	0.0	0.0	27.5	34.2	34.4	6.0	13.7	18.9	16.0	34.2	36.7	3.0	10.0	0.0
50–75%	4.5	5.9	6.1	35.1	0.0	0.0	26.7	29.1	31.8	7.4	12.8	14.2	23.1	44.3	48.0	3.3	7.6	0.0
25–50%	4.8	5.9	6.0	30.3	0.0	0.0	35.8	39.0	41.3	2.3	8.8	10.7	22.2	35.8	42.0	4.7	10.4	0.0
10–25%	2.8	3.5	2.2	29.8	0.0	0.0	29.0	35.0	37.4	1.8	4.7	7.7	32.9	48.3	52.7	3.7	7.4	0.0
5–10%	1.6	2.5	3.3	42.1	0.0	0.0	27.1	31.1	30.0	6.7	19.0	23.3	21.3	40.4	43.3	1.2	7.1	0.0
0–5%	0.3	0.3	0.0	20.0	0.0	0.0	33.6	34.6	36.7	3.3	6.7	6.7	41.6	57.2	56.7	1.2	1.2	0.0
All firms (600)	4.0	5.6	6.3	33.6	0.0	0.0	30.3	33.9	35.6	5.2	11.7	14.9	22.6	38.6	43.2	4.3	9.8	0.0

ᵃ Direct ownership (% of equity)
ᵇ Ultimate ownership (% of equity)
ᶜ Largest ultimate shareholder (% of firms)
Source: Trend, (www.trend.at), own calculations.

Table 3.9 Austrian listed companies: Direct, ultimate ownership, and largest ultimate shareholder by investors and size classes, 1996

Size class	Banks			Domestic firms			Foreign firms			State			Family			Public		
	Dᵃ	Uᵇ	Lᶜ	D	U	L	D	U	L	D	U	L	D	U	L	D	U	L
75–100%	11.3	12.7	25.0	24.3	0.0	0.0	5.5	5.5	0.0	9.6	21.2	43.8	9.6	15.5	31.3	39.8	45.2	0.0
50–75%	16.7	21.4	33.3	31.1	0.0	0.0	24.9	15.2	13.3	3.5	8.9	13.3	2.3	24.0	40.0	21.5	30.5	0.0
25–50%	2.7	2.7	0.0	24.8	0.0	0.0	21.8	21.1	33.3	0.0	0.0	0.0	11.2	38.3	66.7	39.5	37.9	0.0
0–25%	14.6	16.5	25.0	23.8	0.0	0.0	17.2	19.6	31,3	0.0	0.0	0.0	11.9	31.3	43.7	32.6	32.6	0.0
All firms (62)	11.4	13.3	21.0	25.9	0.0	0.0	17.1	15.3	19.4	3.3	7.6	14,6	8.9	27.2	41.7	33.4	36.6	0.0

ᵃ Direct ownership (% of equity)
ᵇ Ultimate ownership (% of equity)
ᶜ Largest ultimate shareholder (% of firms)
Source: Trend. (www.trend.at), own calculations.

Table 3.10 *Ultimate beneficial ownership of the twenty largest companies in Austria in 2015*

Family	Institutional investor	Other financial	Others	State	Widely held	Widely held parent
10	10	5	10	40	5	20

Note: Ownership structure is presented as percentage of the total.
Source: Peev and Yalamov (2020).

While in 1996 the banks were the largest ultimate owners of 21% of listed companies, about twenty years later there were no banks having ultimate control among the top 20 Austrian firms.

3.5 The Determinants of Ownership Change

What are the determinants of the ownership change (or perhaps rather continuity) in large Austrian firms over the past decades? We may document two key determinants. First, Austria witnessed a wave of privatization of state-owned firms and correspondingly a decrease in the role of the state in the biggest Austrian businesses. Second, there also might have been a 'global corporate governance revolution' (Cheffins, 2001), with corporate governance changes coinciding with Austrian accession to the EU in 1995. Since then, the newly created EU single capital market and the numerous policy initiatives for development of a market for corporate control in the EU member states, may have reshaped the corporate governance and ownership landscape in Austria.

3.5.1 The Persistence of Domestic Pyramidal Ownership Structures

We have presented evidence for the persistence of Austrian non-financial firms and holding companies over the past decades. These companies have remained the most important owners in Austria, on average. In 2018–2019, non-financial firms and holding companies together controlled nearly half of the top 100 Austrian firms. Pyramidal ownership structures remained prevalent as of 2018–2019 in Austria. Thus, families and individuals, which stand behind those companies, remain the most important ultimate controlling owners. The rest of the companies are controlled by foreign owners as well as the state. The state retains control predominantly in very large corporations. Of course, the same factors preserving observed ownership and control structures have severely constrained ownership change and the development of widely held companies, especially. What are the major factors driving this persistence? We examine possible factors in Subsection 3.5.2.

3.5.2 *The Increase(?) in Widely Held Companies*

In Section 3.4, we presented evidence that the number of Austrian listed companies with dispersed ownership (widely held companies) increased from around 4% to 20% in the past decades. While there is no denying the fact that ownership concentration has decreased for some companies in Austria, several qualifying comments must be mentioned. First, in terms of absolute numbers and economic significance, there are still very few free-float companies in Austria (eleven in 2018–2019). Second, we applied a rather high threshold for defining widely held companies (largest shareholder having less than 20% ownership stake), and in most of these companies that we defined as widely held there is a large shareholder holding more than 10% (but less than 20%). Finally, overall shareholder concentration remains very high in Austria even for listed companies (with the largest shareholder holding more than 44%, on average).

In the apogee years of the global corporate governance movement in the 1990s and the early 2000s, prominent researchers predicted a convergence to the Anglo-American corporate governance and ownership structure. For example, Hansmann and Kraakman (2001) claimed that despite the apparent divergence in corporate governance and ownership across developed economies, the basic law of the corporate form has already achieved a high degree of uniformity and the ideology of shareholder primacy is likely to press all major jurisdictions towards similar rules of corporate law and practice. Franks and Mayer (2001) argued that competition between stock exchanges, the dismantling of control-enhancing mechanisms and the development of a market for corporate control might gradually produce a convergence of the ownership structures of German and

Anglo-American stock markets. What went wrong with these predictions in general and in the case of Austria in particular? We focus on the development of (1) the Austrian stock exchange and (2) the Austrian market for corporate control.

3.5.2.1 The Austrian Stock Exchange

The Austrian stock exchange has remained less developed over the past decades than in other countries. Stock market capitalization as a percentage of GDP was only 25.65% in 2018. For comparison purposes, in 2018 this indicator was 27.40% in Poland, 44.46% in Germany and 85.18% in France. On the other hand, legal investor protection in Austria has improved somewhat since 1995 (see e.g. the Takeover Act with the mandatory bid). Yet, better shareholder protection in Austria did not result in deeper capital markets. This observation is somewhat at odds with the law and finance literature which finds that higher levels of shareholder and creditor protection are correlated with increased financial development (see e.g. La Porta et al., 1998 and 1999).[6] The lack of correlation between the legal reforms for strengthening shareholder rights and the development of the capital market in Austria supports the evidence presented in a recent study of law and finance of thirty countries. Deakin et al. (2018) showed that legal reforms driven by global standards such as those of the World Bank and OECD do not straightforwardly translate into improved financial outcomes at the country level. The authors argued that where changes to the laws of a given country are triggered by external factors, such as the influence of international standard-setting bodies, the presence of endogenous demand for investor protection, coupled with 'complementary institutions' at country level, will make a difference to the effectiveness of the law in practice, and hence to financial outcomes.

One could speculate which 'complementary institutions' in Austria were not so supportive to the development of the capital market. First, there are both supply and demand side factors constraining the development of (equity) capital markets in Austria. On the supply side, owners in Austrian large companies may not want to relinquish control for a couple of reasons. Perhaps the most important is that controlling family owners have been engaged in long-term

---

[6] It may be that financial development drives shareholder protection and not the other way round.

shareholding and have a vision for the long-term company development, a crucial benefit that appears lacking in widely held companies.
Thus, owners' preferences may stem from efficiency considerations
rather than the ideology of shareholder primacy. Recent studies show
that the efficiency considerations are also a plausible explanation for
the persistence of blockholders, particularly family owners in Germany
(Franks, Mayer and Wagner, 2015).

On the demand side, the risk aversion of people in Austria appears
much higher than in other countries. For example, Ferreira (2018)
examined the differences in risk attitudes and risk perceptions across
thirteen European countries, the United States and Australia with
regard to investments in shares, mutual funds and bonds and showed
that there are significant differences in attitudes to financial risk across
countries. People living in Germany, Austria and the Netherlands are
the most risk-averse, while those in the United States, Turkey,
Australia and the United Kingdom are more ready to accept risk.
Moreover, the author reported that subjective risk preferences have
approximately a ten times greater explanatory power on risky investment holdings than short- and long-term objective measures of financial market performance and volatility.

Second, political factors in Austria may not be favourable for the
development of shareholder capitalism. Meyer and Höllerer (2010)
illustrated how the liberal notion of shareholder value gained significant ground in the 1990s in Austria, a country that is iconic in
Continental Europe's stakeholder and corporatist tradition. They
claimed that in Austria the predominant accounts in favour of shareholder value concerned the stimulation and revitalization of the capital
market and the retreat of the state from economic activity. However,
the authors concluded that shareholder value developments in the
socioeconomic context in Austria were not sustainable and any critical
event (e.g. the global financial crisis in 2008–2009) could bring about a
resurgence of the traditional system in Austria.

The Austrian governments were involved in a number of legal and
regulatory reforms designed to foster domestic capital market development (e.g. reforms from January 1999 through December 2000).
However, political will has appeared to be not sufficiently strong for
more changes supporting shareholders' value. Unlike the tax reform in
Germany in 2000, Austrian governments were reluctant to introduce
shareholder-friendly tax measures in the 2000s. In the Austrian tax

reform of 2012, the treatment of equity holders was not favourable (e.g. there was an increase to the capital gains tax rate as well as an abolishment of the tax exemption due to those with a long holding period).

Consistently, the state has been unwilling to sell the rest of the companies/partial stakes it is still controlling. Austria has one of the largest public sectors among EU member states. For example, a study of the European Commission reveals that over the period 2008 to 2013 the reported share of state-owned enterprises (SOEs) in total turnover in the energy sector was almost 60% in the EU. Cyprus, Luxembourg, Croatia, France and Austria are the member states with the highest share of SOE turnover in total energy turnover, essentially 100% (European Commission, 2016).

Third, there may be good substitutes for outside equity capital. Banks (under the 'Hausbank system') are still important providers of debt. Debt finance dominates external financing for firms in Austria (OECD, 2017a). The internal capital markets of predominantly German multinationals may also substitute for outside equity.

Fourth, there are also other possible complementary institutions not supportive of the development of the capital market in Austria such as the lack of private pension funds, hence less institutional investment, and the lack of representation of Austrian companies in stock market indexes, hence no investment by index funds and others.

3.5.2.2 The Austrian Market for Corporate Control

The Austrian market for corporate control has remained inactive.[7] This is not only a specific Austrian but a typical Continental European phenomenon. A few factors explaining this outcome have been suggested. For example, Gordon (2003) focused on the role of economic nationalism in the EU member states. Mukwiri (2020) argued that the failed attempt to introduce a mandatory board neutrality rule into EU takeover law demonstrates that it is difficult to enact rules that are

---

[7] The causal relationship between the market for corporate control and ownership concentration is not straightforward. For example, Franks et al. (2012) showed that in countries with strong investor protection, developed financial markets and active markets for corporate control, family firms evolve into widely held companies as they age. However, one might argue that the market for corporate control presupposes a free-float, because only then can a hostile bid as a method for obtaining control be successful. Thus, there is no market for corporate control because there is no free-float.

contrary to the corporate law cultures of the majority of the member states.[8] Moreover, the literature on the varieties of capitalism distinguishing between 'coordinated market economies' (CMEs), such as Austria and other countries in Continental Europe, and 'liberal market economies' (LMEs), such as the United Kingdom, has shown the crucial importance of complementary, non-market institutions, which allow for inter-firm coordination and which help regulate the interaction between shareholders, managers, employees and other stakeholders (see e.g. Vitols, 2001). These non-market institutions remain embedded in the Austrian national corporate governance system and may have eventually prevented the development of a market for corporate control in Austria.

Thus, both a fragile (equity) capital market and a missing market for corporate control in Austria have been constraining the predicted rise of widely held companies. The Austrian experience partly confirms the evidence presented in other studies on countries in Continental Europe such as Germany, Italy and France. For example, Franks et al. (2012) showed that family control of companies proved to be relatively stable over time only in countries with weak investor protection, inactive markets for corporate control and less-developed financial markets. Germany, Italy and France were such countries and did not experience declines in family control over time. In contrast, in the United Kingdom, family control clearly tended to diminish as companies aged and became widely held following the firm life cycle.

3.5.3 The Decline(?) of State Ownership

We have documented a remarkable decline of the state control of listed companies in Austria. However, the state has retained its role as a large shareholder in Austrian big business among the top 20 and top 100 firms. How do we explain these findings? Austrian privatization programmes have intended to not only transfer state ownership to private hands (and to raise cash) but also to develop a national equity capital market and a shareholder corporate culture. Privatization of SOEs has been the driving force for fostering shareholder capitalism in Austria and other countries in Western Europe such as France, Italy and Spain in the 1990s (Megginson and Netter, 2001). Thus, privatization has

---

[8] There is a board neutrality rule in Austria for listed companies. However, one might argue that due to the concentrated ownership structure it is not important.

decreased the number of state-controlled listed companies in Austria (Stiefel, 2000). Yet, one might doubt whether privatization programmes have fulfilled their purpose of developing 'shareholder capitalism' in Austria, since we have witnessed a decrease of the share of listed companies in the largest Austrian corporations, and the state has remained a large and controlling shareholder in many of the largest (listed and unlisted) Austrian companies.[9]

In sum, the evidence from Austria does not point to global market competitive forces driving traditional ownership structures in the direction of the dispersed Anglo-American corporate governance model. Despite the great expectations of the 1990s, that is an expected rise of widely held companies as well as a fall in the share of state-controlled listed companies, the results about twenty-five years later have been quite modest. Moreover, the dominant domestic pyramidal ownership structures (non-financial firms and holdings) have persisted. The absence of a market for corporate control and a developed capital, in particular equity, market may partly explain the observed ownership patterns in Austria. The external pressure from the EU and global markets to foster corporate law and market developments in Austria appear to interlace with the domestic institutions belonging to the coordinated market economy family.[10] The globalization and European integration forces in the 1990s did not manage to transform the Austrian coordinated market economy. It appears that the absence of this major transformation led to the failure of the law and corporate governance reforms as well as privatization policies to produce more significant corporate ownership changes in Austria over the past decades.

3.5.4 *The Important Role of Foreign Ownership*

Austria is a small open economy. Ownership and control structures mirror this feature. Thus, while a few decades ago, foreign owners already controlled around 20% of the largest Austrian companies, this

---

[9] For example, the state holds a 31.5% ownership stake in OMV AG (the largest Austrian company); 51% in Verbund AG (the largest electricity company); and 28% in Telekom Austria AG (the largest telecom company). One reason for the still large presence of the 'state' in Austrian corporate governance is the reluctance of the federal states ('Bundesländer') to privatize their companies (e.g. in EVN AG, a very large electricity company, Lower Austria still holds more than 50% of the shares).

[10] For the key features of coordinated market economies, see Section 1.3.5.

percentage if anything has continued to increase. Moreover, foreign investors and companies very often own non-controlling minority stakes in Austrian companies. Consistently, the main way of 'exit' of family controlling owners of companies is not via the stock exchange (e.g. via an initial public offerring) but by directly selling the company to large multinational companies.[11] Thus, while the state and pyramidal owner-ship structures, predominantly used by family owners, hindered an even more prominent role for foreign investors, foreign control remains one of the defining features of Austrian corporate governance.

3.6 Conclusion

This chapter arrives at several conclusions regarding Austria using several samples on listed and unlisted companies in both the mid-1990s and in recent years.

First, like many other European countries, Austria experienced a shake-up in securities law, mainly induced by EU Directives (such as those on shareholder rights, takeovers and transparency). Without going into details, one can safely state that the investor's position has improved, even if not all reforms are up to the highest standards and some are of doubtful efficacy.

Second, and despite investor-favourable changes to securities law, ownership concentration has remained very high in Austria in listed and unlisted companies alike. Thus, large shareholders remain the predominant corporate governance model in Austria. If anything, ownership concentration has increased in the last few decades to average levels of supermajority control in the average top 100 firm.

Third, the identities of the controlling shareholders remained very much the same during the analysed period with one important excep-tion: banks. While there is a lot of stability with state, (family) pyram-idal ownership structures and foreign investors remaining the main ownership and control categories in top Austrian corporations, banks lost their significance in equity holding of companies.

Finally, the widely held corporation does not appear to have become anywhere near a role model for the Austrian corporation. While we

---

[11] For example, in 2015 Adidas, a German multinational, bought the Austrian fitness app Runtastic for €220 million; in 2017 ABB, the Swiss multinational, bought Bernecker + Rainer Industrie-Elektronik Ges.m.b.H. for about €1.8 billion.

have witnessed an increase in the number of widely held firms in the past decades in Austria, their economic significance remains minor.

Thus, in Austria we do not see the kind of convergence to Anglo-American corporate governance and ownership structures predicted by, for example, Hansmann and Kraakman (2001) or Franks and Mayer (2001). We identify a few potential 'complementary institutions' that hinder this convergence e.g. the preferences of controlling both owners as well as prospective buyers and a missing political will to embrace a more shareholder-oriented model.

4 | Germany

EVGENI PEEV

4.1 Introduction

What has been the fate of German corporate insiders thirty years after the global corporate governance revolution in the 1990s? In this chapter, we will shed light on this question, examining the ownership structure of the top 20, the top 100 and listed companies in Germany in 1990 and 2018–2019.

At the end of the 1990s, Martin Hellwig asked whether the internationalization of major German corporations and their shareholders would limit the power of corporate insiders such as large shareholder families, banks, employees, the state and professional managers (Hellwig, 2000). Goergen, Manjon and Renneboog (2008) and Rapp and Strenger (2015) presented reviews of the developments of the German corporate governance system in the 1990s and after the governance reforms in the 2000s. Ringe (2015) documented the ownership structure of DAX-30 companies in 2001 and 2014 and claimed that German corporate ownership patterns have been undergoing a major change: the traditional network between German firms, known as 'Deutschland AG' ('Germany Inc.'), was eroding. He reported three main aspects of ownership change: (1) decreasing ownership concentration and a corresponding increase in equity dispersion, (2) the decline of bank ownership of non-financial equity stakes and (3) an increase in foreign ownership. These changes resulted in some kind of control vacuum that shareholder activists such as hedge funds exploited intensively in the early 2000s (Bessler, Drobetz and Holler, 2015). Franks, Mayer and Wagner (2015), using large samples of *listed* companies, presumably including also mid-sized companies, have reported a similar increase in dispersed ownership and a decline in inter-corporate and bank holdings. They also reported persistence, and even an increase in family-controlled German companies, rising from 21% of listed companies in 1990 to 37% in 2014. In contrast,

Bessler et al. (2021) presented evidence of the sharp decline of founding family firms from 63% of non-financial German Prime Standard companies in 2001 to only 31% of these companies in 2015, as well as a dramatic decline of listed companies subsequent to the global financial crisis.

Most studies focus on DAX-30 listed companies or German listed companies in general. A thorough examination of large unlisted firms is largely neglected in mainstream corporate governance research and especially in studies of the developments of corporate governance and ownership changes in Germany over the last few decades. The common problem articulated by scholars is the lack of data on private firms.

In this chapter, using unique datasets, we have tracked the ownership change or eventual stability of major businesses in Germany, examining the top 20, top 100 and listed companies at two points in time: 1990 and 2018–2019.

We have found that nearly thirty years after the start of the global corporate governance revolution German individuals and families and other German companies still appear to be the key blockholders in the top 20 (65% of firms), top 100 (54%) and listed German companies (53%). Nevertheless, the non-traditional owners of 'Deutschland AG' such as foreign blockholders and widely held companies together account for 25% of the top 20 firms, 36% of the top 100 and 36% of listed German companies. We have also speculated about the possible factors explaining these ownership patterns.

This chapter is structured as follows: Section 4.2 briefly describes the main organizational forms, legal foundations and ownership disclosure rules in Germany. Section 4.3 presents ownership data. Section 4.4 identifies ownership structures in 1990 and 2018–2019, and the main patterns of ownership change. The determinants of the observed ownership changes are discussed in Section 4.5. Conclusions are outlined in the last section.

4.2 Corporate Governance Framework

4.2.1 Organizational Forms

The prevailing types of German company whose shareholders have limited liability are as follows:

a. **Private limited company** (*Gesellschaft mit beschränkter Haftung*) (GmbH). A private limited company is less rigidly regulated by statutory law. The rights of shareholders of a private limited company can be basically determined by the company's articles of association.

b. **Public limited company** (*Aktiengesellschaft*) (AG). The rights of shareholders of a public limited company are mainly statutorily regulated and can be modified by the articles of association only in accordance with the German Stock Corporation Act (*Aktiengesetz*) (AktG). The shares of a public limited company may be listed.

c. **Partnership limited by shares** (*Kommanditgesellschaft auf Aktien*) (KGaA). A partnership limited by shares is managed by a general partner. Its shares may be listed. It is often used by family firms to access equity capital markets.

d. **European company** (*Europäische Gesellschaft*) (*Societas Europaea*) (SE). A European company has limited co-determination. When it has a registered office in Germany, the company is treated as a public limited company formed in Germany subject to Regulation (EC) No 2157/2001 on the Statute for a European Company (SE). The shares of an SE may be listed.

e. **Limited partnership** (*Kommanditgesellschaft*) with a GmbH as general partner (GmbH & Co. KG). A limited partnership provides limited liability and income taxation at the limited partners' level.

f. **Entrepreneurial company** (*Unternehmergesellschaft*) (UG). An entrepreneurial company is a private limited company with minimal share capital.

Public limited companies are a small part of the universe of German enterprises. Only about 11,000 of the approximately 3.7 million enterprises in Germany in 2012 were public limited companies (*Aktiengesellschaften* or *Kommanditgesellschaften auf Aktien*). These public limited companies accounted for about 18% of aggregate revenues and employed just under 9% of employees subject to social security contributions. A small fraction of German public limited companies is listed on the stock exchange. In 2020, shares of about 600 companies were trading at the major trading venues of Deutsche Börse AG.

4.2.2 Legal Foundations

The statutory laws most relevant for the corporate governance of public limited companies are as follows:

(1) the Stock Corporation Act (*Aktiengesetz*, AktG), which sets out the largely mandatory framework for the organization of public limited companies as well as the rights and duties of the corporate bodies, the management board, the supervisory board and shareholders' meetings, as well as the shareholders;

(2) the EU Market Abuse Regulation (MAR), which entered into force on 3 July 2016 and replaces the existing Market Abuse Directive (MAD) and the national laws implementing the MAD, including large parts of the Securities Trading Act. The MAR, inter alia, governs market abuse and market manipulation, disclosure of non-public information and directors' dealings;

(3) the Securities Trading Act, which still contains provisions on the enforcement of violations of the MAR under German law;

(4) the Securities Acquisition and Takeover Act, which contains rules on mandatory and voluntary takeover offers and defensive measures;

(5) the Commercial Code, which, inter alia, sets out the accounting rules applicable to German companies;

(6) the Co-Determination Act and the One-Third Participation Act, granting employees co-determination rights on a supervisory board level; and

(7) the German Corporate Governance Code (Kodex), which was adopted in 2002 and its new version published on 20 March 2020.

4.2.3 Ownership Disclosure Rules

Ownership disclosure rules for public limited companies and private limited companies in Germany can be summarized in a few main points. First, under securities regulations on shareholdings, a shareholder who holds a certain percentage of voting rights (the lowest threshold is 3%, and does not include financial instruments) must notify the public limited company (AG). The public limited company is then obliged to disclose this information to the German Federal Financial Supervisory

Agency (*Bundesanstalt für Finanzdienstleistungsaufsicht*) and publish the notification. Listed companies are required to report the holding of voting rights to the public supervisory authorities if certain thresholds are achieved, exceeded or undercut. The thresholds, based on European law requirements, amount to 3% of total voting rights (voting rights attached to voting shares only, not financial instruments), 5%, 10%, 15%, 20%, 25%, 30%, 50% and 75% of total voting rights (shares with voting rights and/or financial instruments). Second, managing directors of a private limited company (GmbH), or under certain circumstance notaries, must file in the German Commercial Register and keep an up-to-date list of shareholders. This list also has to include specific information on shareholders and their shareholdings. Third, public limited companies and private limited companies as well as other businesses and organizations must provide information to the German Transparency Register. This information includes data on their ultimate beneficial owners (individuals directly or indirectly holding more than 25% of the equity or votes, or otherwise controlling the business entity). Fourth, there are also filings on ownership information required under German Competition Law.

The European Parliament and the European Council adopted the Shareholder Rights Directive II (SRD II) in 2017 to 'encourage long-term shareholder engagement' and tackle the shortcomings exposed by the 2008 financial crisis. EU member states retained a degree of discretion in transposing this directive into national law. The directive was transposed into German law in November 2019 and came into effect on 1 January 2020 (Trif, 2020). The legal and regulatory reform of the German corporate governance system has included important changes to the AktG and Kodex. As a result, institutional investors could expect enhanced transparency from German issuers and stronger rights to exercise effectively their stewardship responsibilities. The reform reflected both the transposition of the EU SRD II into domestic law and a corresponding Kodex change, both aiming to incorporate governance features that are more typically associated with Anglo-American jurisdictions.

The Kodex contains non-binding best practice recommendations regarding the management and oversight of German listed companies, with the latter legally bound to annually report on their adherence to the Code's provisions. The SRD II prompted the need to revise the Kodex to harmonize it with the new corporate governance framework.

Accordingly, the 2020 Kodex was submitted to the Federal Ministry of Justice and Consumer Protection for review and its new version came into force after it was published in the Federal Gazette on 20 March 2020.

4.3 The Data

We have used four datasets on ownership structure of the top 100 non-financial firms (listed and unlisted) and non-financial listed firms in Germany at two points in time: 1990 and 2018–2019 (sample '*Top 100 in T0*', sample '*Listed in T0*', sample '*Top 100 in T1*' and sample '*Listed in T1*'). The construction of these datasets is described in Chapter 1 of this volume. Additionally, we have used a dataset on the *ultimate* ownership of the top 20 non-financial firms (listed and unlisted) in Germany in 2015.

4.4 The Ownership Structures

4.4.1 Listed Companies

Our data show that in 1990 listed companies made up 63% of the top 100 firms and in 2018–2019 this percentage had risen to 94% of the top 100 firms. Since the early 1990s, the number of initial public offerings (IPOs) had started to increase, resulting in more listed companies on the German capital market, but this was mainly due to the 'Neuer Markt' IPO period with more than 326 IPOs between 1997 and 2002. Since then and especially after the global financial crisis the number of listed companies has declined (Bessler et al., 2021a). The trend of decline of the number of listed companies was also observed in the United Kingdom and the United States. Both the United Kingdom and the United States have experienced a sharp drop in the number of domestic companies listed on the main stock exchanges. In the case of the United Kingdom, the fall is around 50% during the last twenty years, and in the United States, the decline is only slightly smaller (Franks et al., 2015). The 'listing gap' in the United States started in 1996 (Doidge et al., 2017), whereas in Germany it began in 2008–2009. The decline in the number of listed companies in Germany is less pronounced in the *Prime Standard* market segment of the Deutsche Börse. The *Prime Standard* is the most strictly regulated segment, requiring the highest disclosure standards in Europe. It focuses on established firms that can meet the highest requirements. The number of listed firms on the *Prime Standard* slightly declined from 372 to 310 over the period 2003–2015, and from 310 to 302 during the period 2015–2020.

4.4.2 *Ownership Structures in 1990*

Table 4.1 reports ownership concentration of the top 20, top 100 and listed companies in Germany in 1990. The largest shareholder held a very high ownership stake. The size of the median largest share block was about 48% in the top 20, about 54% in the top 100 firms and 50% in listed companies. The size of the share blocks of the second- and the third-largest shareholders was also relatively high. The median stake of the second-largest shareholder was about 11% in the top 20 firms and 23% (25%) in the top 100 (listed companies). The third-largest shareholders held about a 12–13% median stake in the three samples. The high ownership concentration of German listed companies has also been observed in other studies (see e.g. Franks and Mayer (2001) examining a sample of the largest 171 German listed companies in 1990). Our scores of ownership concentration of listed companies differ from the results of the study of German listed companies in 1999 by Becht and Boehmer (2001). Their sample included 1,043 domestic German listed companies in 1999. They reported that only 20% of the listed companies had more than two registered shareholders and the average stake of the second-largest shareholder was only 7.4%. The variation between their results and ours seems due to the different sample sizes and years. Our sample includes 192 German listed companies in 1990. Presumably, these are large companies and the potential contestability of control proxied by the ownership stake of the second-largest shareholder has been relatively high.

Who then were the dominant shareholders in large German companies in 1990? Table 4.2 presents the main ownership categories of the top 20, top 100 and listed companies. Other German companies (non-financial and holdings) were the largest shareholders of 30% of the top 20 companies. The state was the second most important shareholder (25% of the top 20). Among the top 100 firms, the most important controlling shareholders (49%) were other German

Table 4.1 *Ownership concentration in 1990 in Germany*

	Number of firms	Largest shareholder (C1)[a]				Second-largest shareholder (C2)[a]				Third-largest shareholder (C3)[a]				All largest shareholders (Largest SH)[b]			
		Min.	Med.	Mean	Max.	Min.	Med.	Mean	Max.	Min.	Med.	Mean	Max.	Min.	Med.	Mean	Max.
Top 100[c]	100	5	53.71	60.42	100	0.01	23.33	22.06	50	0.01	12.5	12.68	30	10	86.05	75.93	100
Top 20[d]	20	5	47.77	47.53	100	2.23	11.29	15.04	25.3	0.01	12.7	11.56	30	10	67.2	62.23	100
Listed[e]	192	5	50.1	55.17	100	1.8	25	22.38	50	2	12.0	14.5	30	10	75	68.36	100

Notes:

[a] C1, C2 and C3 are the shareholdings in % of the largest, second- and third-largest shareholders in a company.
[b] Largest SH is the total share of all shareholders having 10% or more of outstanding shares in a company.
[c] Top 100 are the largest 100 firms (both listed and unlisted) in Germany.
[d] Top 20 are the largest 20 firms (both listed and unlisted) in Germany.
[e] Listed are listed firms in Germany.

Source: Bureau van Dijk (1999), Amadeus database, own calculations.

91

Table 4.2 Largest shareholders by ownership categories in 1990 in Germany

Ownership categories[a]	Top 100					Top 20					Listed				
	(percentage of firms)[b]	Min.[c]	Med.	Mean	Max.	(percentage of firms)[b]	Min.[c]	Med.	Mean	Max.	(percentage of firms)[b]	Min.[c]	Med.	Mean	Max.
Families/individuals	11	22.9	51.5	64.55	100	5	48.1	48.1	48.1	48.1	22	24.7	50	57	100
State	6	20	50.71	50.48	74	25	20	50	45.77	60	3	20	50	45.79	60
Non-financial	36	25	74.6	72.07	100	20	25	60.35	61.42	100	38	20	60.1	61.6	100
Financial	9	25	28.1	38.71	80	5	28.1	28.1	28.1	28.1	6	25	31.8	39.65	75
Holdings	13	30	50	54.38	100	10	30	33.55	33.55	37.1	11	25	53.25	54.34	100
Others	7	23	51	53.89	92	15	34	67.2	64.4	92	3	23	34	33.82	50
Foreign	12	24.5	97.71	78.3	100	10	24.5	62.25	62.25	100	10	24.5	87.5	75.93	100
Dispersed	6	5	10	10.32	18.9	10	5	7.5	7.5	10	7	5	12.7	12.23	19
Total	100					100					100				
Number of firms	100					20					192				

Notes:

[a] We identify the company's direct controlling owner as the largest shareholder holding 20% or more of outstanding shares. When no single entity owned at least 20%, a company was categorized as having dispersed ownership. Ownership categories: Families/individuals, state, non-financial firms, financial (banks, other financial institutions) and holdings are domestic shareholders. Foreign are all foreign shareholders (physical and legal persons).

[b] Percentage of firms: percentage of firms controlled by each ownership category or with dispersed ownership.

[c] Descriptive statistics (min., med., mean and max.) are the percentage of ownership stake of the ownership category in firms controlled by this ownership category.

Source: Bureau van Dijk (1999), Amadeus database, own calculations.

companies (non-financial and holdings), then foreign investors (12%) and families (11%). All these ownership categories had majority control. Banks and other financial firms were the largest shareholders in 9% of the top 100 firms. Interestingly, the median ownership stake of the financial institutions was 28.1%. It appears that banks and other financial firms (e.g. insurance companies) have managed to control companies with minority ownership stakes. Remarkably, in 1990 the state was not an important majority control shareholder in the largest 100 firms. We discuss the role of the state as a blockholder in Subsection 4.5.3.

In the sample of listed companies, other German companies (non-financial and holdings) were the prevailing largest shareholders (49%), followed by families (22%), foreigners (10%) and banks and other financial firms (6%). Our results are similar to the findings of Franks and Mayer (2001), who reported that ownership of 171 German listed companies in 1990 was dominated by three kinds of blockholder: other companies, founding families and banks.

4.4.3 Patterns of Ownership Change or Persistence

How has the ownership structure in large German firms changed over the past thirty years? Table 4.3 reports ownership concentration and Table 4.4 ownership categories of the top 20, top 100 and listed companies in Germany in 2018–2019. As Table 4.3 shows, ownership concentration dropped in all the samples of firms. In each sample, the stakes of the largest, second- and third-largest shareholders also decreased. Yet ownership concentration of large German companies remained relatively higher than in their counterparts in the Anglo-American world. The size of the median largest share block has become 30% in the top 20 German firms, 36.6% in the top 100 firms and 41.5% in listed companies.

As one might expect, ownership concentration was less pronounced in the top 20 companies. In 2018–2019, in these firms the difference between median ownership stakes of the first shareholder (30%) and the second (13%) was smaller than in firms in the other two samples. It appears that in 2018–2019 the relative control of the largest share-holder of the top 20 German firms as compared with the second shareholder has become weaker than in 1990, when the median ownership stake of the first shareholder was 48% and the second 11%.

Table 4.3 *Ownership concentration in 2018–2019 in Germany*

	Number of firms	Largest shareholder (C1)[a]				Second-largest shareholder (C2)[a]				Third-largest shareholder (C3)[a]				All largest shareholders (Largest SH)[b]			
		Min.	Med.	Mean	Max.	Min.	Med.	Mean	Max.	Min.	Med.	Mean	Max.	Min.	Med.	Mean	Max.
Top 100[c]	100	1.48	36.57	44.28	100	1.63	11.2	13.5	35.06	0.01	5	6.98	26.98	10.35	58.39	61.14	100
Top 20[d]	20	3.2	30	43.88	100	3.46	13.35	14.36	31	1.1	7	9.07	26.98	25.48	65.2	64.13	100
Listed[e]	576	0.03	41.49	44.2	100	0.21	10	12.16	49	0.01	5	6.89	33.33	10.02	59.17	59.32	100

Notes:
[a] C1, C2 and C3 are the shareholdings in % of the largest, second- and third-largest shareholders in a company.
[b] Largest SH is the total share of all shareholders having 10% or more of outstanding shares in a company.
[c] Top 100 are the largest 100 firms (both listed and unlisted) in Germany.
[d] Top 20 are the largest 20 firms (both listed and unlisted) in Germany.
[e] Listed are listed firms in Germany.
Source: Bureau van Dijk (2020), Orbis database, own calculations.

Table 4.4 Largest shareholders by ownership categories in 2018–2019 in Germany

Ownership categories[a]	Top 100 (percentage of firms)[b]	Min.[c]	Med.	Mean	Max.	Top 20 (percentage of firms)[b]	Min.[c]	Med.	Mean	Max.	Listed (percentage of firms)[b]	Min.[c]	Med.	Mean	Max.
Families/individuals	17	20.6	31.25	37.33	70.3	25	25.48	29.52	28.61	31	15	20	37.75	43.59	100
State											1	31.35	76	67.51	93
Non-financial	30	20.04	55.95	56.85	100	35	27.89	75.1	73.27	100	29	20	58.6	58.8	100
Financial	6	22.61	51.5	48.14	60						8	20.29	41	43.54	91.69
Holdings	7	37.5	89.88	77.51	100	5	37.5	37.5	37.5	37.5	9	25.13	66.01	62.54	98.85
Others	4	25	31.15	32.82	44	10	25	27.5	27.5	30	2	21	31.74	36.75	75
Foreign	19	22.36	51	51.16	91.5	5	83.1	83.1	83.1	83.1	15	20.04	50.41	52.23	98.18
Dispersed	17	1.48	8.2	9.01	19	20	3.2	11.95	11.53	19	21	0.03	10.26	10.9	19.95
Total:	*100*					*100*					*100*				
Number of firms	**100**					**20**					**576**				

Notes:

[a] We identify the company's direct controlling owner as the largest shareholder holding 20% or more of outstanding shares. When no single entity owns at least 20%, a company is categorized as having dispersed ownership. Ownership categories: Families/individuals, state, non-financial firms, financial (banks, other financial institutions) and holdings are domestic shareholders. Foreign are all foreign shareholders (physical and legal persons).

[b] Percentage of firms: percentage of firms controlled by each ownership category or with dispersed ownership.

[c] Descriptive statistics (min., med., mean and max.) are the percentage of ownership stake of the ownership category in firms controlled by this ownership category.

Source: Bureau van Dijk (2020), Orbis database, own calculations.

What then are the major patterns of ownership change or stability in large German businesses? Have German companies converged to the Anglo-American model of dispersed ownership thirty years later? Table 4.4 presents ownership categories of the top 20, top 100 and listed companies in Germany in 2018–2019. As the table reveals, there is a remarkable increase in the number of companies with dispersed ownership (companies without a controlling shareholder holding 20% or more of total shares). Yet, these widely held companies account for only 20% of the top 20 firms, 17% of the top 100 and about 21% of listed companies.

A few other patterns of ownership change have also emerged. First, there was a decline in other German companies (non-financial and holding companies) as the largest shareholders from 49% to 37% of the top 100 firms and 38% of listed companies, respectively. However, in the sample of the top 20 firms, other German companies have persisted as important large shareholders. We discuss the major determinants of this and other ownership patterns in Section 4.5. Second, the role of families as key largest shareholders has varied by company size. While there was a rise of families in the largest firms (top 20 and top 100), families became less important in listed companies. Third, the role of domestic financial institutions such as banks and insurance companies among the largest blockholders in the top 20 and top 100 non-financial companies has declined over the past decades. Fourth, we have observed a rise of foreign investors in both top 100 and listed companies. However, the process of internationalization measured by foreign direct investment seeking control through blockholdings appeared not as remarkable as the penetration of foreign portfolio investors documented in recent studies on ownership change in Germany (e.g. about 70% of the DAX-30 companies have had foreign owners, such as mutual funds and exchange trade funds). Fifth, the role of the state as the largest shareholder declined in all the samples. The main factor for this was privatization.

Our study has also documented that other German companies and foreign investors have maintained their majority control but the median ownership stake of families as the largest shareholders has dropped from around 50% in all the samples in 1990 to 29.52% in the top 20 (31.25% in the top 100 and 37.75% in listed companies) in 2018–2019. Recent studies of German listed companies confirm the observed trend of decreasing family ownership and control. In 2019, on average, the founding families hold 24.3% of the voting rights in family businesses (down from 35.3% in 2009).[1]

4.5 The Determinants of Change in Ownership Structure

What are the determinants of the ownership patterns of change or stability in Germany over the past thirty years? The interplay between the factors determining ownership structures in Germany appears complex. For example, Ringe (2015) argued that it is an exogenous shock (market pressure plus taxation reform) that leads to changes in ownership structure, which in turn requires an adaptation of legal rules. Thus, the ownership changes have been mainly a response to two key factors. First, global market pressure (e.g. German banks divesting their equity stakes mainly as a consequence of increased international competition in the 1990s). Second, taxation law reform enabling and accelerating the competition process already under way. Thus, legal rules and market competition may be understood as not operating in isolation, but as interactive forces. The initial and main impact of the tax reform was to break the power and influence of the banks. The tax reform offered banks the incentive to reduce their shareholdings by being exempt from paying capital gains taxes. Thus, many banks exited. In this vacuum foreign investors and hedge funds stepped in (see e.g. Bessler et al., 2015).

In what follows, we briefly speculate about the determinants of the observed basic ownership patterns: (1) the decline of ownership concentration, (2) the persistence of traditional German owners in the top 20 firms, (3) the fall of state ownership, (4) the moderate 'erosion' of traditional German owners in the top 100 firms and listed companies and (5) the rise of foreign blockholders.

4.5.1 The Decline of Ownership Concentration

We have presented evidence that (1) ownership concentration dropped in all the samples of firms, (2) the relative control of the largest shareholder of the top 20 firms as compared with the second-largest shareholder has become weaker and (3) there was an increase in the

---

[1] Stiftung Familienunternehmen, Borsennotierte Familienunternehmen in Deutschland (2009 and 2019).

number of companies with dispersed ownership (companies without a controlling shareholder holding 20% or more of total shares) in all the samples of firms. How can we explain these findings?

First, following the key hypothesis of the influential "law and finance" literature established since the mid-1990s (La Porta et al., 1997, 1998), one answer is that the enhancing of shareholders' legal protection in Germany since 1990 has encouraged minority shareholders to invest in German listed companies. (For the shareholders' protection index in Germany over the period 1990–2013, see e.g. Siems, 2016.) However, our results reveal that there was no straightforward relationship between the improvement of shareholder protection and the rise of widely held companies in Germany. Families and other German companies have only moderately decreased their stakes but still preserved their dominant position in 2018–2019. It appears that minority shareholders (mainly institutional investors) have been motivated to invest in German companies despite the presence of the country's traditional largest blockholders.

Second, Mark Roe (2003) has argued that the positive effects of blockholdings are associated with limited competition because monitoring by blockholders prevents managers from rent-seeking under limited competition and, therefore, leads to positive returns. Following these considerations, one may conclude that the increased global competition in the 1990s severely constrained rent-seeking and blockholders were motivated to sell their stakes because the costs of blockholding started exceeding the private benefits of control. In the German capital market context, firms tried to keep the private benefits of control by delisting from the *Prime Standard* and moving to the *General Standard* or even delisting altogether. The *General Standard* does not require information in English and therefore has been less attractive for foreign investors. A problem of keeping control when still being listed is that in Germany shares with multiple voting rights have been not allowed since 1998 (Bessler and Vendrasco, 2019). Thus, the increased global competition in the 1990s may only partly explain the decline in ownership concentration.

4.5.2 The Persistence of Traditional German Owners in the Top 20 Firms

We have documented the persistence and even the rise in the importance of the traditional blockholders in the top 20 German firms.

Families and other German companies have been the key blockholders of 35% (65%) of the top 20 firms in 1990 (2018–2019). The persistence of families and pyramidal ownership groups shows that powerful forces have been playing a pivotal role over the past thirty years in Germany other than global market competition, better legal protection of minority shareholders and taxation law reform. One might speculate what these 'other powerful' forces are.

Recent studies examined the impact of path dependency and the initial conditions for corporate governance development (Bebchuk and Roe, 1999). According to path-dependence hypothesis, corporate governance has been embedded in the national legal system and in patterns of ownership, control and monitoring. Consequently, notwithstanding the impact of globalization pressure, the rate and extent of convergence to the Anglo-American model of widely held companies would be constrained by the forces of path dependency (Gordon and Roe, 2004). We speculate that forces of path dependency stemming from the German national system of coordinated market economy appear to be more powerful than the pressure coming from the exogenous shocks of global markets and legal reforms in the 1990s.

Why have the forces of path dependency been overcoming globalization pressure in Germany? We can suggest at least three major reasons. First, as Douglas North argued, ownership and institutional change is a slow process (North, 1990). The change of the German national system of a coordinated market economy and any economic system, in general, require substantial reforms, such as the changes that occurred in Eastern Europe after World War II and since the collapse of communism in 1989. Presumably, there was no political will for a radical *system change* to a liberal market economy in Germany. For example, one of the fundamental features of the German corporate governance system is the co-determination (the involvement of employees in the company's strategic decision-making process). German labour unions have persistently chosen to oppose nationalization (starting as early as 1918 with the Stinnes–Legien Agreement), opting in favour of co-determination and powerful union representation (and thus contrary to the Russian approach, which had large-scale nationalization and a disempowerment of unions). The practice of co-determination was expanded after World War II, when capital and labour had to join forces to rebuild the country. German labour co-determination is unique in requiring that half of the supervisory board members to be labour representatives in companies with workforces of at least 2,000. Studies on the effects of co-determination have presented mixed results (see e.g. Jirjahn, 2011). Co-determination is essentially incompatible with Anglo-Saxon-style corporate governance because it turns hostile takeovers into a near hopeless undertaking (see e.g. Davies and Hopt, 2013). However, there have been no serious government attempts to change co-determination in Germany. The German labour unions continue to exert a strong influence both inside the Christian Democratic Union of Germany (CDU) and the Social Democratic Party of Germany (SPD). In sum, Germany continues to retain a number of special path-dependent features that characterize the German corporate governance system, in particular labour co-determination, two-tier boards and a codified law of groups (Hopt, 2015b). Thus, it appears that market forces and legal changes alone (e.g. the introduction of the EU single capital market and corporate law and corporate governance reforms) were not enough to cause a radical change to a liberal market economy in Germany. Consequently, the emerging ownership patterns of large German companies thirty years later have become a mixture of traditional blockholders (a dominant part) and new structures such as foreign and dispersed ownership stemming from the forces of globalization.

Second, corporate scandals in the United States in 2000–2002, the global financial crisis in 2008–2009 and other US problems have revealed serious problems in the Anglo-American model.[2] Thus, economic efficiency may play a critical role in the persistence of the traditional German ownership structures. In the 1990s, the global corporate revolution aimed at the development of the more efficient dispersed ownership structures and global corporate governance standards of the Anglo-American model. Paradoxically, recent studies explain the persistence of blockholders in German companies, particularly family ownership, with the main benefits of blockholders providing long-term shareholding that is often found to be deficient in the dispersed ownership systems of the United Kingdom and the United States (see e.g. Franks et al., 2015).

---

[2] For the purpose of 'footloose' companies with diffused ownership and their effects on inequality, environmental degradation, poor innovation and other societal issues, see, for example Mayer (2018).

The question about the effects of corporate governance and the ownership model is by no means trivial. While in the 1980s, studies stressed the advantages of the German or Japanese 'insider system' of corporate governance, in the 1990s and the early 2000s most studies presented evidence of the primacy of the Anglo-Saxon 'outsider system'. Another strand of theory argues that ownership structure does not matter in good times, when firms have access to financial resources, but ownership structure is important in bad times, when firms have more constraints (Schönfelder, 2020). Over the last two decades the potential of the US capital market to support the growth of large companies appeared enormous and much more impressive than the potential of the German capital market, which remained relatively small for the size of the German economic output and less competitive compared to other countries. While in both 2002 and 2020, seven out of the ten largest publicly traded companies by market capitalization in the world were US companies, in 2002 there was only one German company among the top 10 and there were only five German companies among the top 100 companies, and in 2020 no German company was in the top 10 and only two German companies were in the top 100 (Bessler and Book, 2021b). While US banks experienced dramatic declines in the immediate aftermath of the global financial crisis, they recovered much faster than their German and European counterparts, and essentially retain their long-run profit potential (Gugler and Peev, 2018). Thus, it appears that economic efficiency considerations may only partly explain the persistence of traditional German owners in the largest German companies.

Third, there is another answer as to why the forces of path dependency have overcome the pressure of globalization in Germany. Leaving aside the question about the (in)efficiency of blockholders or dispersed ownership systems, we may assume that *rent-seeking* of corporate insiders and economic entrenchment factors appear important variables explaining the persistence of the traditional ownership structures in Germany. Thus, vested local interests have used political tools to play against convergent legal, corporate governance and ownership changes. Germany has been a leading economy in Europe and German corporate insiders have had both the resources and political will to protect themselves. Interestingly, it appears that these vested interests have managed to maintain family and other German companies' ownership. However, they were not capable enough or not interested enough in preserving the role of the state in the largest German firms.

4.5.3 The Fall of State Ownership

We have presented evidence concerning the decline of the state's role as the largest shareholder in German companies. Privatization was the driving force for this result. Privatization of state-owned enterprises played a critical role in the development of capital markets and ownership changes in several Western European countries (e.g. the United Kingdom, France, Italy, Austria) in the 1980s and 1990s (Megginson and Netter, 2001). However, it was not so important in Germany, the main reason being that most of the largest German companies were already privately owned. Nevertheless, following the major privatization movement in Europe in the 1990s, German governments have initiated privatization of a few state enterprises (e.g. Deutsche Telekom). As a consequence, the state has sold its majority stake in the largest German firms. Yet the state has maintained minority ownership participation in a number of companies. For example, in 2018 the German government owned about 20% of the outstanding shares of Deutsche Post and about 30% of the shares of Deutsche Telekom, respectively, and the state of Lower Saxony still owned about 20% of the outstanding shares of Volkswagen. State participation is regularly reviewed. The results of these reviews are presented in reports published by the Federal Ministry of Finance. The trend in reducing the minority state-owned stakes has been pronounced since the privatization of German firms over the past few decades (Bundesministerium der Finanzen, 2001, 2020).

4.5.4 The Moderate 'Erosion' of the Traditional German Owners in the Top 100 Firms and Listed Companies

We have documented an ambivalent development amongst family blockholders and other German companies (non-financial and holding companies) in the top 100 firms and listed companies. The importance of families has slightly increased in the top 100 firms but there has been a moderate decline of family blockholders in listed companies. We have also observed a moderate decline in other German companies (non-financial and holding companies) as blockholders in both the top 100 firms and listed companies. How do we explain these findings?

First, following the previous discussion on the persistence of traditional German owners in the top 20 German firms, one may speculate that path-dependence factors are less pronounced in relatively smaller firms and listed companies. For listed companies especially, studies show that capital market development and the improvement of shareholder protection appear as key factors in the drop in family ownership (see e.g. Franks et al., 2012).

Some studies have focused on a much broader picture, identifying the long-term trends in the rise and eventual fall of the capital network among German non-financial firms, banks and insurance companies (for a short overview of the developments of this network, see e.g. Höpner and Krempel, 2004). The authors claimed that while in the 1950s and 1960s, the core of the company network was characterized by a commonly shared national orientation, from the 1970s onward, there has been a gradual erosion of this national economic orientation. Competition in the domestic financial sector increased in the 1980s, when there were attempts by banks to enter into the insurance market. In the 1990s, the increased competition in the domestic financial sector and global market pressure led to a reorientation of the large banks towards investment banking. This reorientation produced further tensions that called the industrial ownership of banks into question. Höpner and Krempel (2004) argued that: 'the government change in 1998 placed the company network back on the political agenda. In contrast to previous decades, both network participants and politicians questioned the rationale for its existence' (p. 352).

Second, the decline in the importance of other German companies (non-financial and holding companies) as blockholders in both the top 100 and listed companies may be partly attributed to law reforms, for example the tax reform introduced by the Schroeder government in 2000. Ringe (2015) argued that the 2000 tax reform abolishing taxation on the divestiture of equity holdings created incentives for equity dispersion and prompted an acceleration of competitive forces. Weber (2009) presented evidence on the dropping mean size of the largest voting block in all industries in the non-financial sector, except real estate, from 1999 to 2005. Thus, one might speculate that the complex interlacing between global market pressure, lobbying by network participants (e.g. German banks and firms), the political strategy of the social democratic government of Chancellor Schroeder, law reforms (e.g. the Corporate Governance and Transparency Act in 1998) and tax reforms have eventually impacted the traditional German blockholders such as banks and other German companies.

How radical have the ownership changes been in Germany following the legal reforms since 1998? Our findings have documented a *moderate* change. Our results are partly supported by previous studies. For example, Weber (2009) reported that the role of banks changed between 2001 and 2005 as the major banks such as Deutsche Bank sold many of their equity stakes in listed companies. However, it appeared that the corporate tax reforms had a once-and-for-all effect on ownership concentration, since the decrease in ownership concentration slowed between 2003 and 2005 compared to 2001 to 2003. Weber (2009) claimed that the 2000 corporate tax reforms did not revolutionize corporate governance in Germany because ownership concentration overall still remained very high among listed companies in 2005 and there was no active market for corporate control. Hackethal, Schmidt and Tyrell (2005) also suggested that the changes in the German corporate governance system were a modernization of the old system rather than a convergence towards the Anglo-America model.

However, other authors have argued that German ownership change was more considerable. For example, Höpner and Krempel (2004) argued that in the early 2000s there was an 'erosion' of the German company network. Wolf-Georg Ringe examined the DAX-30 companies in 2001 and 2014 and claimed that German corporate ownership patterns were undergoing a major change (Ringe, 2015). The differences between the results presented by Wolf-Georg Ringe and the results of this chapter are partly based on the different study periods and different sample selection. We have compared large German companies (both listed and unlisted) in 1990 and 2018–2019. It appears that the global market forces proxied by the rise of foreign and institutional investors have been more pronounced among the largest listed companies such as DAX-30 companies (Ringe, 2015) but the persistence of traditional German owners (e.g. families and other German firms) can be distinctly observed if one examines ownership development of both listed and unlisted firms over time. The main difference between the conclusions presented in Ringe (2015) and our explanation of ownership change or persistence in Germany is that we have emphasized the importance of path-dependence factors stemming from the existing coordinated market economy in Germany. The roots of the German economy can be found about a hundred years ago in the early decades of the twentieth century. According to Alfred Chandler, at this time the key advantage of Germany compared with the United Kingdom was that family owners in large German companies were much more supportive in establishing managerial hierarchies and professional management. Concentrated ownership and managerial sophistication have correspondingly produced beneficial economic results (Chandler, 1990). The presence of blockholders such as families and other German companies have had other competitive advantages stemming primarily from continuity and a long-term orientation.

In sum, it appears that globalization forces such as the EU single capital market and pressures for developing a market for corporate control in the 1990s and 2000s were not so politically powerful or efficient in changing the German corporate governance model. Market, legal and political pressure, including also German corporate insiders' pressure for corporate governance reform in the 1990s, impacted the corporate ownership of other German firms and families as blockholders but the resulting ownership changes were rather moderate.

4.5.5 The Rise of Foreign Blockholders

We have observed a rise in foreign investors as the largest shareholders in the top 100 and listed companies. Foreign ownership has increased to 19% of the top 100 firms and 15% of listed firms in 2018–2019. The process of internationalization measured by foreign direct investment seeking control through blockholdings appears not as remarkable as the penetration of foreign portfolio investors documented in recent studies on ownership transformation in Germany (see e.g. Ringe, 2015; Bessler et al., 2021a). The cross-border activity of institutional investors are the main reason for the significant share of portfolio foreign ownership on the German capital market, especially on the main share price index, DAX.[3] Even though a significant fall in foreign holdings of German equities was observed after the collapse of Lehman Brothers in 2008, the trend towards cross-border securities investments rebounded relatively quickly. The foreign ownership share of the market capitalization of German public limited companies was 58.8% at the end of 2007, it receded to 51.6% in the wake of the

---

[3] The German share price index, the DAX, is calculated by Deutsche Börse and tracks the share price developments of the thirty largest German public limited companies which are admitted to trading on the Frankfurt Stock Exchange.

collapse of Lehman Brothers in 2008 and increased to 57.1% in 2014 (Deutsche Bundesbank, 2014). Subsequently, North American investors have continued to grow and accounted for 37.6% of the regional DAX holdings in 2020 (up from 32% in 2013), while investors from Europe (excl. Germany) reduced their ownership to 16.9% in 2020 (down from 19% in 2013).[4]

Our study shows that the increase in direct foreign investment is another important pattern of ownership change in Germany over the past three decades. There are a number of factors determining this ownership pattern, such as global market forces and the launch of the EU single capital market. Yet the presence of foreign investors as the largest shareholders of the largest German companies still appears not to be that significant a few decades after the beginning of German corporate law and governance reforms in the 1990s.

4.6 Conclusion

We have presented evidence that ownership change in large German companies in the past few decades appears not to be that significant. Examining samples of the top 20 and top 100 (listed and unlisted companies) and a sample of listed companies, we have documented a moderate decline of other German companies in the top 100 and listed firms, and their persistence in the top 20 firms. In fact, other German companies have still maintained their role among the key shareholders in large German firms in 2018–2019. The role of families as key shareholders has been maintained in the top 20 and top 100 firms and there was a slight decline in the share of family largest shareholders of listed companies. Thus, our results do not corroborate the predictions of the theory of convergence to the Anglo-American model of widely held companies (Hansmann and Kraakman, 2001); both other German firms and families have appeared to be in decline, but still persist in the German corporate landscape.

We have partly answered the question, posed by Hellwig (2000) at the beginning of this chapter, about whether the internationalization of German large corporations and their shareholders will limit the power of corporate insiders. German individuals, families and other German companies still appear to be the key blockholders in the top 20 (65% of

---

[4] See Ipreo und DIRK (2015); IHS Markit and DIRK (2021).

firms), top 100 (54%) and listed German companies (53%). Nevertheless, the non-traditional owners for 'Deutschland AG' such as foreign block-holders and widely held companies together account for 25% of the top 20 firms, 36% of the top 100 and 36% of listed German companies. The emergence of a hybrid ownership landscape incorporating both the traditional and non-traditional owners for 'Deutschland AG' may challenge future corporate law and governance developments in Germany.

5 | Switzerland

ALEXANDER F. WAGNER AND CHRISTOPH
WENK BERNASCONI

5.1 Introduction

This chapter analyses the ownership of Swiss corporations from the 1990s to the late 2010s. A main finding is that in listed companies there has been a substantial decrease in the percentage of ownership held by the top three shareholders. For example, for the listed companies ranked 21 to 100, the median stake of the three largest shareholders dropped from 42.5% in 2008 to 36.6% in 2018. More generally, the concentration of the disclosed shareholders has decreased. Non-domestic investors hold large stakes in companies listed in Switzerland and have become more important in the largest, most mature companies; not only has their share ownership significantly increased, but they are also more active in exercising their voting rights and in engaging with companies. We also provide some evidence, drawing on a series of surveys of market participants, that these developments, especially the presence and increasing activity of non-domestic investors, have direct implications on the governance practice of companies listed in Switzerland.

This chapter is structured as follows. In Section 5.2, we first provide an overview of the most prevalent organization structures in Switzerland and a summary of the legal foundations and shareholder rights. Section 5.3 provides summary statistics of the long-term development of shareholder patterns in a broad sample of listed and non-listed companies in Switzerland. The main analysis is conducted in Section 5.4. There, we analyse the shareholder structure of the 100 largest companies listed in Switzerland and its development over the past decade. The determinants and consequences of changes in this structure are discussed in Section 5.5. Section 5.6 concludes the chapter.

5.2 Corporate Governance Framework and Recent Legal and Institutional Reforms

5.2.1 *Corporate Demography of Switzerland*

The Swiss Federal Statistical Office classifies Swiss businesses into eight different groups of legal structures. In the following, we provide an overview of the structures most prevalent in today's market.

a. **Individual Ownership Company.** This structure is by far the most commonly used in Switzerland, accounting for 52.3% (Federal Statistical Office, 2019) of all registered companies in Switzerland. It has very limited legal set-up requirements and entails limited bureaucratic effort to establish. In this structure, ownership and management are not separated and the founder of the company is liable with his/her entire personal wealth. There are no minimum requirements with respect to capital or people involved to form such a company. By the end of 2017, 11.6% of the Swiss workforce was employed by an individual ownership company.[1]

b. **Public Limited Company (AG).** This structure, the classical stock corporation, accounts for 21.6% of registered companies in Switzerland. This organizational structure formally limits the liability of shareholders to the capital individually invested in shares of the entity, while allowing an effortless trading of the individual ownership certificates of the company. The bureaucratic efforts as well as the formal requirements to incorporate such a public limited company are higher than for the limited liability company. To originate a public limited company, a minimum of three founding shareholders and CHF 100,000 of capital are required. In 2017, AGs employed 59.6% of the Swiss workforce.

c. **Limited Liability Company (GmbH).** This is the third most-widely used structure, accounting for 20.1% of all registered companies in Switzerland. This organizational structure formally limits the liability of the founder(s) to the company's paid-in capital, but does not facilitate the splitting of ownership certificates into easily tradable shares the same way the public limited company does. Compared to the public limited company, the minimum capital requirement to

---

[1] All data on employment and spread of the different corporate structures are sourced from the Federal Statistical Office (2019).

form a limited liability company is smaller (CHF 20,000), and a less formal process to register the entity applies. In 2017, GmbHs employed 12.1% of the Swiss workforce.

d. **Other Forms.** Besides the earlier mentioned most prominent legal forms of business, there exist other forms such as associations/ foundations (2.6%), partnerships (2.3% of all companies), or cooperatives (0.6%). In particular, the associations/foundations and cooperatives differ in terms of their ownership and economic goal. Most associations/foundations do not have a 'for-profit' mandate and cooperatives generally have equal uniform voting rights for each member. Despite only playing a minor role in terms of the number of registered entities, some of the best-known brands in Switzerland are either cooperatives (e.g. Migros, Coop) or associations (e.g. FIFA).

5.2.2 Legal Foundations

Switzerland is a constitutional direct democracy, with a separation of power into three pillars, consisting of the Federal Council (the executive), the parliament, which is split into the national council and the council of states (together the legislature) and the federal courts (the judiciary). The Swiss people elect the parliament, which in turn elects the executive as well as the judiciary and passes laws.

A peculiarity of the Swiss political system is that the Swiss people have a direct democratic instrument in the form of the popular initiative. Any Swiss citizen can, together with at least six other citizens, launch such a popular initiative. If the initiators succeed in securing the support of at least 100,000 Swiss citizens eligible to vote within an eighteen-month time frame, the proposal of the popular initiative will be subject to a popular vote. If the majority of the Swiss people overall, as well as the majority of the twenty-six cantons individually vote in favour of the initiative, its content becomes part of the Swiss constitution. The popular initiative was established in 1891 and since then 228 initiatives have been voted on, though the public has voted in favour of only twenty-five of them. In many of the unsuccessful instances, however, parliament has taken up the initiative's demands and provided its own counter-proposal to the initiative. Hence, popular initiatives may be successful overall, despite not being approved themselves in a national ballot. However, for Swiss corporations, in particular their boards of directors, management and shareholders, it is important to realize that the public in Switzerland has a much more direct way to bring forward regulation on issues that it deems are not appropriately dealt with by lawmakers. An important initiative that ultimately had a significant impact on corporate governance in Switzerland was the Minder Initiative, formally the Ordinance against Excessive Compensation (OaEC), which is discussed in more detail subsequently. As pointed out in Roe (2006) and Vatiero (2017), the Swiss legal origin is quite particular, presenting a unique case with respect to legal origin theory. This is ultimately carried over to the Swiss corporate governance framework, which presents a middle ground between the Anglo-Saxon and the Continental European system and as such presents an interesting case to consider.

In the following, we provide a high-level overview of the main codes and rules applied to businesses in Switzerland.

a. **Swiss Code of Obligations/Financial Market Infrastructure Ordinance.** The Swiss Code of Obligations (CO) forms the basis of how businesses in Switzerland are organized and sets the basic rules on how companies should conduct their business. The CO is amended from time to time. The latest revision of the code was approved by the Swiss parliament in June 2020 and has become fully effective in 2023. Since 1992, the code requires that listed companies have to disclose in their annual report any shareholders owning more than 5% of a company's outstanding shares. In 1995, the Federal Act on Stock Exchanges and Securities Trading was enacted, requiring listed companies to disclose shareholdings of individual parties whenever they cross the thresholds of 3, 5, 10, 15, 20, 25, 33⅓, 50 or 66⅔%. The reporting obligation remains unchanged, but has since then been transferred to the Financial Market Infrastructure Ordinance (FMIO). There are no requirements for the disclosure of shareholders for non-listed companies (which is important for the analysis conducted in Section 5.3).

Besides this disclosure requirement, the CO further sets the minimum standards that guide the structuring and organization of businesses in Switzerland. The most important ones with respect to shareholder rights are discussed in the following subsections.

i) **Right to Call a Shareholders' Meeting/Include an Item on the Agenda of the Meeting.** The CO provides shareholders the right to call a shareholders' meeting or include items in a regular Annual

General Meeting (AGM) agenda. According to the revised CO, one or a group of shareholders representing at least 5% of the share capital can ask the board of directors to call a shareholders' meeting. Shareholders (alone or in groups) owning at least 0.5% of equity or voting rights can ask the board of directors to include additional agenda items including supplementary information in a shareholders' meeting agenda. These requests must be in writing and reach the company in a timely manner. The board may ask shareholders to lower the thresholds in their articles of association. The board of directors has to organize such a meeting or include the agenda items in due time.

ii) **Share Classes.** A company may issue different share classes. The CO requires, however, that each share, independent of its class, has to carry one vote. To differentiate voting power among different share classes, the company may vary the nominal value of a share across different share classes. For example, for each CHF 1 in nominal value, a company's A shares may carry one voting right, while the B shares represent one voting right per CHF 0.10 in nominal value. Hence, for the same amount invested, holders of B shares have ten times the voting rights of holders of A shares. Moreover, the CO allows public limited companies to issue participation capital (PC). This PC is split into participation certificates with a nominal value, but does not provide the holder with voting rights. The nominal value of PC may not be more than twice the capital of the registered share capital. Besides PC, the articles of association may also allow the company to create profit participation certificates. The articles also need to define who should benefit from these certificates and what fraction of the company's profit or liquidation proceeds shall be allocated to the holders of these certificates. Profit participation certificates do not have a nominal value.

iii) **Mandatory Bid Offer.** The Financial Market Infrastructure Act (FMIA) stipulates that if a single shareholder or a group of shareholders acting in concert acquire more than $33^1/_3$% of a company's shares, they must make an offer to all other shareholders to acquire the remaining shares outstanding. The offer price has to be at least as high as the higher of the stock exchange price or the highest price that the acquirer has paid for equity securities of the target company in the preceding twelve months. The company may raise ('opt up') or abolish ('opt out') the threshold for the mandatory bid offer in its articles of association, subject to shareholder approval. An opting up or an opting out is generally done in companies with a large anchor shareholder to avoid an unintended triggering of the bid offer due to changes in the capital structure.

iv) **Subscription Rights in Capital Increases.** A listed company generally has three possibilities to increase its capital, all of which are subject to shareholder approval: (i) an ordinary increase, which needs to be conducted within three months after shareholder approval, (ii) an authorized capital band, which provides the board of directors with the possibility, but not the obligation, to increase/decrease capital up to a maximum defined amount (50% of the current capital at most) within a five-year time frame[2], and (iii) a conditional increase, which is linked to convertible bonds, stock options and the like that trigger the issuance of new shares through their conversion. While conditional capital will always lead to a dilution of existing shareholders in terms of voting rights, the board may also decide to issue ordinary or authorized capital without a rights offering to existing shareholders. While this will also lead to a dilution of the voting power of existing shareholders, the CO considerably limits the transactions and issuance conditions for transactions in which rights offerings are excluded, effectively protecting existing shareholders from value dilution.

The CO is revised and amended from time to time. In 2005, the parliament decided to amend the existing code with a requirement to disclose compensation amounts (CO 663b) for each member of the board of directors individually as well as the overall compensation amount for the executive management. Additionally, the compensation of the highest paid executive needs to be disclosed. A company is further required to publish any compensation to former executives and former board members, as well as loans granted to members of these two bodies. These disclosure requirements apply only to listed companies, not to privately held corporations. The disclosure requirement came into force as of 1 January 2007.

---

[2] The capital band is newly introduced with the revised CO. So far, the authorized capital only lasted for two years and only covered transactions that increase the equity capital. Every decrease in equity capital was subject to a shareholder approval.

b. **Ordinance against Excessive Compensation.** The OaEC is the consequence of a 2008 public initiative, the so-called 'Anti rip-off' or 'Minder' (after its initiator) initiative, which constituted a major development in the corporate governance regulation in Switzerland. The initiative's key demands concerned compensation matters for management as well as the board of directors. In particular, the most notable request of the initiative was the introduction of a binding say-on-pay for shareholders regarding the compensation amounts to be allocated to the executive management as well as the board of directors (see Wagner and Wenk (2022) for a detailed analysis). With the successfully completed revision, the OaEC has been formally transferred into the CO. In the process of this transfer, three additional items have been added to the original OaEC: (i) if a company opts for a prospective shareholder vote on variable compensation elements, it is mandatory to provide shareholders with an advisory vote on the compensation report; (ii) a gender quota of 30% for boards of directors and 20% for executive committees is introduced on a comply-or-explain basis, whereas explanations on why the quota has not been reached and what kind of measures are taken need to be included in the compensation report, at the latest five years (for the board) and ten years (for the executive committee) after the revised CO takes effect; and (iii) only the independent proxy, representing all the shareholder votes that were submitted prior to the AGM, is allowed to share information about general voting trends with the company and this information may be shared no earlier than three days before the AGM.

c. **Listing Regulations of the Swiss Stock Exchange (SIX).** The annual and interim financial reporting of companies listed on the SIX Swiss Exchange is regulated by the 'Listing Rules', the 'Directive on Financial Reporting' (DFR) and the 'Directive on Regular Disclosure Obligations' (DRDO), issued by the regulatory body of the SIX Swiss Exchange (Regulatory Board). Reporting under these rules must be in accordance with a financial reporting standard that the regulatory board recognizes, such as IFRS, US-GAAP or Swiss GAAP. Companies listed on the SIX Swiss Exchange are further required to complement the business report with a corporate governance report outlining information based on the requirements of the 'Directive on Information Relating to Corporate Governance'.

Since 2015, listed companies are required by law to provide to their shareholders a separate and audited compensation report. The Corporate Governance Directive (DCG) further requires information on the principles and elements of compensation as well as on the compensation procedures to be disclosed in the governance or compensation report. At this time, there is no formal requirement for publishing a sustainability report, but listed companies may opt in to publish such a report in line with SIX Swiss Exchange's standards.[3]

d. **Swiss Code of Best Practice.** In 2002, the Swiss industry organization Economiesuisse introduced the first version of the 'Swiss Code of Best Practice for Corporate Governance' (Swiss Code), a self-regulatory code for Swiss companies to establish a best practice corporate governance framework. The Swiss Code is subject to a comply-or-explain principle and widely followed by companies listed on the Swiss stock exchange. The code was amended in 2013 to reflect the increased priority of sustainable corporate success and to provide a general understanding of corporate social responsibility. The revision also focused on the board of directors, in particular related to diversity (including gender representation), and extended the sections on risk management and compliance.

5.2.3 Shareholder Rights

The rights of shareholders of Swiss-listed companies include in particular:

(1) **Annual board of directors' elections:** shareholders have to elect annually and individually each board member.
(2) **Annual chairperson election:** shareholders have to elect annually and individually the chairperson of the board of directors.

---

[3] To be recognized as a sustainability report by the SIX Swiss Exchange and to be included in the SIX officially published sustainability reporting overview, a company's sustainability report has to follow one of the following internationally recognized standards: the Global Reporting Initiative, the Sustainability Accounting Standards Board Standard, the UN Global Impact or, in the case of real estate companies, the European Public Real Estate Association Best Practices Recommendations on Sustainability Reporting.

(3) **Annual compensation committee elections:** shareholders have to elect annually and individually each member of the compensation committee.

(4) **Annual votes on compensation amounts:** each year, shareholders have to approve the (maximum) amount of compensation allocated to the executive committee, the board of directors and advisory boards, if any. Shareholder approval can be given ex ante (prospectively) in the form of a maximum budget for the current or future period or ex post (retrospectively) on the maximum amount for the past period. If companies opt for an ex ante vote on variable compensation elements, according to the revised CO it is mandatory to also have an advisory vote on the compensation report.

(5) **Approval of the articles of association, which include amongst others:**
   - The maximum tenure/age limit for board members
   - The maximum outside mandates each member of the board of directors or executive committee may hold
   - A description of the compensation scheme for the executive committee and the board of directors
   - Exceptions to the mandatory offer bid that is generally applied if a shareholder crosses the 33.33% threshold (opting up in case this threshold is increased or opting out if this threshold is abandoned altogether)

(6) **Annual election of the independent proxy and the external auditor:** shareholders have to elect annually (i) the independent proxy, who will represent shareholder votes that have been cast in advance at the AGM, and the (ii) external auditor, who conducts the annual audit on the company's financial statements.

5.3 Broad Developments in Corporate Ownership from the 1990s to the Late 2010s

This section provides an overview of ownership concentration over a roughly thirty-year time period, starting from as early as 1988 and extending to 2018. The sample considered here consists of the largest 100 companies overall, the largest 20 or all listed companies. The largest 100 are not necessarily listed companies, but also include cooperatives and other legal forms. Given that Switzerland does not have disclosure requirements regarding ownership of non-listed companies, these data should be considered with care, as they include self-reported ownership from a group of companies that choose to disclose their ownership. The tables in this section are based on data whose collection and construction are described in Chapter 1 of this volume. Although the financial sector of Switzerland is very sizable, for consistency with the other chapters of the book, financial companies are not included in this analysis.

Despite these data composition limitations, Tables 5.1 to 5.4 reveal some interesting basic insights. First, to obtain insights into the size of the largest shareholders, consider Tables 5.1 and 5.3. In the full sample, the median size of the three largest owners fell slightly over these thirty years. For example, the median stake of the largest owner was 37.6% in 1990, and 35.79% in 2018. However, the median share of all the shareholders holding more than 10% increased from 54.35% to 67.25%. Among the listed firms,[4] developments are clearer. Here, the ownership of the largest shareholders has decreased (e.g. the largest shareholders at the median held 33% in 1990, and held 29.4% in 2018), and the median share of all the shareholders holding more than 10% also fell from 52.7% to 50.01%.

Second, to obtain insight into who the main shareholders are, consider Tables 5.2 and 5.4. While in 1990, in almost a quarter (24%) of the largest 100 firms, the biggest shareholder was a family or an individual (Table 5.2, column 1), that was the case in only 6 of the largest 100 firms in 2018. Compared to other countries where influential families sometimes use pyramidal structures to control a number of companies, family ownership in Switzerland is largely confined to a single company, in which the family has been involved over generations. While those companies where family members continue to be actively involved in management remain persistently in family control, it is mostly the second group, those in which families are disentangled from operations and only hold a financial stake, which has seen a decline over the years. Overall, the empirical findings on economic entrenchment of families, therefore, only apply to a limited extent in Switzerland. The by far most frequent ownership structure (at least

---

[4] Notice that the included number of listed firms grew from 87 in 1990 to 228 in 2018. As we discuss in Section 5.4, this makes a direct comparison difficult as different sized companies saw different developments in their shareholder structure.

Table 5.1 *Ownership concentration in the 1990s in Switzerland*

	Number of firms	Largest shareholder (C1)[a]				Second-largest shareholder (C2)[a]				Third-largest shareholder (C3)[a]				All largest shareholders Largest SH[b]			
		Min.	Med.	Mean	Max.	Min.	Med.	Mean	Max.	Min.	Med.	Mean	Max.	Min.	Med.	Mean	Max.
Top 100[c]	100	3.50	37.62	43.33	100.00	3.00	11.00	15.53	50.00	3.00	7.20	8.33	22.30	10.00	54.35	56.12	100.00
Top 20[d]	20	6.30	49.50	44.65	100.00	5.50	11.00	18.71	50.00	3.20	9.25	8.77	13.90	10.70	65.50	63.17	100.00
Listed[e]	87	3.50	33.00	39.96	96.90	3.00	11.00	14.09	40.00	3.00	5.90	7.62	22.30	10.00	52.70	51.43	96.90

Notes:

[a] The table shows ownership for the first year with available ownership data in the 1990s. C1, C2 and C3 are the shareholdings in % of the largest, second- and third-largest shareholders in a company.

[b] Largest SH is the sum of shareholdings of all shareholders having 10% or more of outstanding shares in a company.

[c] Top 100 are the largest 100 firms (both listed and unlisted) in Switzerland.

[d] Top 20 are the largest 20 firms (both listed and unlisted) in Switzerland.

[e] Listed are listed firms in Switzerland.

Source: Bureau van Dijk (1999), Amadeus database, own calculations.

Table 5.2 *Largest shareholders by ownership categories in the 1990s in Switzerland*

Ownership categories[a]	Top 100 (% of firms)[b]	Min.[c]	Med.	Mean	Max.	Top 20 (% of firms)[b]	Min.[c]	Med.	Mean	Max.	Listed (% of firms)[b]	Min.[c]	Med.	Mean	Max.
Families/individuals	24.00	20.00	41.87	43.18	88.00	10.00	31.00	41.00	41.00	51.00	28.74	20.00	40.73	41.30	88.00
State	3.00	44.90	49.00	53.13	65.50	10.00	49.00	57.25	57.25	65.50	2.30	44.90	55.20	55.20	65.50
Non-financial	19.00	20.00	69.70	63.41	100.00	30.00	22.46	43.50	52.05	100.00	12.64	35.70	76.60	72.38	96.90
Financial	4.00	22.60	29.00	39.05	75.60	5.00	75.60	75.60	75.60	75.60	5.75	20.00	30.00	40.52	75.60
Holdings	16.00	23.23	43.12	50.58	92.00						11.49	23.23	63.61	58.55	90.70
Others	1.00	64.00	64.00	64.00	64.00						3.45	29.00	64.00	52.33	64.00
Foreign	11.00	25.00	50.10	61.13	100.00	20.00	50.00	56.50	65.75	100.00	6.90	25.00	40.50	49.52	88.10
Dispersed	22.00	3.50	10.35	10.49	17.80	25.00	6.30	9.28	9.14	11.40	28.74	3.50	12.00	11.79	18.50
Total	*100*					*100*					*100*				
Number of firms	100					20					87				

Notes:

[a] The table shows results for the first year with available ownership data in the 1990s. We identify the company's direct controlling owner as the largest shareholder holding 20% or more of outstanding shares. When no single entity owned at least 20%, a company is categorized as having dispersed ownership. Ownership categories: Families/individuals, state, non-financial firms, financial (banks, other financial institutions) and holdings are domestic shareholders. Foreign are all foreign shareholders (physical and legal persons).

[b] Percentage of firms: percentage of firms controlled by each ownership category or with dispersed ownership.

[c] Descriptive statistics (min, med., mean and max.) are the percentage of ownership stake of the ownership category in firms controlled by this ownership category.

Source: Bureau van Dijk (1999), Amadeus database, own calculations.

Table 5.3 *Ownership concentration in 2018 in Switzerland*

	Number of firms	Largest shareholder[a]				Second-largest shareholder[a]				Third-largest shareholder[a]				All largest shareholders[b]			
		Min.	Med.	Mean	Max.	Min.	Med.	Mean	Max.	Min.	Med.	Mean	Max.	Min.	Med.	Mean	Max.
Top 100[c]	100	0.00	35.79	42.48	100.00	1.68	9.77	12.51	43.10	0.40	5.10	7.32	21.32	10.00	67.25	66.15	100.00
Top 20[d]	20	0.00	15.36	33.31	100.00	2.99	6.13	11.26	39.30	1.10	4.08	5.34	14.03	11.20	72.17	66.82	100.00
Listed[e]	228	3.02	29.42	33.46	97.89	0.88	8.70	10.55	39.30	0.40	5.10	6.49	25.84	10.00	50.01	49.16	99.96

Notes:
[a] The table displays descriptive statistics for the shareholdings of the largest, second- and third-largest shareholders in a company in 2018.
[b] All largest shareholders is the total share of all shareholders having 10% or more of outstanding shares in a company.
[c] Top 100 are the largest 100 firms (both listed and unlisted) in Switzerland.
[d] Top 20 are the largest 20 firms (both listed and unlisted) in Switzerland.
[e] Listed are listed firms in Switzerland.
Source: Bureau van Dijk (2020), Orbis database, own calculations.

Table 5.4 *Largest shareholders by ownership categories in 2018 in Switzerland*

Ownership categories[a]	Top 100 (% of firms)[b]	Min.[c]	Med.	Mean	Max.	Top 20 (% of firms)[b]	Min.[c]	Med.	Mean	Max.	Listed (% of firms)[b]	Min.[c]	Med.	Mean	Max.
Families/individuals	6.00	35.20		69.40	100.00	10.00	45.00		72.50	100.00	10.09	23.70	48.15	46.96	77.00
State	13.00	38.60		75.40	100.00	10.00	50.95		75.48	100.00	1.32	33.50	38.60	41.02	50.95
Non-financial	7.00	27.40		53.05	100.00						3.07	34.32	57.28	64.28	95.60
Financial	13.00	20.43		47.86	100.00	10.00	39.71		44.86	50.00	18.86	20.00	41.34	43.27	96.27
Holdings	8.00	31.44		71.46	100.00						8.77	22.07	53.85	52.39	72.70
Others	5.00	21.06		45.47	66.29	5.00	32.30		32.30	32.30	3.95	21.06	50.75	49.00	66.29
Foreign	12.00	20.92	50.66	55.69	100.00	10.00	55.36	77.68	77.68	100.00	16.23	20.28	48.62	46.51	97.89
Dispersed	36.00	0.00	8.49	8.08	18.41	55.00	0.00	8.20	8.44	18.41	37.72	3.02	10.11	10.52	19.90
Total	100					100					100				
Number of firms	100					20					228				

Notes:

[a] We identify the company's direct controlling owner as the largest shareholder holding 20% or more of outstanding shares. When no single entity owned at least 20%, a company is categorized as having dispersed ownership. Ownership categories: Families/individuals, state, non-financial firms, financial (banks, other financial institutions) and holdings are domestic shareholders. Foreign are all foreign shareholders (physical and legal persons).

[b] Percentage of firms: percentage of firms controlled by each ownership category or with dispersed ownership.

[c] Descriptive statistics (min., med., mean and max.) are the percentage of ownership stake of the ownership category in firms controlled by this ownership category.

Source: Bureau van Dijk (2020), Orbis database, own calculations.

relatively speaking) in 2018 was dispersed ownership (which, here, is defined as the case when the largest shareholder holds less than 20% of the shares): for 36 out of 100 companies, this applied, whereas this was true for only twenty-two companies in 1990. Similar patterns apply for the top 20 and listed companies. In 2018, in 13 of the 100 companies considered, the state was the largest owner, whereas that was so in only three companies in 1990. This is likely not a general trend, but rather a consequence of the data selection process and structural development in Switzerland. In the 2018 sample, a significantly higher number of power plants and utilities, which are increasingly organized as individual entities instead of being kept on the books of Cantons or the Country of Switzerland, were among the largest 100 companies. The low fraction of state-owned enterprises amongst the largest companies, mostly restricted to infrastructure such as utilities, telecommunications or transportation, reflects the Swiss government's generally liberal approach towards the economy. This is further underpinned by an increase in a partial floating of the shares of so far fully state-owned cantonal banks in recent years. Throughout the period, in slightly more than 10% of the companies, the largest shareholder was a foreign, non-domestic shareholder.

Third, the data show a considerable increase in listed companies amongst the top 20 companies over time. While approximately only one in three companies was listed in 1990, this fraction increased to 75% in 2018. A possible driver of this development in the largest companies is the increased globalization of the world that could be observed in the last decades. Many of the top 20 companies in Switzerland belong to the largest companies in their industries worldwide, an achievement that required substantial capital investments, which would arguably only be raised through access to the capital market. Moreover, the formation of these large companies in Switzerland is likely not a consequence of changing laws and regulations, but to the contrary, rather due to the stable, open and liberal economic environment that has been prevalent in Switzerland for decades. For the top 100 sample, the percentage of listed companies remained basically unchanged (with a slight increase from 57% to 62%).

Overall, this thirty-year view suggests some stability and some change in the ownership of Swiss companies. Section 5.4 will now take a deeper look at the developments in the most recent decade, focusing on listed firms, for which clear disclosure requirements exist.

5.4 Main Results: Shareholder Structure and Shareholder Behaviour in Swiss-Listed Companies 2008–2018

This section analyses the shareholder structure of publicly listed companies in Switzerland between 2008 and 2018 as well as the behaviour of shareholders in these companies. We draw on two sources of data.

First, data on listed companies' shareholders are provided by Orbis, which sources data from official ad hoc announcements by listed companies, filings of institutional investors or fund fact sheets. Thus, they cover not only the legally required disclosures, but also voluntary disclosures below the legal threshold. Besides an investor's holding in a specific company, Orbis further reports the name of the investor, the country of origin of the investor and the investor type (e.g. bank, insurance, private owner etc.). The data obtained from Orbis were screened manually to avoid double counting of investors' holding as multiple entries for the same investor are prevalent in this database. The data used here originates from a different data source than that reported in Section 5.3. Also, the focus in this section is on listed companies only. Nonetheless, there are clearly parallels in the findings across both samples. However, the richer data available for listed companies allow a more detailed analysis. Financial data on companies are from Thomson Reuters Datastream and index member data from the SIX Swiss Exchange.[5]

The sample covers the 100 largest companies listed in Switzerland in each year. It consists of the Swiss Performance Index® Large, representing the twenty highest capitalized stocks in Switzerland, more commonly known as the Swiss Market Index® (SMI), and the Swiss Performance Index® M, representing the next eighty highest capitalized stocks in Switzerland ('medium-index shares'). Only companies for which shareholdings are available are included. Because some companies have multiple listed share classes, or due to missing data,

---

[5] Several other academic papers use samples of Swiss companies drawn from similar data sources to study ownership-related research questions. For example, Becht et al. (2017) focus on activist shareholders across different countries, including Switzerland; Puca and Vatiero (2017) use Switzerland to study the relation between corporate ownership and innovation; Loderer and Waelchli (2010) use the Swiss case to investigate whether the decision of being a listed/unlisted company impacts minority shareholder protection; and Nenova (2003) provides an analysis of voting rights and corporate control across different countries, including Switzerland. None of these papers provides as detailed an account of the changes in ownership structure as this chapter.

Table 5.5 *Sector overview, Switzerland*

	2008	2018
Company ICB sector[a]	Number of companies	Number of companies
Basic materials	8	3
Industrials	23	32
Consumer goods	9	9
Health care	12	12
Consumer services	8	4
Telecommunications	1	2
Utilities	1	1
Financials	27	25
Technology	5	6
No Data[b]	6	6
Total	100	100

Notes:
[a] Corresponds to the main sector classification as reported to the SIX Swiss Exchange.
[b] No shareholder information is available for these companies and they were dropped from the top 100 sample.
Source: The data sources are described in Section 5.4.

for example due to limited disclosure as a consequence of being incorporated outside Switzerland, the actual sample used in the analysis may be lower than 100 observations per year.

As shown in Table 5.5, a significant number of the largest 100 companies in Switzerland are in the financial sector, which contributed almost 30% to the sample in 2008 and only slightly less in 2018. The second-largest sector is industrials (about every third company in 2018). Health-care companies are the third-largest group in the top 100 of listed companies.

Second, we draw on a unique annual survey on corporate governance in Switzerland (the 'Survey' in what follows), which we conducted together with SWIPRA Services, a governance consultancy and governance think tank for the Swiss market.[6] Since 2013, this survey has gathered views of Swiss-listed issuers as well as asset managers and

---

[6] Surveys can provide important insights on the preferences and behaviour of market participants. For example, McCahery, Sautner and Starks (2016) present results of a comprehensive survey of institutional investors. They find that investors engage both in voice and exit.

Table 5.6 *Sample coverage SWIPRA Surveys 2013–2019 in Switzerland*

	Coverage			
Year	Institutional investors[a] equity AuM (%)[b]	N	Listed SPI® companies market cap (%)[c]	N
2013	n/a	77	n/a	31
2014	n/a	54	n/a	53
2015	18.8	95	77.9	58
2016	21.2	74	81.3	98
2017	20.8	63	79.3	83
2018	26.0	74	77.0	80
2019	30.0	75	78.0	78

Notes:
[a] Including asset managers, fund managers and asset owners.
[b] Percentage of equity assets under management calculated on the basis of the worldwide Top 400 Asset Managers' list issued annually by *Investment & Pensions Europe*.
[c] Relative to the total market capitalization of all Swiss Performance Index® constituents.
Source: The data sources are described in Section 5.4.

asset owners over time (SWIPRA Surveys, 2013–2019). In the first two years (2013 and 2014), the Survey focused on Swiss-based asset managers and asset owners on the investor side. Foreign institutions were first asked to participate in 2015. Table 5.6 provides an overview to the Survey's coverage. In recent years, it was approximately 80% of the market capitalization of Swiss-listed companies and around 30% of the global equity assets managed by the 400 largest asset managers in the world. The three key advantages of the Survey are, therefore, that (1) it asks the same (or suitably rephrased) questions to both issuers and institutional investors, (2) it covers several years, allowing some changes to be observed for a few questions that are asked multiple times and (3) it covers almost the whole public equity market of the country.

5.4.1 Observation 1: Signs of Decreasing Concentration of Shareholders in the Full Sample

Table 5.7 covers for each year the largest 100 companies listed on the Swiss Performance Index® and for which shareholder information is

Table 5.7 *Shareholdings in the full sample, Switzerland*

Panel A: Full sample

	2008					2018				
	Min.	Med.	Mean	Max.	N	Min.	Med.	Mean	Max.	N
Market capitalization (CHF million)	15.2	1,641.0	8,557.0	1,59,327.8	93	474.7	3,627.4	14,177.0	2,44,427.3	91
Shareholder coverage[a]	4.4%	66.9%	62.3%	98.0%	94	25.9%	64.3%	65.0%	100.0%	94
Largest shareholder	2.0%	20.3%	28.3%	80.3%	94	3.8%	18.2%	28.3%	100.0%	94
Top 3 shareholders[b]	4.4%	35.7%	39.3%	86.6%	94	8.8%	31.9%	38.5%	100.0%	94
Swiss shareholders[c]	0.0%	36.6%	45.5%	100.0%	92	0.9%	39.0%	43.9%	100.0%	92
Shareholder concentration[d]	0.5%	11.1%	19.2%	80.3%	94	-8.3%	7.4%	17.6%	84.5%	93

Panel B: Non-financial companies[e]

	2008					2018				
	Min.	Med.	Mean	Max.	N	Min.	Med.	Mean	Max.	N
Market capitalization (CHF million)	15.2	1,475.0	9,600.2	1,59,327.8	67	474.7	3,286.6	15,827.0	2,44,427.3	66
Shareholder coverage[a]	13.0%	68.0%	64.4%	98.0%	67	29.4%	67.0%	67.8%	100.0%	69
Largest shareholder	3.6%	20.3%	25.8%	70.5%	67	3.8%	20.4%	28.2%	100.0%	69
Top 3 shareholders[b]	9.4%	32.3%	37.8%	82.2%	67	10.0%	35.5%	39.6%	100.0%	69
Swiss shareholders[c]	0.0%	36.0%	44.6%	100.0%	66	0.9%	35.9%	42.7%	100.0%	69
Shareholder concentration[d]	1.4%	11.0%	15.8%	60.3%	67	-8.3%	7.8%	15.9%	70.0%	68

Panel C: Financial companies[f]

	2008					2018				
	Min.	Med.	Mean	Max.	N	Min.	Med.	Mean	Max.	N
Market capitalization (CHF million)	399.0	2,045.1	5,869.0	43,519.3	26	615.7	4,442.3	9,820.9	47,170.2	25
Shareholder coverage[a]	4.4%	59.0%	57.2%	94.7%	27	25.9%	57.7%	57.2%	96.4%	25
Largest shareholder	2.0%	29.8%	34.4%	80.3%	27	4.0%	10.7%	28.5%	84.5%	25
Top 3 shareholders[b]	4.4%	46.3%	42.9%	86.6%	27	8.8%	26.2%	35.6%	84.5%	25
Swiss shareholders[c]	0.0%	57.9%	47.9%	100.0%	26	2.2%	42.0%	47.4%	100.0%	25
Shareholder concentration[d]	0.5%	15.7%	27.8%	80.3%	27	1.2%	5.1%	22.2%	84.5%	25

Notes:

[a] Sum of all disclosed shareholdings.

[b] Sum of the shareholdings of the three largest disclosed owners.

[c] Sum of all disclosed shareholdings of Swiss shareholders in a company relative to the company's disclosed total shareholdings.

[d] Normalized Herfindahl coefficient [0,1], calculated on the basis of shareholder coverage.

[e] Companies not belonging to the ICB Industry Classification 'Financials' (6000).

[f] Companies belonging to the ICB Industry Classification 'Financials' (6000).

Source: The data sources are described in Section 5.4.

available. Panel A provides an overview of the shareholder structure of all the companies. Our shareholdings data covers approximately two-thirds of a company's shareholders (median coverage of 66.9% in 2008 and 64.3% in 2018). Thus, these data provide a representative view of the ownership in these companies in terms of power to take decisions at general shareholder meetings. It is important to note that any evaluation of ratios is always done with respect to the disclosed ownerships. For example, the percentage of Swiss investors is calculated as a percentage of the *disclosed* holdings.

In this aggregate view, some tendencies of decreasing concentration are already visible. The median stake of the largest shareholder has decreased slightly from 20.3% in 2008 to 18.2% in 2018. On average, the stake of the largest shareholder remained unchanged over this period at 28.3% and the three largest shareholders held 39.3% in 2008 and 38.5% in 2018. These numbers are notably lower than those provided in Aminadav and Papaioannou (2020) for 2012, which is mainly due to their larger Swiss sample, covering 276 companies, many of which were not actively and regularly traded as a result of a very small free float. The three largest shareholders held in 2018 on average 38.5% in Switzerland (Panel A of Table 5.7). This is notably lower than in other markets such as Germany and France, where the average holding of the largest three shareholders was above 50% (de la Cruz, Alejandra and Yun, 2019), but above markets such as the United Kingdom or the United States in which the largest three shareholders on average command between 20% and 30%.[7]

Shareholder concentration, as measured by the Herfindahl index – ranging from 0% (low concentration) to 100% (monopoly) – has come down, too, from 11.1% in 2008 to 7.4% in 2018. However, as discussed in detail in Edmans and Holderness (2017), it is not sufficient to just identify the presence of a large shareholder (or in their terminology, blockholder) as different blockholders generally vary significantly in their objectives. We discuss the presence and impact of some of these blockholders, such as families and private individuals or institutional investors, in more detail in the following subsections.

---

[7] The samples used by de la Cruz et al. (2019) for the markets discussed above generally have a slightly wider coverage than our Swiss sample but are, in terms of market capitalization covered within each individual country, approximately comparable to our top 100 Swiss companies.

An interesting finding with respect to companies with large, controlling shareholders emerged from the 2019 Survey. In this survey, 60.3% of the participating investors stated that they generally see a better governance and disclosure quality in widely held companies than in companies with a large anchor shareholder. This suggests that a lower concentration in the shareholder base is associated with a more transparent disclosure and more interaction between the company and its shareholders. Indeed, it provides qualitative evidence of a potential conflict of interest arising between different kinds of shareholders, namely blockholders and minority shareholders.

The median stake held by Swiss investors was 39% in 2018 (Panel A of Table 5.7). This suggests a very high participation of non-domestic investors in the Swiss market, comparable to the highest international levels shown in de la Cruz et al. (2019). However, the Swiss shareholder base is arguably larger than these numbers suggest, because disclosure rules only require shareholders with equity stakes above 3% to disclose their holdings. Consequently, unlike their peers in the United States or the United Kingdom, many Swiss institutional investors do not have to publicly disclose their holdings in Swiss-listed companies. This can also be seen by the unaccounted for fraction of investors in Swiss companies that represent about a third of the shares outstanding (the fraction that is not included in *coverage*[8]), which is significantly higher than for example in the United Kingdom or the United States, as pointed out in de la Cruz et al. (2019). Ownership of domestic investors has actually increased somewhat since 2008. In the next subsection, we take a closer look at how investors' origins actually changed in the subsample of companies that have been amongst the 100 largest Swiss companies since 2008.

5.4.2 Observation 2: Concentrated Young Companies and Widely Held Old Companies

Of the analysed companies, sixty-one remained in the sample over the entire period from 2008 until 2018 ('full-period companies'). Table 5.8

---

[8] Coverage measures the percentage of disclosed shareholdings, i.e. shares of a company that can be assigned to a specific shareholder, relative to the total share capital issued by a company. For the percentage of issued share capital that is not included in coverage, i.e. (100% − coverage), no information on these shareholders is available.

Table 5.8 *Shareholdings in the full-period sample, Switzerland*

Panel A: Full sample

	2008					2018				
	Min.	Med.	Mean	Max.	N	Min.	Med.	Mean	Max.	N
Market capitalization (CHF million)	407.1	2,351.4	12,106.4	1,59,327.8	60	474.7	6,209.4	20,001.5	2,44,427.3	60
Shareholder coverage[a]	4.4%	66.8%	62.7%	98.0%	61	25.9%	62.2%	61.1%	100.0%	61
Largest shareholder	2.0%	19.6%	25.8%	70.5%	61	3.8%	13.9%	24.1%	75.4%	61
Top 3 shareholders[b]	4.4%	32.3%	37.2%	86.6%	61	8.8%	27.5%	34.2%	83.4%	61
Swiss shareholders[c]	0.0%	35.5%	42.8%	100.0%	61	2.2%	30.2%	40.5%	98.3%	61
Shareholder concentration[d]	0.5%	9.5%	16.7%	60.3%	61	1.2%	5.9%	15.7%	59.3%	61

Panel B: Non-financial companies[e]

	2008					2018				
	Min.	Med.	Mean	Max.	N	Min.	Med.	Mean	Max.	N
Market capitalization (CHF million)	407.1	2,465.4	13,882.1	1,59,327.8	42	474.7	7,650.8	24,214.6	2,44,427.3	41
Shareholder coverage[a]	27.6%	70.6%	67.2%	98.0%	42	29.4%	63.9%	64.0%	100.0%	42
Largest shareholder	3.6%	22.4%	26.1%	70.5%	42	3.8%	16.1%	23.4%	71.1%	42
Top 3 shareholders[b]	9.4%	37.5%	38.3%	82.2%	42	10.0%	27.8%	34.7%	83.4%	42
Swiss shareholders[c]	0.0%	32.8%	41.4%	95.5%	42	9.8%	27.8%	38.9%	94.8%	42
Shareholder concentration[d]	1.4%	11.4%	15.8%	60.3%	42	1.6%	6.2%	13.9%	56.9%	42

Panel C: Financial companies[f]

	2008					2018				
	Min.	Med.	Mean	Max.	N	Min.	Med.	Mean	Max.	N
Market capitalization (CHF million)	614.7	2,305.9	7,963.2	43,519.3	18	1,544.8	5,713.5	10,910.2	47,170.2	19
Shareholder coverage[a]	4.4%	58.2%	52.6%	94.7%	19	25.9%	57.7%	54.7%	96.4%	19
Largest shareholder	2.0%	14.1%	25.3%	67.0%	19	4.0%	10.0%	25.8%	75.4%	19
Top 3 shareholders[b]	4.4%	25.8%	34.8%	86.6%	19	8.8%	20.4%	33.1%	83.2%	19
Swiss shareholders[c]	0.0%	56.9%	45.9%	100.0%	19	2.2%	35.0%	44.1%	98.3%	19
Shareholder concentration[d]	0.5%	6.7%	18.9%	57.2%	19	1.2%	4.2%	19.7%	59.3%	19

Notes:
[a] Sum of all the disclosed shareholdings.
[b] Sum of the shareholdings of the three largest disclosed owners.
[c] Sum of all disclosed shareholdings of Swiss shareholders in a company relative to the company's disclosed total shareholdings.
[d] Normalized Herfindahl coefficient [0,1], calculated on the basis of shareholder coverage.
[e] Companies not belonging to the ICB Industry Classification 'Financials' (6000).
[f] Companies belonging to the ICB Industry Classification 'Financials' (6000).
Source: The data sources are described in Section 5.4.

131

covers the 61 companies among the largest 100 companies that remained in the sample over the entire observation period (2008–2018). As can be seen in Panel A, these companies are generally larger than the overall sample companies. This should not, however, bias our analysis of the dynamics over time as these companies belong to the largest sample companies in the first year (2008) as well as in the last year (2018).

While the shareholder structure of the full-period sample of companies does not differ significantly from the overall sample in 2008, their development until 2018 seems much more accentuated than for the overall sample. For example, median holdings of the largest shareholder in the full-period sample companies drop from 19.6% in 2008 to 13.9% in 2018 (compared to 18.2% in the general sample). This tendency towards a decreasing shareholder concentration and a decreasing number of voting share companies in Switzerland contrasts with the observations of Morck, Wolfenzon and Yeung (2005), who draw a picture of entrenched families and private individuals controlling large parts of the economy through superior voting shares (i.e. multi-class share structures) instead of invested capital.[9] Indeed, an additional analysis (not tabulated) of the Swiss top 100 sample reveals that in 2018 only a very small fraction of the companies is actually controlled by individuals and families (this observation is consistent with the findings in the long-term sample discussed in Section 5.3). They only hold 0.5% in the median and 19.6% in the highest quartile of companies (in 2008, private individuals controlled 5.4% in the median and 29.3% in the top quartile). The data are more in line with the hypothesis of Franks et al. (2012) who postulate a life-cycle theory for family firms. Accordingly, in countries with strong investor protection, high financial development and active markets for corporate control (all of these characteristics apply to the Swiss market), the fraction of equity owned by the family becomes smaller as investment opportunities, external financing requirements and high merger and acquisition activity increase the share of external shareholders. In other words, these markets experience a general development over time away from family firms to widely held companies.

---

[9] Of course, decreasing concentration could also mean that it is easier to preserve managerial entrenchment because it becomes harder for shareholders to coordinate in actions against entrenched management.

Interestingly, the proportion of Swiss shareholders in these full-period companies dropped from 35.5% in 2008 to 30.2% in 2018. This suggests that the newly included companies of the SPI top 100 differ substantially from the companies remaining in the index for the entire period, with the largest shareholder commanding a much higher equity stake in the newly included firms relative to the full-period companies. Similarly, the proportion of domestic Swiss shareholders is much higher in the newly added companies than in the full-period companies. A reason for this is, as we will point out in the next subsection, company size. Companies that remain within the sample over the entire period are generally the largest and most mature ones that are well established in international capital markets. On the other hand, many of the newly included companies went through a recent IPO and, due to a widely observed home bias of investors (Coval and Moskowitz 1999), generally have a much higher percentage of Swiss investors, in many instances also the company's founders, in their shareholder base.

5.4.3 Observation 3: Opposite Trajectories in Shareholder Concentration in Financial and Non-financial Companies

As pointed out at the outset of this subsection, companies in the financial sector contribute approximately 30% of the companies in our sample and are an important pillar of Switzerland's economy. A closer look at these companies and a comparison with the non-financial sector is warranted.

Panels B and C of Table 5.7 provide an overview of the shareholder structure and its development for both groups. In 2008, financial companies' shareholder structure used to be much more concentrated, with the three largest shareholders controlling a median 46.3% of the shares, compared to 32.3% in their non-financial counterparts. Yet, while the shareholdings of the three largest shareholders remained almost unchanged in the non-financial companies, they dropped by 20 percentage points in the financial sector. Therefore, by 2018, the tables have turned and concentration in non-financial companies is now higher than in financial ones. Similar results apply for the largest shareholders and shareholder concentration in general.

Interestingly, financial companies' shareholder base has historically been dominated by Swiss investors. Despite a large increase in non-Swiss shareholders over the last ten years, financial companies continue to have a higher fraction of Swiss shareholders than their non-financial counterparts. (Part of this is due to real estate companies, which are classified as financial companies, and for which legal restrictions made it very difficult for non-Swiss investors to purchase.)

In Panels B and C of Table 5.8, a similar picture emerges for the full-sample companies with respect to the development from 2008 to 2018. However, when looking at the holdings of the largest as well as the three largest shareholders in 2008, it is striking to see that their holdings were already lower in financial companies than in non-financial companies, contrary to what we have seen in Table 5.7. Thus, the large concentration in the shareholder base of financial companies in 2008 was largely driven by companies that dropped out of the sample, for example by being acquired or taken into private companies.

5.4.4 Observation 4: Company Size Matters for Shareholder Concentration

Table 5.9 differentiates between the largest twenty listed companies versus the eighty next largest listed companies. This split is motivated by the fact that these two groups of companies are fundamentally different in terms of their overall size and, therefore, international visibility and exposure to large non-domestic shareholders. Using this split, some intriguing trends can be observed. In particular, while the impact of the largest shareholder has remained largely unchanged over the years in the largest companies (median shareholding of 9.9% in 2008 and 10.7% in 2018), it dropped somewhat, from 25.1% to 23.6%, in the eighty next largest companies. This observation is accentuated when considering the median stake of the three largest shareholders. This stake decreased markedly for the medium-index shares, from 42.5% in 2008 to 36.6% in 2018. This is still significantly above the 22.1% for the top 20 (SMI) companies in 2018, for which the holdings also changed only slightly (25.8% in 2008).

A similar result can be found with respect to shareholder concentration, measured by the normalized Herfindahl coefficient. As can be seen in Panel A of Table 5.9, concentration in the SMI companies has remained largely unchanged, while for the medium companies, it has decreased by about 30%, from 12.6% to 9.3%. Hence, compared to 2008, medium companies seem to have more medium-sized shareholders

Table 5.9 *Developments in different companies groups by size, Switzerland*

Panel A: Largest 20 SPI companies

	Coverage[a] (%)	Largest shareholder (%)	Second-largest shareholder (%)	Third-largest shareholder (%)	Top 3 shareholders[b] (%)	Swiss shareholders[c] (%)	Shareholder concentration[d] (%)
2008	58.2	9.9	5.6	2.9	25.8	20.1	4.1
2018	62.2	10.7	5.2	3.8	22.1	18.5	4.0

Panel B: Next 80 SPI companies

	Coverage[a] (%)	Largest shareholder (%)	Second-largest shareholder (%)	Third-largest shareholder (%)	Top 3 shareholders[b] (%)	Swiss shareholders[c] (%)	Shareholder concentration[d] (%)
2008	67.5	25.1	6.6	5.0	42.5	47.8	12.6
2018	65.0	23.6	5.4	4.1	36.6	45.0	9.3

Notes:
[a] All statistics in this table are medians and cover the largest 100 companies of the Swiss Performance Index® (SPI) in each year for which shareholder information is available, split into the twenty largest companies (Swiss Market Index®) and the remaining eighty companies (SPI Mid Index). Coverage is the sum of all the disclosed shareholdings.
[b] Sum of the shareholdings of the three largest disclosed owners.
[c] Sum of all disclosed shareholdings of Swiss shareholders in a company relative to the company's disclosed total shareholdings.
[d] Normalized Herfindahl coefficient [0,1], calculated on the basis of shareholder coverage.
Source: The data sources are described in Section 5.4.

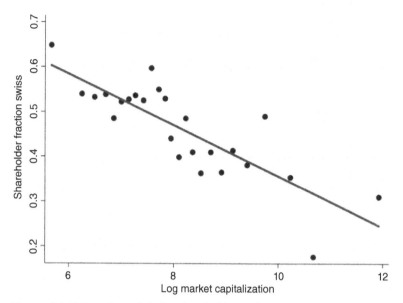

Figure 5.1 Proportion of Swiss shareholders relative to company's market capitalization among top 100 companies, 2008–2018.
Source: The data sources are described in Section 5.4.

with similarly large stakes, but fewer shareholders holding a large stake by themselves nowadays.

As Figure 5.1 shows, larger Swiss-listed companies have a far more non-domestic shareholder base. However, the mild trend towards internationalization of the shareholder base in Swiss-listed companies is not only confined to the largest stocks, as seen above in Table 5.9.

An interesting finding with respect to how different-sized companies interact with their shareholders was revealed in the SWIPRA Survey of 2019. While 44.4% of Swiss and 40.0% of non-domestic institutional investors stated that they had sufficient access to the boards of the largest Swiss companies included in the Swiss Leader Index (SLI®, covering the largest thirty stocks in the Swiss market), a home bias seems to emerge for the non-SLI companies within the largest 100 stocks. For these companies, board access is deemed sufficient for 55.6% of Swiss institutional investors, but only for 15% of non-domestic institutional investors.

5.4.5 Observation 5: Passively Invested Institutional Investors Are, in Fact, Active

Academia and market commentators have increasingly paid attention to passive institutional shareholders as the managed assets by these market players have increased significantly over the last ten years (see e.g. Bebchuk and Hirst, 2019). With low fees and a broad diversification promise, these funds have attracted trillions of dollars from asset owners. The name of their investment strategy, 'passive', has for a long time tricked many market participants into thinking that these funds also behave passively in terms of their shareholder rights. On the contrary, passively invested asset managers belong to the most active ones in terms of casting shareholder votes and thereby influencing companies and their governance framework. Indeed, passive institutional investors have become very active stewards, upholding the interests of their beneficial owners. For example, Appel, Gormley and Keim (2016) show that passive investors significantly influence the governance framework of their investee companies and are positively associated with long-term firm performance. Similar evidence is provided by McCahery, Sautner and Starks (2016) in their survey of large institutional investors. Their survey suggests that institutional investors use 'behind-the-scenes' engagements with their investee company to shape the governance framework as a complementary resource to the standard-theory exit strategy. Fahlenbrach and Schmidt (2017) argue, however, that an increase in passive investors leads to higher agency conflicts and, therefore, impairs firm value. Thus, whereas the actual impact of those large passive investors on firm value does not seem entirely clear, it is undisputed that their presence impacts a company's governance.

A recent development with a noticeable impact on listed companies is not explicitly visible in the data for disclosure reasons, but supported by various pieces of survey evidence. Until the OaEC (see Subsection 5.2.2) was enacted, it was common for Swiss pension funds to invest at least a portion of their portfolio directly into shares of listed companies. As the Ordinance included provisions requiring pension funds with direct equity investments to more comprehensively exercise their fiduciary duties, for example by actively voting their shares, pension funds amended their investment approach. Assets were no longer invested directly, but through external asset managers for which the

Ordinance's fiduciary rule did not apply. With this shift in assets from pension funds, in Switzerland generally passive owners, to the largest, often passively investing asset managers, which at the time developed into more active owners in terms of fiduciary duty, listed companies were increasingly confronted with higher requirements regarding their corporate governance. Thus, interestingly, the Ordinance's aim to increase pension funds' fiduciary duties was circumvented at first, but the shift to external asset managers eventually led to a more comprehensive exercise of fiduciary duties. Yet, the fact that most of the largest investors managing Swiss pension fund assets are located in the United Kingdom or the United States led to pressure for Swiss-listed companies to adapt a more Anglo-Saxon kind of corporate governance (see Section 5.4.6).

The asset management industry is all about size in terms of assets under management (AuM). This has led to a considerable concentration, which we also see in the Swiss data. By the end of 2018, the 'Big 3' of asset management, BlackRock (EUR 5.3 trillion AuM), Vanguard (EUR 4.3 trillion AuM) and State Street Global Advisors (EUR 2.2 trillion AuM) together control about 18% of the AuM of the 400 largest asset managers in the world (Investment & Pensions Europe, 2019). UBS is the largest Swiss asset manager with EUR 0.7 trillion AuM.

Panel A of Table 5.10 shows that the median holdings of the Big 3 in the Swiss stock market have increased notably. While the median holding of BlackRock in the largest 100 stocks in Switzerland was 0% in 2008, this increased to a median holding of 2.6% in each of the largest 100 Swiss-listed shares. This development is particularly accentuated for the largest twenty Swiss-listed companies, which are often constituent companies in pan-European or global industry-leader indices that form the basis of the largest passively managed funds.

This rise of large passive investors to become medium-sized shareholders comes at a time when the ownership of the single largest shareholder generally decreases. Consequently, as contrasted in Panels A and B of Figure 5.2, BlackRock predominantly built its stake in companies that are not controlled by a single large shareholder. Hence, the passive investors, shown here by the example of BlackRock, generally have their stakes in companies that cannot rely on a single controlling shareholder. As a result, they have a lot of impact on the board of directors of these companies. A very similar picture arises when the holdings of the largest shareholder measure is considered

Table 5.10 *Passive investors development, Switzerland*

Panel A: Largest 100 SPI companies

	BlackRock (%)	Vanguard (%)	State Street (%)	UBS (%)
2008	0.0	0.0	0.0	1.0
2018	2.6	2.1	0.2	1.6

Panel B: Largest 20 SPI companies

	BlackRock (%)	Vanguard (%)	State Street (%)	UBS (%)
2008	0.2	0.4	0.2	1.5
2018	4.1	2.6	0.3	1.8

Panel C: Next 80 SPI companies

	BlackRock (%)	Vanguard (%)	State Street (%)	UBS (%)
2008	0.0	0.0	0.0	0.8
2018	2.4	2.0	0.2	1.5

Note: All statistics in this table are medians and cover the largest 100 companies of the Swiss Performance Index® (SPI) in each year for which shareholder information is available, split into the twenty largest companies (Swiss Market Index®) and the remaining eighty companies (SPI Mid Index).
Source: The data sources are described in Section 5.4.

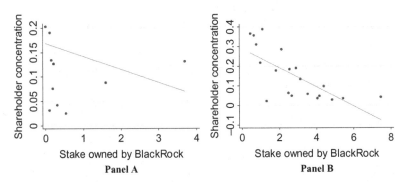

Figure 5.2 Development of BlackRock's shareholdings in Swiss companies.
Note: Shareholdings of the largest owners relative to BlackRock's stake (%) in a company's share ownership. Sample: Top 100 companies in 2008 (panel A) and 2018 (panel B).
Source: The data sources are described in Section 5.4.

instead of the shareholder concentration (available on request). In companies where BlackRock's stakes are high, the shareholder structure is generally more equally distributed.

The power of these shareholders is also reflected in the choices companies make in terms of structuring their governance. According to the Survey of 2018, 57% of the institutional investors agreed that international governance standards, in particular from the EU, the United Kingdom and the United States have a large or rather large influence in how AGM agenda items are assessed. The perception of Swiss-listed issuers is similar, 63% agreeing with the rather large to large influence. Hence, while national legislation is, due to its binding nature, indeed a key pillar of the governance framework of domestic listed companies as suggested by Gordon (2018), to the extent that one observes a convergence in governance practices, this effect does not seem to be driven by changing legal frameworks, but rather by the export of governance practices from key markets such as the United Kingdom or the United States through the major global institutional investors that are based in these markets. This trend is particularly accentuated in Switzerland, where the binding legal requirements in terms of governance structures are fairly limited, allowing for a notable impact of these large shareholders.

5.4.6 Observation 6: Rising Participation and Strong Behavioural Differences between Domestic and Non-domestic Investors

How do changes in regulation and shareholder structure affect Swiss-listed companies? First, participation in AGMs of Swiss-listed issuers has increased substantially over the last ten years, from an average value of 52.3% in 2010 to 71.1% in 2018 (Figure 5.3). About half of this increase (approximately the jump that can be observed from 2013 to 2014) can be attributed to the OaEC (see earlier discussion), which legally requires Swiss pension funds to exercise their voting rights in direct investments.

Second, do Swiss and non-Swiss investors behave differently? Aggarwal et al. (2011) argue that a high proportion of non-domestic shareholders generally impacts the governance frameworks of domestic companies. Indeed, the 2015 Survey reveals striking differences in this respect. Despite the relatively small sample, the tendencies are very

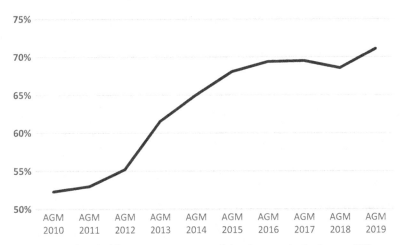

Figure 5.3 Shareholder AGM average participation rate in the largest 100 companies listed on the Swiss Performance Index.
Source: The data sources are described in Section 5.4.

clear. As depicted in Figure 5.4, 90% of the arguably larger non-Swiss asset managers stated that exercising shareholder voting rights might, overall, generate value over the medium term. By contrast, only 56.3% of Swiss asset managers and 43.8% of Swiss pension funds shared this view. Hence, having more non-Swiss institutional shareholders implies higher participation rates at AGMs and increased pressure on the board of directors due to a more active and informed shareholder base.

Besides assigning a higher value to voting rights, non-Swiss investors also indicated in the 2016 Survey that they are more likely to engage with companies over governance issues. While all the participating non-domestic investors (100%) indicated that they participate in engagement meetings, only 58.3% of Swiss asset managers and 24.2% of Swiss pension funds do so.

Additionally, in the 2017 Survey, 55.6% of non-domestic asset managers stated that their engagement meetings with Swiss portfolio companies have increased or strongly increased. This applies only to 22.7% of the participating Swiss asset managers. Hence, these non-domestic asset managers not only impact companies listed in Switzerland with a more dedicated AGM voting, but also through a more substantial dialogue with the company, predominantly the board of directors, during the year.

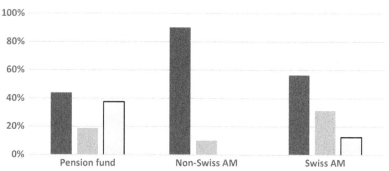

Figure 5.4 Value of voting rights in Swiss companies, 2015.
Note: This graph is based on the answers to the SWIPRA Survey 2015 question: 'In your opinion, what is the general value of shareholder voting rights for your organization?' Non-Swiss and Swiss asset managers (AMs) are classified according to the registration of the headquarters.
Source: The data sources are described in Section 5.4.

According to the 2017 Survey, investors predominantly use engagement meetings to better understand AGM agenda items and the individual company, but also to influence a company's governance framework. This approach seems to be successful, two-third of the companies indicating that they have adjusted their governance framework following engagement discussion, while only 41.9% of the issuers have done so to react to the previous year's AGM voting results. Interestingly, the largest companies indicated that they generally make larger adjustments following engagements than smaller companies. No such differential between different-sized companies is found in reactions to AGM voting outcomes.

Several papers have looked at the value impact of such engagements. Dimson, Karakaş and Li (2015) find an average positive abnormal return to engagement of 2.3% in the year after the engagement initiation, going up to 7.1% where these engagements are successful. A very similar effect was found by Barko, Cremers and Renneboog (2017), who put a higher emphasis on environmental and social engagement topics.

Thus, these research papers and survey findings suggest that the development in shareholder structure we have documented in the earlier subsections have a real impact on companies and their policies. In particular, the largest and most mature companies listed in Switzerland have not only seen an increase in shareholdings of non-domestic investors, but their influence on Swiss companies has grown disproportionally due to their active approach to AGM voting and engagement. The 2018 Survey further suggests that the increase in non-domestic investors leads to a significant spill-over of regulation enacted in the United Kingdom, the EU or the United States to companies listed in Switzerland. At least 56.9% of the investors believe that regulatory developments outside Switzerland have a rather large or large influence on how non-domestic asset managers analyse AGM agenda items of companies listed in Switzerland. This is generally aligned with the theory of converging corporate governance due to institutional investors striving for a global model, as suggested by Gordon and Roe (2004).

As an illustration of the concrete impact on the company of the presence of Swiss and non-domestic investors, consider the case of advisory votes on compensation reports. These votes have historically been the most controversial agenda item.

Table 5.11 shows that issuers with a below-median proportion of domestic investors (top line), that is, those with more international

Table 5.11 *Swiss companies' AGM voting outcomes on compensation report items, 2008–2019*

		SPI size index	
AGAINST votes (%), medians		M	L
Proportion Swiss	Below median	9.70%	11.33%
	N	171	129
	Above median	9.33%	3.44%
	N	148	23

Note: The table shows the median percentage of 'against' votes and the number of AGM votes on the compensation report item. The sample covers all AGM votes on compensation reports from 2008 to 2019 for the top 100 companies of the Swiss Performance Index® for which voting data is available. The sample is split into the twenty largest companies (L; Swiss Market Index®) and the remaining eighty companies (M; Swiss Performance Index Mid®).
Source: The data sources are described in Section 5.4.

investors, have historically received more 'against votes' at AGMs on their compensation reports. This is particularly accentuated for the largest companies, in which non-domestic investors generally have a majority stake (recall Table 5.9). For medium-index companies, the against votes difference between Swiss and non-domestic dominated companies is very small. A possible explanation for this difference between large and small companies may be the public perception of the largest companies, which are generally much more in focus and, therefore, subject to a higher level of scrutiny. Moreover, the largest companies also account for a higher proportion of the institutional investors' holdings, in particular if they passively follow an index, and are, therefore, analysed in more detail and subject to higher standards.

5.4.7 Observation 7: Corporate Social Responsibility as a Broad Governance Theme

A very topical, investor-driven development concerns corporate social responsibility (CSR), often also referred to as 'ESG' (environmental, social and governance). In its latest report, Eurosif collected information on the largest asset managers in the EU with respect to how their socially responsible funds are invested, specifically which socially responsible investment (SRI) strategy is used in managing these funds (Eurosif, 2018). Investors domiciled in the large mainland EU countries such as Germany and France, but also Switzerland, indicated that they mostly apply exclusion restrictions in their SRI funds, meaning that they abstain from investing in certain industries or countries. On the other hand, the fraction of engagement-based investments, which use shareholder rights to steer a company into a more responsible behaviour, is very small in these countries. Exceptions are investors from the United Kingdom and the Netherlands, for whom the proportions of engagement-based and exclusion-based investments are balanced. The 2019 Survey provides additional evidence in support of this behaviour. Nine out of ten non-domestic institutional investors (mainly UK- and US-based) participating in the survey indicated that they conduct governance engagements with their portfolio companies, while only 54.7% of Swiss institutional investors said that they conduct such meetings. The main reason given by those investors abstaining from such engagements is the direct costs of this approach. This cost argument is perhaps best interpreted in light of the assets managed. While the global equity universe is largely the same for all investors, the average amount of AuM is higher for non-domestic than for domestic investors in our sample. Consequently, relative to the assets managed, domestic investors face higher direct costs than their non-domestic counterparts.[10] However, engagements could help to reduce another particular friction with respect to ESG that was revealed by the survey: only 41% of the companies participating in the survey stated that they understand or somewhat understand to what extent CSR information is reflected in institutional investors' investment decisions and 48.1% understand or somewhat understand how this information influences their investors' AGM voting behaviour.

Accordingly, the different investment approaches that the Swiss and non-domestic investors are following towards a higher CSR or better ESG behaviour ultimately impact how they invest and interact (if at all) with their investee companies. Consequently, the composition of a company's shareholder base arguably has an impact on how the company ultimately deals with and prioritizes its CSR.

5.5 Drivers of Change in Shareholder Structure

In the previous sections, we have shown that specific groups of listed Swiss companies have seen developments in their shareholder structure over the past decade and more. Dispersion in the shareholder base has generally increased, family shareholdings have decreased and non-domestic investors have increased their ownership in Swiss companies. While it is difficult to pinpoint specific drivers of these developments, overall the pattern is consistent with the life-cycle hypothesis of Franks et al. (2012). Switzerland's economy is largely export oriented, governed by a relatively liberal business legislation with a reliable and stable rule of law, and it can depend on a very open and well-reputed capital market that also offers a functioning market for corporate control. Despite the country's small size, it has, therefore, been able to serve as home to some of the world's largest corporations. Moreover, the openness of Switzerland has limited the potential for insiders to coordinate to keep companies tightly under their control (Rajan and Zingales 2003). Switzerland has furthermore historically

---

[10] This effect is particularly pronounced in the asset management industry due to its significant concentration, described in Section 5.4.5.

not seen a prevalence of influential and entrenched families controlling large stakes of the economy through cross-shareholdings or particular control structures as discussed in Morck et al. (2005), but mostly relied on a functioning financial market to finance companies' growth. In light of the fast-moving globalization of the world economy during the periods we studied, these companies needed ample capital to stay top of their industries. This capital is increasingly provided by non-domestic investors who consequently own larger fractions of Swiss companies and also support worldwide expansions of so far family-owned companies. This heavy international focus of Swiss companies is not only reflected in their shareholder structure; these companies also have quite diverse boards of directors in terms of nationalities repre-sented.[11] They generally live up to the increasingly high corporate governance standards requested by the large institutional investors.

The revised Swiss CO will likely increase this international focus of the Swiss capital market even more, as listed companies are now allowed to (1) hold their AGMs outside Switzerland, (2) hold virtual-only meetings ('cyber meetings'), (3) denominate their capital in a currency other than the Swiss franc and (4) pay interim dividends.

5.6 Conclusion and Outlook: Active, Not Activist Shareholders

The analysis of ownership data in Switzerland over ten, but also over thirty years, initially indicates stability, Swiss style. Yet, alongside major developments of shareholder rights and governance regulation, movement can be observed in particular groups of companies. Notably, the proportion of listed companies among the twenty largest Swiss companies has increased substantially over the time period stud-ied. Moreover, listed companies face a fairly different shareholder base than ten or twenty years ago. Specifically, these companies have seen a development towards a more evenly distributed shareholder base over time, largely driven by non-domestic, so-called passive investors that have seen a considerable inflow of funds over the past years. With a less concentrated shareholder base that is unengaged and also remains

---

[11] See Schneider, Wagner and Bernasconi (2016) for an overview through 2016. According to Egon Zehnder (2018), the percentage of international directors among the largest Swiss companies is 66.1%. This compares to 48.7% in the United Kingdom, 21.3% in Germany, 23.8% in France and 26.7% globally.

passive in the exertion of their governance rights, entrenchment can actually become easier for a company's leadership team. However, the new shareholders are actually building pressure on the board of directors to search for a more active dialogue with the company's key shareholders. These shareholders have been given significantly more rights and have become more active in using their rights. This 'active share ownership' clearly has become a new reality for listed companies, forcing boards of directors to communicate more actively, become more transparent and be more aware of their shareholders' views. This active share ownership, largely driven by asset owners' demands for a more accountable fiduciary duty, also clearly differs from the classic 'activist shareholder'. These new active owners have much longer-term horizons (in the case of passive investors, essentially infinite) and continuously interact with the board of directors, contrary to the event-driven interactions of classic activists. Successful corporate managers need to learn to engage with this new type of shareholder.

PART III

Scandinavian Countries

6 | Sweden

JOHAN EKLUND AND EVGENI PEEV

6.1 Introduction

This chapter examines the ownership and control of Swedish corporations since the 1990s. The Swedish experience is particularly important in the light of the corporate scandals in 2000–2002 and the global financial crisis in 2008–2009, both demonstrating failures of the Anglo-Saxon corporate governance model. Recently researchers argued that the 'Scandinavian' governance model may present examples of the best corporate governance practice (see e.g. Mayer, 2018).

Studies on corporate ownership and control in Sweden in the 1990s noted remarkable changes. For example, Agnblad et al. (2001) using data in 1998 concluded their study of Swedish listed companies with a section labelled 'The Swedish Model under Attack'. They wrote: 'Given the traditional stability of the ownership structures in Sweden over the last 60 years, the recent changes have become dramatic; more has happened during the last few years than over the previous 60 years' (Agnblad et al., 2001, p. 255). The authors expected the domestic pyramidal holding companies to recede and eventually be abolished, challenged by both international institutional investors and industrial competitors.

In this chapter, we compare the ownership and control structure of three samples of firms (top 20, top 100 – both listed and unlisted non-financial firms – and all the domestic listed non-financial firms in Sweden) in the mid-1990s and at the end of the 2010s. We present evidence of the substantial persistence of traditional controlling shareholders, such as well-known families and holding companies' closed-end investment funds. Our study also documents the increase in foreign owners and the rising importance of institutional investors. The chapter is structured as follows. Section 6.2 briefly outlines the corporate governance framework and legal reforms in Sweden. Section 6.3 describes the data. Section 6.4 presents the ownership structure in large

Swedish companies in the 1990s and at the end of the 2010s. Section 6.5 discusses the determinants of the ownership patterns of change or persistence. Section 6.6 concludes.

6.2 Corporate Governance Framework and Legal Reforms

6.2.1 Corporate Governance

Studies on corporate governance in Sweden have documented the importance of the 'Swedish model' of corporate ownership (Agnblad et al., 2001; Henrekson and Jakobsson, 2005; Hogfeldt, 2005). The social model of a 'good compromise' in Sweden has created a particular corporate governance landscape, which has interacted with globalization forces, the liberalization of domestic markets and legal reforms since the mid-1980s.

By the early 1990s the Swedish corporate governance model was characterized by a high degree of concentration of corporate control (La Porta et al., 1999; Agnblad et al., 2001; Faccio and Lang, 2002).Voting rights had been separated from cash-flow rights by considerable use of dual-class shares and pyramid structures. The two most influential closed-end investment funds organized as pyramid-holding companies were Investor AB, privately controlled by the Wallenberg family, and Industrivärden AB, institutionally controlled. These funds used dual-class shares and controlled a great share of market capitalization of the Stockholm Stock Exchange. Since the 1990s institutional investors have been growing in importance in Swedish public companies (see e.g. Wiberg (2008) for factors behind the rise of institutional investors in Sweden). Studies in the early 2000s reported an increasing role for institutional investors, mainly Swedish financial institutions such as pension and mutual funds (see e.g. Henrekson and Jakobsson, 2005). The tendency for an increase in the role of domestic institutional investors (e.g. national pension funds [AP1–4]) was preserved in the 2010s.

Agnblad et al. (2001) stressed three major future challenges to the traditional Swedish corporate governance model stemming from the globalization of capital markets and the structural changes fuelled by innovation and increasing international competition. First, the fundamental problem for the Swedish model was how to attract more institutional, particularly foreign, capital while maintaining a closely held, family dominated governance structure. Second, it was expected that the pivotal pyramidal holding companies would recede and eventually be abolished, challenged by both international institutional investors and industrial competitors. Third, the Swedish model was also challenged by the attempts to reactivate the harmonization efforts within the EU in the area of corporate law. Authors concluded that there were clear signs that the old governance structures were already breaking down in response to the pressures from international and domestic institutional investors, the OECD and the US government to harmonize global corporate governance structures. A few studies examine recent ownership and control development in Sweden. Henrekson and Jakobsson (2012), using data up to 2010, presented mixed evidence about the decline of the Swedish corporate control model. Henrekson et al. (2020), using data up to 2018, documented the decline of industrial foundations as controlling owners of Swedish listed firms and the rise of direct family ownership.

The capital markets in Sweden were liberalized in a number of steps. Domestic credit markets had become fully deregulated by 1986. Until 1990, there were legal constraints on foreign investors owning more than 5% of the total shares outstanding. After that, reforms to open the country to international competition started and the deregulation of capital markets, including the abolishment of the restrictions on foreign ownership, was completed in 1993. Regulated product markets have also been liberalized, e.g. domestic airlines (1992), the financial sector (1993), telecommunications (1993), postal services (1993) and electricity (1996). At the same time the tax system was reformed and became more market friendly (Henrekson and Jakobsson, 2005). These reforms led to a revival of the Swedish financial markets in the 1990s. From January 1980 to January 2000, the stock market index of the Stockholm Stock Exchange increased fifty-six times, which was more than five times the US and UK increases in the same period (Henrekson & Jakobsson, 2012). The number of listed companies on the Stockholm Stock Exchange increased remarkably in the 1980s and 1990s, after which there was a slight decline and recently it has increased again. The number of companies listed on the main market of the Nasdaq Stockholm AB, formerly known as the Stockholm Stock Exchange, reached 383 on 31 March 2021.

6.2.2 Organizational Forms

We briefly provide an overview of the basic forms of business organization in Sweden.

6.2.2.1 Limited Company (*Sw. Aktiebolag*, AB)

A limited company (*Sw. Aktiebolag*, AB) is a legal person owned by its shareholder or shareholders and with its own rights and responsibilities. There are two types of limited company in Sweden: private limited companies and public limited companies. A private limited company is usually owned by one or two people. The shareholders elect the board of directors, which must consist of at least one member, and appointing a managing director is optional. A public limited company issue shares which can be sold to the public. A public limited company must have a board of directors consisting of at least three elected board members. One of the members must be appointed chair of the board. A managing director must also be appointed. The managing director can be a board member but not chair of the board. A public limited company must also appoint an auditor. The only company form that requires deposited funds is the limited company. For private limited companies, effective as of 1 January 2020, the minimum capital requirement was changed to 25,000 SEK (previously 50,000 SEK). For public limited companies the minimum capital requirement is SEK 500,000.

6.2.2.2 Trading Partnership (*Sw. Handelsbolag*, HB)

Under the Partnership and Non-registered Partnership Act a trading partnership (*Sw. Handelsbolag*, HB) is constituted by an agreement between two or more individuals and/or legal entities to conduct business in association. The trading partnership's basic advantage is its flexibility. Partners are free to organize their relations without the restraints of a corporate form. The partners in a trading partnership are personally liable for the partnership's agreements and debts.

6.2.2.3 Limited Partnership (*Sw. Kommanditbolag*, KB)

A limited partnership (*Sw. Kommanditbolag*, KB) is a form of trading partnership in which one or more partners have reserved the right not to be liable for its obligations in excess of the sum he or she has contributed to the partnership. Such a partner is referred to as a limited partner (*Sw. Kommanditdelägare*). Other partners in a limited partnership are referred to as general partners (*Sw. Komplementär*). A limited partnership must have two or more partners: at least one general partner and one limited partner.

6.2.2.4 Societas Europaea (SE)

A Societas Europea (SE) or European company (*Sw. Europabolag*) has a legal structure which resembles that of a public limited company. An SE is formed as a public limited company regulated by EU law. The shares of an SE may be listed on a stock exchange. The shareholders' liability is limited to their subscribed capital of an SE. The minimum amount of subscribed share capital of an SE is EUR120,000.

6.2.3 *Corporate Governance Legal Reforms*

The Swedish corporate governance legal reform started at the beginning of the 1990s with work on a revision of the Companies Act, which brought about the new Companies Act coming into force on 1 January 2006. The Swedish Shareholders Association published the first Swedish ownership policy in March 1993, consisting of guidelines for the role of owners in listed companies. Since then, a few Swedish institutional investors have issued similar guidelines. A number of corporate governance guidelines and recommendations were also published by self-regulating bodies, such as the Swedish Industry and Commerce Stock Exchange Committee and the Swedish Securities Council. The Stockholm Stock Exchange also presented a number of corporate governance rules in its listing requirements. The Swedish Academy of Directors published Guidelines for Good Board Practice, the first code of practice for boards of directors of Swedish companies, in January 2003. A working group was set up to devise a Swedish corporate governance code in September 2003 and the Code came into force on 1 July 2005. The Swedish Corporate Governance Board was set up in 2005 in order to monitor and analyse the Code implementation. The Code was revised in 2008 and 2010, and a further revised version came into force on 1 December 2016.

The corporate governance framework of Swedish companies whose shares are trading on a regulated market (i.e. listed companies) includes:

(1) the Swedish Companies Act,
(2) the Swedish Annual Accounts Act,
(3) the Swedish Corporate Governance Code (the Code) and
(4) the rules of the stock exchanges.

The framework also includes:

(5) statements and recommendations issued by the Swedish Financial Reporting Board,
(6) statements by the Swedish Securities Council concerning what is regarded as accepted practice on Swedish securities markets, and
(7) the Council for Swedish Financial Reporting Supervision's review of financial reports of Swedish listed companies.

The Swedish Companies Act contains fundamental rules about company organization. The Act stipulates the required corporate bodies, the tasks of each of these bodies and the responsibilities of the people within each body. The Code complements the law by setting higher requirements in some areas, while allowing companies to deviate from the code rules if it would lead to better corporate governance in the individual case ('comply or explain').

A particular characteristic of the Swedish corporate governance model is that Swedish listed companies must have a governance structure consisting of a shareholders' meeting, a board of directors and a chief executive officer (CEO), which are in a hierarchical relationship, and a controlling body, an auditor, appointed by the shareholders' meeting. Another distinct feature of the Swedish corporate governance model is the engagement of shareholders in the nomination process for boards of directors and auditors, which occurs through their participation in companies' nomination committees. Nomination committees of Swedish listed companies are not regulated by the Companies Act but by the Code. A Swedish nomination committee is not a subcommittee of the board, but a preparatory body for the shareholders meeting because it is considered that a board of directors should not nominate its own members and that this task would be better performed by a structure representing the company's owners. The Swedish corporate governance model assumes that large shareholders must take responsibility for companies' affairs by participating on boards of directors in order to have an active impact on companies' management. At the same time, the Companies Act contains a number of provisions for the protection of minority shareholders, such as requiring qualified majorities for a number of decisions at the general meeting of shareholders.

6.2.4 *Ownership Disclosure of Listed Companies*

Major shareholders are obliged to submit major shareholding notifications concerning changes to their holdings in companies whose shares are admitted for trading on a regulated stock market (e.g. Nasdaq Stockholm AB and NGM Main Regulated). The obligation to submit a major shareholding notification arises when an ownership change leads to reaching or passing, upwards or downwards, certain set thresholds. The thresholds are 5%, 10%, 15%, 20%, 25%, 30%, 50%, 66% (two-thirds) and 90% of the voting rights or number of shares in a company. When these thresholds have been reached or passed, the natural or legal person whose holding has changed should inform the company and the Financial Supervisory Authority (Finansinspektionen) in Sweden. The provisions concerning the major shareholding notification obligation are contained in the Transparency Directive and have been implemented through Chapter 4 of the Financial Instruments Trading Act. The major shareholding notification regulations also apply to listed companies with a registered office outside the European Economic Area that have chosen Sweden as their home member state. The Financial Supervisory Authority publishes major shareholding notifications and stores them in the stock exchange information database. The shareholder is responsible for the content of the major shareholding notification.

In accordance with the Annual Accounts Act and the Code, listed companies must disclose an annual corporate governance report consisting of information on their corporate governance and their compliance with the Code. If a company chooses to deviate from a certain provision of the Code, it must state the reasons ('comply or explain'). Moreover, a corporate governance report must include information about internal controls and risk management concerning financial reporting, and how the annual evaluation of the board of directors has been administered and reported.

Swedish companies, associations and other legal entities are obliged to register their ultimate beneficial owners at the Swedish Companies Registration Office. There are a few exceptions to this obligation, including government bodies and listed companies. The ultimate beneficial owner is the natural person, or persons, who ultimately owns or controls a legal entity. A natural person is presumed to exercise this control if he or she, directly or indirectly, holds or controls more than 25% of the votes, or holds or controls the right to appoint or remove a majority of the members of the board of directors. Moreover, a legal entity may not have any beneficial owner or may, under certain conditions, be relieved from the obligation to report its beneficial owner due to complex ownership structures, as investigation obligations are limited.

6.3 The Data

We examine the ownership structure of the top 20, the top 100 and listed non-financial companies in Sweden in the early 1990s and at the end of the 2010s. In a few cases, we include data from 1987 to 1989. First, we have constructed four datasets on the ownership of the top 100 non-financial firms (listed and unlisted) and non-financial listed firms in Sweden at two points in time: sample *'Top 100 in T0'*, sample *'Listed in T0'*, sample *'Top 100 in T1'* and sample *'Listed in T1'*. The data collection and samples construction are described in the introductory chapter of this volume. Second, we have also prepared datasets of *ultimate* ownership of the top 20 and top 100 Swedish non-financial firms (listed and unlisted) in 2018–2019.

6.4 The Ownership Structures

Corporate governance studies in the 1990s documented that Swedish ownership structures were undergoing a major transformation (Henrekson and Jakobsson, 2003, 2005). A few ownership trends were documented: the decreasing ownership concentration by the abolishment of golden shares and dual-class shares, the increase in foreign ownership and the rising importance of domestic private financial institutions following the changes in the Swedish pension system. The Swedish corporate governance system has been remarkably successful in generating internationally competitive companies, so that the stock exchange was largely constituted of a few very large Swedish-based multinational firms. Most Swedish large firms were closely held, ultimately controlled by a single family. In our study we examine the top 20 and top 100 Swedish firms (both closely held and listed) as well as listed companies.

6.4.1 Ownership Structures in the Mid-1990s

We examined the ownership concentration of three samples of firms in the mid-1990s: the top 20, top 100 and listed companies. Table 6.1 displays the results. The average stake held by the largest shareholder in the top 20 firms was 21.36% and the median was 16.4%. The corresponding numbers for the second- and the third-largest shareholders were 9.73% (median 8.65%) and 7% (median 6.4%), respectively. The total share of all shareholders having 10% or more of outstanding shares in a company was 33.21% (median 30.45%). Not surprisingly, in both the top 100 firms and listed companies, equity ownership concentration was slightly higher. In these companies, the average stake held by the largest shareholder was about 27.5% and the total share of all shareholders having 10% or more of outstanding shares in a company was about 40–41%.

The documented equity ownership concentration of Swedish large firms in the mid-1990s was much lower than ownership concentration of their counterparts in countries in Continental Europe such as Germany (see Chapter 4 in this volume). For example, in 1990 the average stake held by the largest shareholder in the top 20 German firms was 47.53% (median 47.77%). Listed German companies were typically under majority control with the average size of the largest shareholder at 55.17% (median 50.1%). In Sweden, the equity ownership concentration appeared moderate, but there were important instruments for maintaining corporate control such as dual-class shares combined with cross-holding and pyramid-holding companies (closed-end investment funds). In fact, Sweden was among the few countries simultaneously using these three instruments in the 1990s (La Porta et al., 1999).

Table 6.2 reports the largest shareholders by ownership categories. The prevailing number of firms were companies with dispersed ownership. These are companies that do not have a shareholder owning at least 20% of total outstanding shares. In the sample of listed firms, 43.69% of companies fall into this category.[1] Swedish institutions (non-financial firms and holdings, and financial firms) were the largest shareholder in 35% of the top 100 firms (30% of listed companies).

---

[1] This number was slightly higher than that provided by Faccio and Lang (2002) using data on 245 Swedish listed companies in 1998 and reporting that 37.43% of companies do not have a shareholder controlling at least 20% of votes.

Table 6.1 *Ownership concentration in the 1990s in Sweden*

	Number of firms	Largest shareholder (C1)[a]				Second-largest shareholder (C2)[a]				Third-largest shareholder (C3)[a]				All largest shareholders (Largest SH)[b]			
		Min.	Med.	Mean	Max.	Min.	Med.	Mean	Max.	Min.	Med.	Mean	Max.	Min.	Med.	Mean	Max.
Top 100[c]	100	0.6	23.5	27.47	74.5	3	10.2	12.04	38.5	1.1	6.91	7.2	19.1	10	37.35	40.76	100
Top 20[d]	20	0.6	16.4	21.36	51.4	5.15	8.65	9.73	20.3	3.2	6.4	7.06	12	10	30.45	33.21	66.7
Listed[e]	103	3.3	23.3	27.66	79	2	10	11.17	35.1	1.1	6.5	6.76	19.1	10	36.4	39.82	83.1

Notes:

[a] The table shows results for the first year with available ownership data in the 1990s. C1, C2 and C3 are the shareholdings in % of the largest, second- and third-largest shareholders in a company.

[b] Largest SH is the total share of all shareholders having 10% or more of outstanding shares in a company.

[c] Top 100 are the largest 100 firms (both listed and unlisted) in Sweden.

[d] Top 20 are the largest 20 firms (both listed and unlisted) in Sweden.

[e] Listed are listed firms in Sweden.

Source: Bureau van Dijk (1999), Amadeus database, own calculations.

Table 6.2 *Largest shareholders by ownership categories in the 1990s in Sweden*

Ownership categories[a]	Top 100 (percentage of firms)[b]	Min.[c]	Med.	Mean	Max.	Top 20 (percentage of firms)[b]	Min.[c]	Med.	Mean	Max.	Listed (percentage of firms)[b]	Min.[c]	Med.	Mean	Max.
Families/individuals	11	31.1	35.5	40.85	62.7	5	50.24	50.24	50.24	50.24	15.54	23.7	36.15	44.46	70.3
State	2	25	37.62	37.62	50.24	15	20.1	43.5	38.33	51.4	1.94	25	32	37.62	79
Non-financial	19	20.1	33.3	38.38	74.5	5	45	45	45	45	12.62	21.3	39.2	40.05	70.6
Financial	12	21.3	35.3	39.23	70.6						13.59	20	28	28.63	38.5
Holdings	4	20	19.67	26.88	31.5						3.88	22.7	24.75	24.75	26.8
Others	1	22.7	22.7	22.7	22.7						1.94				
Foreign	9	22.3	35	40.01	61	10	22.3	28.65	28.65	35	6.8	23.4	35	39.91	61
Dispersed	42	0.6	13	12.67	19.3	65	0.6	13.2	12.28	19.3	43.69	3.3	13.3	12.99	19.3
Total	*100*					*100*					*100*				
Number of firms	100					20					103				

Notes:

[a] The table shows results for the first year with available ownership data in the 1990s. We identify the company's direct controlling owner as the largest shareholder holding 20% or more of outstanding shares. When no single entity owned at least 20%, a company was categorized as having dispersed ownership. Ownership categories: Families/individuals, state, non-financial firms, financial (banks, other financial institutions) and holdings are domestic shareholders. Foreign are all foreign shareholders (physical and legal persons).

[b] Percentage of firms: Percentage of firms controlled by each ownership category or with dispersed ownership.

[c] Descriptive statistics (min., med., mean and max.) are the percentage of ownership stake of the ownership category in firms controlled by this ownership category.

Source: Bureau van Dijk (1999), Amadeus database, own calculations.

Financial firms include e.g. closed-end investment funds, mutual funds and banks. Previous studies showed that the closed-end investment funds were organized as pyramid-holding companies and were an important vehicle for corporate control of the largest firms on the Stockholm Stock Exchange (Agnblad et al., 2001). Families and individuals appeared the largest *direct* shareholders in only 11% of the top 100 firms (15.5% of listed companies), and were not presented as the largest *direct* shareholders among the top 20 Swedish firms. Foreign owners were the largest shareholders in 9% of the top 100 firms (6.8% of listed companies). Interestingly, foreign shareholders have owned blocking minority median stakes (35%).

As we mentioned earlier, the high level of separation of ownership and control in Swedish companies was one of the key features of the Swedish corporate governance model. For example, in 1999 the Wallenberg family through Investor AB owned 19% of capital and controlled 41% of votes of Swedish firms (Investors AB, 1999). Thus, using 20% as the criterion for control for our samples of the top 20, top 100 and listed firms would underestimate the actual dominant shareholders and overestimate the 'dispersed ownership' category. Following previous studies, we use also a 10% cut-off value. Table 6.3 shows the results. Using the 10% definition of control, 37% of Swedish companies

Table 6.3 *Largest shareholders by ownership categories in the 1990s (10% cut-off) in Sweden*

Ownership categories	Top 100 (percentage of firms)	Top 20 (percentage of firms)	Listed (percentage of firms)
Families/individuals	15		22
State	2	5	2
Non-financial	22	20	15
Financial	30	25	31
Holdings	5	5	5
Others	3	10	4
Foreign	13	15	11
Dispersed	10	20	10
Total:	100	100	100
Number of firms	100	20	103

Source: Bureau van Dijk (1999), Amadeus database, own calculations.

were family controlled or controlled by non-financial firms in each of the samples of the top 100 and listed firms, about 30% of companies were controlled by financial firms in all the samples, and the share of firms with dispersed ownership was negligible.

6.4.2 Patterns of Ownership Change

Table 6.4 displays the ownership concentration for the three samples of firms in 2018–2019: the top 20, top 100 and listed companies. Equity ownership concentration remained virtually the same in listed companies. There was a significant increase in ownership concentration in the samples of the top 20 and top 100 firms. The largest shareholder had a median stake of 50.5% in the top 20 firms and 64.5% in the top 100 firms. Why do we observe the increase in ownership concentration in the samples of the top 20 and top 100 firms? The structure of our samples provides an answer to this question. Our data shows that in 2018–2019 the percentage of fully owned subsidiaries had increased from zero in the mid-1990s to 25% (36%) for the top 20 (top 100) companies. Foreign investors made acquisitions in which Swedish firms became subsidiaries to the foreign parent companies and were delisted from the Nasdaq Stockholm AB. For example, among the top 20 firms, foreign-owned subsidiaries were Astrazeneca AB (owned by a British company) and Volvo Car AB (owned by a Chinese holding company). There were also state-owned companies with 100% state participation (e.g. among the top 20 companies these were Stockholms Stadshus AB owned by the city of Stockholm and Vattenfall AB owned by the state). Among the top 20 firms, there was also a subsidiary of a domestic holding company.

Table 6.5 reports the largest shareholders by ownership categories using the 20% cut-off value of control for the three samples of firms in 2018–2019. Two important patterns may be documented. First, the persistence and even increase in the share of families, non-financial firms and financial firms in the top 100 (listed companies) from 42% (41.75%) in the 1990s to 51% (43.85%) in 2018–2019. Second, there is an increasing share of foreign controlling shareholders (from 9% in the initial period to 18% in the top 100, and from 6.8% to 9.02% in listed companies).

Table 6.6 presents the largest shareholders by ownership categories using the 10% cut-off value of control for the three samples of firms in

Table 6.4 *Ownership concentration in 2018–2019 in Sweden*

	Number of firms	Largest shareholder (C1)[a]				Second-largest shareholder (C2)[a]				Third-largest shareholder (C3)[a]				All largest shareholders (Largest SH)[b]			
		Min.	Med.	Mean	Max.	Min.	Med.	Mean	Max.	Min.	Med.	Mean	Max.	Min.	Med.	Mean	Max.
Top 100[c]	100	2.8	64.5	63.3	100	1.4	7.28	9.79	50	0.8	4.23	5.92	25	10.3	99	73.06	100
Top 20[d]	20	2.8	50.51	60.96	100	1.7	7.8	11.21	25	1.7	4.12	6.81	25	12.3	93.4	72.91	100
Listed[e]	244	2.8	22.65	26.31	82	1.6	9.46	10.54	37.2	1.01	6.1	6.56	19.2	10	35.91	39.01	89.99

Notes:

[a] C1, C2 and C3 are the shareholdings in % of the largest, second- and third-largest shareholders in a company.

[b] Largest SH is the total share of all shareholders having 10% or more of outstanding shares in a company.

[c] Top 100 are the largest 100 firms (both listed and unlisted) in Sweden.

[d] Top 20 are the largest 20 firms (both listed and unlisted) in Sweden.

[e] Listed are listed firms in Sweden.

Source: Bureau van Dijk (2020), Orbis database, own calculations.

Table 6.5 *Largest shareholders by ownership categories in 2018–2019 in Sweden*

Ownership categories[a]	Top 100 (percentage of firms)[b]	Min.[c]	Med.	Mean	Max.	Top 20 (percentage of firms)[b]	Min.[c]	Med.	Mean	Max.	Listed (percentage of firms)[b]	Min.[c]	Med.	Mean	Max.
Families/individuals	7	51	71	67.89	100	15	51.00	71.00	74.00	100	9.84	20.10	30.75	36.55	71.80
State	7	39.5	100	91.36	100	15	39.50	100.00	79.83	100	18.85	21.00	30.00	36.32	72.70
Non-financial	21	30	100	79.14	100	10	47.89	48.89	48.89	49.9	15.16	20.00	29.98	36.23	79.50
Financial	23	21.77	30	46.96	100	25	21.77	25.00	39.73	100	2.87	20.60	29.23	39.28	72.00
Holdings	7	100	100	100	100	5	100	100	100	100	2.46	20.40	26.35	37.32	82.00
Others	2	42.95	44.88	44.89	46.82	5	42.95	42.95	42.95	42.95	9.02	20.51	30.25	34.32	64.00
Foreign	18	29.1	100	87.42	100	20	50.01	99.00	87.25	100					
Dispersed	15	4	10.3	10.18	16.9	5	12.3	12.3	12.3	12.3	41.80	2.80	11.80	12.52	19.80
Total	100					100					100				
Number of firms	100					20					244				

Notes:

[a] We identify the company's direct controlling owner as the largest shareholder holding 20% or more of outstanding shares. When no single entity owned at least 20%, a company is categorized as having dispersed ownership. Ownership categories: Families/individuals, state, non-financial firms, financial (banks, other financial institutions) and holdings are domestic shareholders. Foreign are all foreign shareholders (physical and legal persons).

[b] Percentage of firms: Percentage of firms controlled by each ownership category or with dispersed ownership.

[c] Descriptive statistics (min., med, mean and max.) are the percentage of ownership stake of the ownership category in firms controlled by this ownership category.

Source: Bureau van Dijk (2020), Orbis database, own calculations.

Table 6.6 *Largest shareholders by ownership categories in 2018–2019 (10% cut-off) in Sweden*

Ownership categories	Top 100 (percentage of firms)	Top 20 (percentage of firms)	Listed (percentage of firms)
Families/individuals	9	15	11
State	7	15	1
Non-financial	30	10	27
Financial	19	30	24
Holdings	8	5	2
Others	2	5	3
Foreign	19	20	21
Dispersed	6		11
Total	*100*	*100*	*100*
Number of firms	100	20	244

Source: Bureau van Dijk (2020), Orbis database, own calculations.

2018–2019. The table shows that there was virtually no change in the share of companies with dispersed ownership since the 1990s. Thus, the hypothesis for the convergence to the Anglo-American ownership structure, discussed in the introductory chapter of this volume, has not been corroborated for our three samples of large Swedish firms. We discuss possible reasons for this result in Section 6.5. The table also confirms the findings presented in Table 6.5 about the persistence of the key largest shareholders (families, non-financial firms, and financial firms) in Sweden over this period.

So far, we have examined the *direct* ownership and control structures of large Swedish companies. We also studied the *ultimate* ownership for our samples of the top 20 and top 100 companies. Table 6.7 reports the results. We show that using the 10% definition of control for the sample of the top 20 firms, 35% of the firms were family controlled, 25% were controlled by financial firms, 20% were under foreign control and the remaining 20% were divided between state-controlled (15%) and holdings (5%). For the sample of the top 100 firms using the same 10% cut-off, the corresponding shares were 29% for family-controlled firms, 20% for firms controlled by financial firms, 21% for firms under foreign control and the remaining 30% were divided between the

Table 6.7 *Ultimate ownership of the largest shareholders in 2018–2019 (10% cut-off) in Sweden*

Ownership categories	Top 100 (percentage of firms)	Top 20 (percentage of firms)
Families/individuals	29	35
State	10	15
Non-financial	8	
Financial	20	25
Holdings	5	5
Others	1	
Foreign	21	20
Dispersed	6	
Total	*100*	*100*
Number of firms	100	20

Source: Bureau van Dijk (2020), Orbis database, own calculations.

residual categories.[2] We have documented a great deal of stability in ownership structures over the period studied. For example, among the family-controlled firms in the top 20, the bulk of firms are controlled by well-established families, such as Wallenberg, Lundberg, Olsson and Persson. There are also firms controlled by a new generation of entrepreneurs such as Carl Bennet and Erik Selin. Among the firms controlled by financial firms in the top 20, 60% of financial owners are Industrivärden AB (closed-end investment funds) and 40% are national pension funds (AP1–4).

Thus, our data does not corroborate some expectations in the 1990s about the abolishment of the pyramid-holding companies (closed-end investment funds). The ownership structures at the end of the 2010s appeared more nuanced. We have documented both the persistence of corporate insiders and ownership changes, such as an increase in foreign ownership and the establishment of new domestic largest individual shareholders. We also show the importance of financial firms that are domestic institutional investors, such as closed-end investment funds, mutual and pension funds, insurance companies and others.

---

[2] We also used the 20% cut-off value of control and the results were essentially the same.

6.4.3 Continuity of Ownership Structure: A Long-Term View

Glete (1994) examined ownership structure in the twenty-five largest industrial firms in Sweden in 1925, 1970 and 1990 and reported a remarkable persistence of owners of Swedish companies in the turbulent twentieth century. Our analysis covering ownership data in the mid-1990s and the end of the 2010s has also revealed the persistence of corporate insiders. One might speculate that fundamental *long-term* country factors have impacted the ownership structure of large Swedish firms in the past few decades. What are these country factors? We briefly discuss this and other questions about the determinants of ownership structure in the next section.

6.5 The Determinants of Ownership Change

6.5.1 The Persistence of Corporate Insiders

Despite the enormous impact of global market forces in the Swedish open economy in the past decades, family-controlled non-financial firms and holdings have shown notable persistence. This evidence is at odds with the predictions of influential studies of the effects of globalization on corporate governance, which present economic efficiency considerations regarding global market-driven ownership changes (Gordon and Roe, 2004). Globalized markets also induce countries to converge to 'the best' Anglo-Saxon corporate governance and ownership model.[3] Global market forces have crucially influenced the Swedish economy in the 1990s (Svensson, 2002). Yet the Swedish corporate ownership structure has remained relatively stable. Why do we observe this ownership persistence?

We might speculate about a few reasons for the persistence of corporate ownership in Sweden. First, the largest companies controlled by prominent Swedish families have established a long-term reputation as efficient global players. These are large multinational companies participating in the global market for many years. For example, controlling owners such as the Wallenberg family have owned hundreds of firms in virtually all sectors of the economy. This family and other controlling families such as the owners of H&M and IKEA have already

---

[3] See e.g. Hansman and Kraakman (2001) and Ringe (2015).

demonstrated an efficient business model. Thus, some of the theoretical considerations on the effects of globalization on economic efficiency through corporate governance and ownership change presented by Gordon and Roe (2004) appear not to apply to the largest Swedish companies. Second, the economic power of big Swedish business does not stem from its natural monopoly position in Sweden. Furthermore, *economic entrenchment* of the type described by Morck, Wolfenzon and Yeung (2005) is not observed. Large Swedish companies eventually get support from the government for their global expansion but they do not constrain the development of domestic small entrepreneurial firms and the entry of potential new competitors. Third, in Sweden the legal environment (e.g. patent law) is more favourable for large firms. The successful start-ups in the high-tech sector are usually acquired by large Swedish companies. Thus, innovation activities are carried out in large firms and they become highly competitive in global markets. In Sweden, big business stability and innovation appear closely connected. Fourth, financial constraints are not severe in large Swedish companies. In the early 1990s, financial issues and the risk of bankruptcy were key driving forces for corporate governance and ownership change. For example, large Swedish companies such as Electrolux and Ericsson were pressed by external providers of capital such as foreign institutional investors to adjust their peculiar dual-class shares structure (1 share = 1,000 votes) to a more accepted dual-class shares structure (1 share= 10 votes). Since 1990s, however, financial liquidity has not been a major problem for large Swedish companies. Thus, there has been less demand for ownership change than in the early 1990s. Fifth, among important factors supporting the local ownership structure has been also media hostility to the development of shareholder capitalism in Sweden. We also speculate that in the future an eventual change of ownership structure of large Swedish firms might happen as a result of unpredictable events, such as a financial crisis with similar magnitude to the financial crisis in Sweden at the beginning of the 1990s, or a change in labour market conditions.

We can suggest at least two theoretical explanations for the persistence of corporate insiders and the lack of convergence to dispersed ownership in Sweden. First, it appears that the traditional strong social democratic politics substantially influences ownership development in Sweden. Roe (2003) examined the political determinants of ownership structure and showed that Sweden is a country where the impact of strong social democracy and ownership concentration (measured by control rights) is greater than in most other countries. By the beginning of the 1990s, social democratic governments pursued policies that fostered the concentration of corporate control. Since then, these policies have become more neutral but they have still worked against an expansion of diffused ownership and managerial control (Henrekson and Jakobsson, 2001, 2005). Thus, the theory of political determinants of ownership structure may partly explain the observed ownership stability over the period studied. Second, the forces of path dependence appear more powerful than the globalization pressures for convergence to the Anglo-American corporate governance structures. For example, the Swedish corporate governance model has preserved its essential features, such as the superior position of the shareholders' meeting in relation to the company's board and CEO, the board of directors consisting predominantly of members who are not employed by the company and who can be dismissed by the shareholders' meeting at any time and a CEO who is appointed and may be dismissed by the board at any time (Carlsson, 2007). The weak formal position of management kept by Swedish corporate law appears a serious impediment to the development of managerial control and dispersed ownership structure in Sweden. The law reflects the long-term corporate culture where management is subordinate to shareholders (Pacces, 2007; Henrekson and Jakobsson, 2012). Hence, country cultural, legal and financial factors in Sweden empirically support the path-dependence theory of ownership and control structure.

6.5.2 *The Rise in Foreign Ownership*

We have presented evidence of the increase in foreign investors as the largest shareholders in large Swedish companies. We may outline two major policy factors accounting for this result. First, Sweden has followed the global trend of financial deregulation prevailing in OECD countries since the mid-1980s and the early 1990s. The abolishment of capital control had already dramatically increased foreign ownership in the 1990s (Henrekson and Jakobsson, 2003; Wiberg, 2008). Second, there were a series of reforms of the tax system over the period 1985–1994 (see e.g. Agell, Englund and Södersten, 1998). Tax policy had strongly positive effects on the rise in foreign ownership in Sweden from the beginning of the 1990s (see e.g. Henrekson and Jakobsson, 2005).

6.6 Conclusion

This chapter has documented the major ownership and control patterns of large Swedish companies from the early 1990s to the late 2010s. Researchers of the 'global corporate governance revolution' in the 1990s claimed that the Swedish corporate governance model was under attack and expected the pivotal pyramidal holding companies to eventually be abolished (Agnblad et al., 2001). The evidence presented in our study cannot confirm these expectations. We compare several samples of listed and unlisted companies in the mid-1990s and in 2018–2019 and arrive at a few conclusions. First, large shareholders remained the dominant corporate governance model in Sweden. Second, the largest shareholders, such as families and holding companies (closed-end investment funds) have persisted in the top 20, top 100 and listed companies over the decades studied. Third, there was an increase in the share of foreign owners as the largest shareholders in both the top 100 and listed companies. Fourth, there was also an emergence of new entrepreneurs as the largest shareholders in large Swedish companies. We have also shown the importance of financial firms that are domestic institutional investors, such as closed-end investment funds, mutual and pension funds, insurance companies and others. In sum, we have presented evidence of both the persistence of corporate insiders and ownership changes, such as an increase in foreign ownership and the establishment of new domestic largest individual shareholders. Finally, we have discussed a few reasons why ownership structure has remained stable in Sweden despite the substantial influence of global market forces, the liberalization of domestic markets and corporate governance and legal reforms.

PART IV

Mediterranean Countries

7 | Italy

LAURA ABRARDI AND LAURA RONDI

7.1 Introduction: Corporate Governance, Legal and Institutional Framework

Compared with most industrialized countries, the structure of Italian industry is characterized by a very large share of small and medium-sized enterprises (Bianchi et al., 2005).[1] In 1996, manufacturing firms in Italy with less than 100 employees accounted for more than 70% of employment. In contrast, US data from 1992 shows that firms with less than 100 employees accounted for only approximately 20% of employment (Traù, 1999). Many observers have pointed to the proliferation and success of small firms in Italy as an important factor in the development and growth of the economy (Piore and Sabel, 1984; Putnam, 1993). Small and medium-sized firms were praised for competing successfully in the export market and for contributing positively to the balance of trade. But while small Italian firms did not appear to suffer from cost disadvantages associated with their small scale until the end of the 1990s, from the start of the twenty-first century and especially after joining the European Monetary Union in the year 2000, their growth and productivity performance have started to stutter (Calligaris et al., 2016). Some researchers have suggested that underdeveloped financial markets and weak investor protection have been an impediment to the growth of Italian small and medium-sized firms (Demirguc-Kunt and Levine, 2001; Guiso, Sapienza and Zingales, 2004; Pagano and Volpin, 2005; Carpenter and Rondi, 2006).

A second important feature of the Italian industrial structure is the existence of pyramidal groups, among listed as well as unlisted companies. These groups are typically headed by a parent company that holds equity stakes in a number of firms and are often identified as

---

[1] See Carpenter and Rondi (2000) for a detailed account of the Italian corporate governance system and industrial structure at the beginning of the period studied in this chapter.

family-controlled groups. A survey conducted by the Bank of Italy suggests that the majority of Italian economic activity takes place within firms affiliated with groups (Bianchi et al., 2001). The proportion of firms affiliated with groups has generally grown between the late 1980s through the mid-1990s. We present evidence later to show that a large proportion of firms are affiliated with groups and how adoption of pyramidal structures has changed over time.[2]

Italy exhibits many features consistent with a bank-based financial system, as firms rely more on bank debt than on bonds, equity markets are thin and publicly traded firms are sparse. Indeed, bank debt is by far the most important source of outside funds for Italian firms. Non-bank sources of debt, such as bonds or commercial papers, are still scarcely used. Although the presence of institutional investors, such as investment funds, has increased since the year 2000, banks still provide most of the external finance used by Italian firms, especially private (unlisted) ones.[3]

Like other Continental European countries, the stock market is not an important source of finance in Italy. Very few Italian companies are traded publicly, even companies that are quite large and well-known abroad (e.g. Ferrero, Barilla, Esselunga and Mapei). However, over time, the Italian public equity market has acquired a more important role. According to Consob, the National Commission for Companies and the Stock Exchange, only 227 firms were traded on the stock exchange in Milan in 1991 (141 in 1980) and the total capitalized value of firms was EUR115 billion, approximately 12.5% of GDP.[4] In 2017, 231 companies were listed on the MTA market (Mercato

---

[2] The literature has examined the potential reasons for firms becoming affiliated with groups (see Morck, Wolfenzon and Yeung, 2005 for a comprehensive survey). Most explanations centre on how groups affect corporate governance and the intra-group allocation of financial resources. Large parent companies or group member firms may form special relationships with banks, thus accessing funds at a lower cost than a constrained stand-alone company. Groups allow the formation of internal capital markets, which are particularly helpful when the financial system is not well developed, but they also facilitate the separation between ownership and control in economies with weak investor protection.

[3] Notably, until 1993 (Second Directive on Banking), banks were not allowed to hold equity in firms. Moreover, the entire banking system was mostly state owned and heavily regulated, until the EU prompted the deregulation of capital markets at the beginning of the 1990s.

[4] In contrast, there were over 3,000 new listings in the United States during the same period (Loughran and Ritter, 1995).

Telematico Azionario, i.e. Borsa Italiana's main market), with a market capitalization of EUR634 billion, equal to 39.6% of GDP. Almost one in two companies operates in the industrial sector, while the others are equally distributed in the financial and services sectors. Although the market capitalization to GDP ratio has increased since 1991, the number of listed firms does not appear to budge, confirming that the Italian capital market is still relatively underdeveloped and excessively biased towards debt financing compared to other European countries.

The capital market evolution has been accompanied by reforms of the rules governing corporate law (the Consolidated Law on Finance, Law 58/1998-Draghi Law, *Testo Unico della Finanza*, henceforth TUF), of the functioning of the MTA (the privatization of the stock market and its acquisition, first by the London Stock Exchange and then by EuroNext) and of corporate governance (through the issuing of the first Voluntary Corporate Governance Code in 1999), which are analysed below. The following subsections describe the main organizational forms adopted by Italian companies and the main features of the legal and institutional framework. The rest of the chapter describes the changes in corporate ownership and governance of Italian firms over almost three decades, from 1990 to 2017, and the effects of the aforementioned reforms and laws. Section 7.2 describes the data. Section 7.3 conducts a descriptive analysis of the landscape of Italian firms and their corporate governance structures, finding that firms are still characterized by high levels of ownership concentration and a strong reluctance to go public. The Italian dominant control model remains the 'family' firm, with stakes that are inexplicably high (well beyond the 50% threshold that would ensure uncontested majority) and a strong involvement of the family in the management of the firm (most family firms are run by a member of the controlling family). The limited recourse to equity finance is a significant constraint to growth, as testified by the prevalence of small and medium-sized enterprises even in recent years. Section 7.4 discusses the determinants of change in corporate ownership and control and shows that although reforms have not fundamentally changed the Italian ownership and control model, they did have a notable impact on its functioning, making it more modern and efficient, increasing market transparency, reducing the gap between ownership and control and resulting in more balanced boards of directors and more active institutional investors. Since they are a peculiar feature of the Italian corporate governance system, in Section 7.5, we focus on Italian listed family firms, analysing their ownership and control characteristics from 2000 to 2017. Section 7.6 concludes.

7.1.1 Organizational Forms

The Italian legal system allows for six different types of company, within two large classes: partnerships and limited liability companies (S.r.l., limited liability companies; S.p.a., joint-stock companies; S.a.p. a., limited partnerships).

Following reform in 2003, firms may choose among three models of corporate governance: the traditional or 'Latin' model, existing only in Italy; the monistic model of Anglo-Saxon origin; and the dualistic, German-style model. The 'Latin' model is the traditional Italian corporate governance system, and it is applied by default in the absence of a different statutory choice. The shareholders' meeting has the power to appoint the board of directors, the board of statutory auditors and the external auditor, while administration and control are delegated, respectively, to the board of directors (or sole director) and to the board of statutory auditors. The advantage of this model is a well-defined division of functions between the various bodies. However, a potential drawback is that the supervising and controlled bodies are both appointed by the same shareholders' meeting, so that the control committee is not always able to operate autonomously and independently.

Notably, almost all Italian listed companies remained within the traditional governance model, while only two companies switched, one to the monistic model and one to the dualistic model.

7.1.2 Legal and Institutional Framework

Since 1990, the legal and institutional framework in Italy has undergone several important changes, partially as a consequence of the requirements to join the European Monetary Union. We focus on the three cornerstones of these reforms, which were most expected to affect the corporate governance and ownership structure of Italian companies: the equity market, company laws and the voluntary corporate governance code.

7.1.2.1 The Stock Exchange and the Financial Markets

The Milan Stock Exchange was established in 1808 under a public ownership regime, which characterized the Italian equity market until 1998, when it was privatized. Manufacturing companies initially remained unlisted due to their small size. It was only at the turn of the twentieth century that the country's rapid industrial growth led the manufacturing sector to seek the necessary funding on the stock exchange. The number of shares listed in Milan went from 23 to 54 between 1895 and 1900 and to 160 in 1913, when the law defined supervisory and management boards' competences, which survived until the closing of the traditional floor exchanges in 1992.

The period following World War II was characterized by a long expansion, particularly for insurance, financial and electricity companies. In this phase, financial holdings began to be listed alongside the operating companies controlled through cross-shareholdings, becoming the ancestors of pyramidal groups. In the early 1970s, the stock exchange had almost completely lost its function of financing industrial growth. Savings were diverted towards government and treasury bonds, supported by high interest rates. The equity market was thin and illiquid and trading activity for equities was reduced to transfers of controlling stakes and to transactions of a purely speculative nature. In this context, Law 7/6/1974 n. 216 established the Consob, the National Commission for Companies and the Stock Exchange, the supervisory and regulatory authority for the Italian financial market, which supervises the stock exchange and issues the listing procedures and by-laws regulating the functioning of the stock and bond markets and the like. Finally, to improve market transparency, the law also introduced the first corporate disclosure requirements for listed companies.

In the early 1990s, the stock market received an injection of liquidity with the privatization of state holdings. The state listed some public giants, such as Ina (insurance) and Eni (energy), as well as the three largest state banks (Banca Commerciale Italiana, Credito Italiano and Banco di Roma). In that period, policymakers became increasingly aware that Italy needed a more developed equity market. First, in 1992, out of the need to improve transparency conditions, Consob began to publicly disclose the identity of listed companies' shareholders with at least 2% ownership, their equity holdings (percentages of both ordinary and non-voting shares) and their changes. Second, in 1994, a tax incentive was offered to small and medium-sized companies to entice them to go public. Third, in 1997, less restrictive criteria to be admitted for quotation were issued.[5] During the years 1998–2000, the 'dot-com mania' led, in Italy as elsewhere, to a bubble in the price of technology stocks, the establishing of the Nuovo Mercato, similar to the Nasdaq in the United States, and to a leap in the number of listed companies. A few years after the burst of the bubble in 2000, many of those firms had disappeared and the market itself was closed.

From 2003 to the end of 2006 there was a new positive cycle in the stock market, culminating in the acquisition of the Italian Stock Exchange by the London Stock Exchange in 2007. However, 2007 was also the start of the global financial and economic crisis, which resulted in a significant drop in the number of listed companies and related market capitalizations. In fact, while at the end of 2007 there were 301 Italian listed companies and market capitalization had reached 48% of GDP, following the financial crisis there was a reduction to 242 companies listed in 2018 on the main market of the Italian Stock Exchange (MTA) and market capitalization of EUR543 billion, equal to just 33% of GDP.

7.1.2.2 Company Law Reform

The turning point of the transition towards developed financial markets in Italy is the Consolidated Finance Act (TUF) of 1998, which systematically addresses some important issues of corporate governance and corporate controls such as market supervision, regulation of takeover bids, brokerage and regulated markets, and insider trading.

The most important changes concern the privatization of regulated markets, the possibility of direct access to the stock exchange for banks and an entire body of investor protection rights. As regards listed companies, the TUF redefined the role and duties of the board of statutory auditors, modified the operating procedures of company meetings, by allowing proxy vote by mail for the first time and introducing the possibility of a liability action against directors by a qualified group of shareholders. Moreover, the new law allowed cumulative voting and proportional representation, introduced an oppressed minority clause and eliminated the blocking of shares before a

---

[5] See Carpenter and Rondi (2006) for a discussion of the evolution of the Italian stock market and the barriers to going public in the 1980s and 1990s.

shareholders' meeting. Furthermore, the efforts to rationalize corporate tax and property income regulations significantly contributed to the development of the stock exchange market.

Despite the new law, however, the beginning of 2000 was plagued by a series of corporate scandals in Italy as in the United States (e.g. Enron and WorldCom). In particular, the bankruptcy of Parmalat and Cirio involved a large number of small investors. These scandals ultimately triggered a further debate on the regulation of listed companies, particularly centred on accounting and financial fraud and the responsibility of auditors, which resulted in the so-called consolidated law on savings (Law 262/2005) to further improve transparency and investor protection.

7.1.2.3 The Corporate Governance Code

In Italy, the Corporate Governance Code (Codice Preda, or 'Self-Discipline' Code) was issued in 1999 and has been periodically updated up to the current 2020 version.[6] Its adoption is voluntary, hence not a source of legal obligation, but since 2011, companies that decide not to comply with the Code are required to give an explanation to the market ('comply or explain').

The Preda Code pays great attention to the appointment of independent directors on the board of directors and to the compensation policy for the CEO and the board of directors. Independent directors cannot stay in charge for more than nine years, cannot maintain commercial or professional relationships with the company or with the auditing firm and cannot be a former manager or a director of a subsidiary of the company. The Code also recommends the adoption of incentive compensations to relate executive pay and firm performance. The remunerations of the chair, vice-chair, CEO and general managers are to be proposed by a Remuneration Committee, made up of independent and non-executive directors, which specifies the objectives, the criteria for evaluation and the compensation policy for the managers and the CEO. Finally, in 2012, the Consob mandated listed companies to disclose information about stock options, equity holdings and the equity-based component of CEO pay. This request

---

[6] https://www.borsaitaliana.it/comitato-corporate-governance/homepage/homepage.en.htm

came relatively late compared to other countries because stock options and equity-based compensations are not very common in Italy.[7]

7.2 The Data

As mentioned in Section 7.1, the structure of Italian industry is characterized by a very large share of small and medium-sized enterprises, and many small, but also large, firms are organized in groups. Moreover, the disclosure of reliable information on firm ownership is relatively recent, also for large and listed companies. Therefore outlining the economic and legal group entity as well as the identification of the controlling agent/ shareholder is a particularly difficult task that requires very detailed, sensitive, often publicly unavailable, information such as that available only to the Consob or the Bank of Italy. For these reasons, we provide our evidence based on data sourced from annual reports and papers by the Bank of Italy and the Consob, merging information and data from various reports in order to cover a period of almost thirty years.[8] Notably, these data are unique. They allow us to reconstruct consistently the time series for the main ownership variables and to follow the evolution along the observation period adopted by this volume. Finally, for listed family and non-family firms and the evolution of ownership and control structures, we rely on an original database with detailed, hand-collected firm-level variables for the period 2000–2017 (see Section 7.5).

7.3 The Ownership Structures: Descriptive Analysis

7.3.1 The Largest Firms in Italy in 1990 and in 2018

In Tables 7.1 and 7.2, we report the list of the top 20 Italian non-financial firms as recorded yearly by Mediobanca, an investment bank.

---

[7] See Zattoni and Minichilli (2009) for a comprehensive account of the adoption of equity-based compensation in Italy.

[8] The Bank of Italy uses its own INVIND data on companies with more than fifty employees and data from Infocamere to obtain information on ownership structures, ownership concentration, identity of owners and control instruments of listed and unlisted Italian firms. Infocamere is the association of local Chambers of Commerce that collects data on company registrations and the like, thus making it a reliable and consistent source. Bianchi and Bianco (2006) and Baltrunaite, Brodi and Mocetti (2019) provide comprehensive analyses of Italian corporate governance based on these data.

Table 7.1 *Top 20 Italian non-financial firms in 1990 by sales*

	State-control	Listed	Name	Sector	Sales (bill Lire)
1	Yes		IRI	Miscellaneous – Industrial	61760
2		Yes	FIAT	Motor vehicles	52513
3	Yes		Eni	Oil and gas	50034
4	Yes		ENEL	Energy	24321
5		Yes	Ferruzzi Finanziaria	Agricultural – Sugar	16739
6		Yes	Pirelli	Wires, cables and tyres	10139
7		Yes	Olivetti	Computers	9037
8			Fininvest	Media – Publishing	7219
9	Yes		EFIM	Metallurgy	5008
10			Fintermica	Energy	3326
11			RCS Editori	Publishing	2438
12			Barilla	Food	2389
13		Yes	Mondadori	Publishing	2328
14		Yes	Cartiere Burgo	Paper	1813
15		Yes	Italcementi	Cement – Concrete	1557
16		Yes	Falck	Steel	1506
17			Piaggio	Motor vehicles	1501
18		Yes	SMI	Metallurgy	1495
19			GFT	Clothing	1491
20			Marzotto	Textile	1437

Notes: At the end of 1990, the exchange rate ECU/Italian Lira (ITL) was 1 ECU = 1545.8 ITL.
Source: Data from Mediobanca (1990).

Comparing the two lists, we note several differences. First, at the top of the list in 1990 was IRI (Istituto per la Ricostruzione Industriale, the public holding company established in 1933 by the Fascist regime to bail out, restructure and finance banks and private companies that went bankrupt during the Great Depression). This was the largest 'pyramidal group' ever, which used to control all state-owned companies in Italy, from RAI (radio and TV) to Alitalia (airways), from Fincantieri (shipping) to Banca Commerciale (and many other main banks), from STET

Table 7.2 *Top 20 Italian non-financial firms in 2018 by sales*

	State-control	Listed	Name	Sector	Sales (bill EUR)
1	Yes	Yes	Eni	Oil and gas	75.8
2	Yes	Yes	ENEL	Energy	73.1
3	Yes		GSE – Gestore Servizi Energetici	Energy	32.3
4			FCA Italy	Motor vehicles	27.2
5		Yes	Telecom Italia	Telecom	18.7
6			Edizione	Miscellaneous	12.6
7	Yes	Yes	Leonardo (ex-FINMECCANICA)	Aircraft and aerospace	12.2
8	Yes		Ferrovie dello Stato Italiane	Railways	11.6
9		Yes	SARAS – Raffinerie Sarde	Oil and gas	10.3
10		Yes	Prysmian	Wires and cables	10.1
11			ESSO Italiana	Oil and gas	9.5
12		Yes	EDISON	Energy	9.2
13		Yes	Luxottica Group	Eyewear and lenses	8.9
14	Yes	Yes	Poste Italiane	Mail service	8.8
15	Yes	Yes	SAIPEM	Engineering	8.5
16			Supermarkets Italiani	Retail	7.7
17			API – Anonima Petroli Italiana	Oil and gas	6.7
18			Kuwait Petroleum Italia	Oil and gas	6.7
19	Yes	Yes	A2A	Energy	6.3
20		Yes	Parmalat	Food	6.2

Source: Data from Mediobanca (2018)

telecommunications (now privatized Telecom Italia) to ASPI, Autostrade per l'Italia (motorways, privatized in 1999 and sold to Edizione Holding, controlled by the Benetton family) to Finmeccanica (mechanical, aircraft, aerospace and defence industry, now named Leonardo and partially privatized).

Second, in spite of the privatization wave of the early 1990s, the number of state-controlled firms has increased over time. The Italian government still owns eight out of the twenty largest non-financial companies (four in 1990, but they also acted as financial holdings). Among these companies many are partially privatized public utilities that result from the unbundling of the vertically integrated natural monopolies (i.e. ENEL and Eni) such as A2A (municipal multi-utility, mainly energy), GSE and Edison (an electric utility company acquired by Electricité de France in 2012). Other companies (Ferrovie dello Stato, Poste Italiane) were fully state-owned legal entities and are now incorporated as joint-stock companies and partially privatized. Many of the partially privatized top 20 companies are carve-outs from IRI or Eni (while EFIM went bankrupt and was liquidated in 1993).

Third, while the top 20 companies in 1990 were owned by Italian shareholders, either the government (IRI, Eni, ENEL, EFIM) or private individuals or family groups, in 2018 at least four of the largest companies are controlled by foreign investors or subsidiaries of foreign multinationals, namely ESSO Italiana, Kuwait Petroleum Italia, Edison, Parmalat and, notably Prysmian, which includes in its portfolio the cable and wire operations of Pirelli, formerly the sixth largest company in 1990 and now no longer in the top list.

Fourth, the diversification of the portfolio of activities has substantially dropped over time, shifting from manufacturing to utilities and services. In 2018, nine out of the twenty companies operated in the energy, oil and gas sectors (there were three in 1990); moreover, purely manufacturing firms have much reduced their importance, leaving room for service companies. Firms operating in the food (Barilla and Ferruzzi), paper (Cartiere Burgo), rubber and tyres (Pirelli), textile/apparel (GFT and Marzotto), publishing (RCS and Mondadori) and metallurgy (SMI and Falck) are no longer in the top 20 list, though most of them still exist.

Fifth, the number of firms that are publicly traded on the Italian stock exchange market has increased, but not by much, even when we account for the four state holdings in 1990, which were entirely controlled by the government. Excluding government-controlled firms and multinational subsidiaries, only two Italian privately owned companies were listed on the stock exchange in 2018, the eyewear and lenses Luxottica Group, and the oil refinery SARAS. In 1990, there were nine publicly traded companies.

Table 7.3 *Ownership concentration of Italian non-listed companies in 1993, 2005 and 2016*

	1993	2005	2016
Largest shareholder (average %)	66.0	66.9	66.0
2nd- and 3rd-largest shareholders (average %)	27.0	25.0	25.0

Source: Data for 1993 and 2005 are from Bianchi and Bianco (2006); data for 2016 are from Baltrunaite et al. (2019)

To sum up, the reshuffling in the top 20 list is characterized by a larger presence of state-controlled utilities, energy, service and foreign companies. Companies owned by Italian private investors, typically leaders in manufacturing, have shifted to the lower ranks. The role of the public equity market appears to be stalling.

7.3.2 Ownership Structure of Non-listed Firms (1993–2016)

This section describes the evolution of ownership structures in Italian non-listed companies over the period from 1993 to 2016.[9] Overall, the data suggest that there are no significant changes in either the governance structure or the ownership concentration of non-listed companies over the entire period. The most evident changes in Italian non-listed firms rather concern the use of control-enhancing mechanisms by the controlling shareholders to maintain control of the company.

7.3.2.1 Ownership Structure and Identity of the Controlling Shareholder

Table 7.3 provides an overview of the ownership concentration of Italian non-listed companies. The average stake of the largest shareholder was 66% in both 1993 and 2016. This confirms the anecdotal description of Italian corporate governance structure, namely its high and stable ownership concentration. The aggregate stake of the second- and third-largest shareholders was 27% in 1993 and 25% in

---

[9] In this section, we leverage the data and analysis presented in two different studies. The first study is by Bianchi and Bianco (2006), who exploit the INVIND database by the Bank of Italy for the period 1993–2005. The second study is the one by Baltrunaite, Brodi and Mocetti (2019), who use the information provided by Infocamere (the national association of local chambers of commerce) for the period 2005–2016.

Table 7.4 *Type of ownership in Italian non-listed companies in 1993, 2005 and 2016*

	1993 (%)	2005 (%)	2016 (%)	
Individual	50.9	51.0	Family	36
Holding	20.8	24.6	Coalition	20
Private non-financial	13.6	9.0	Private non-financial	34
State	6.9	0.7	State	3
Foreign company	7.8	12.3		
Bank and other financial	0	2.01	Bank and other financial	7

Source: Data for 1993 and 2005 from Bianchi and Bianco (2006); data for 2016 from Baltrunaite et al. (2019)

2005, thus leaving to minority shareholders a residual 7–9% of the entire equity. Notably, in 2005 the average number of shareholders per company is three.

Focusing on the identity of the controlling shareholder, Table 7.4 shows that in the period 1993–2005 about half of Italian non-listed companies were controlled by an individual. The second-largest shareholder (20.8% in 1993, rising to 24.6% in 2005) is a holding company that usually has a family at the top, followed by private non-financial companies (13.6% in 1993, decreasing to 9% in 2005). Since individuals typically own micro or small businesses while holding and private non-financial companies often represent the top of pyramidal groups of medium and large firms (ultimately belonging to a group of shareholders related by family ties), the data in Table 7.4 suggest that the large majority of non-listed companies are controlled by an individual or a family group. Indeed, in 2005, 84.6% of firms were controlled either by an individual, a holding or a private non-financial company, and 85.3% in 1993, pointing once again to a very stable model of concentrated ownership.

The main evidence of change between 1993 and 2005 is within foreign companies and state ownership as foreign-owned companies increased while state-controlled enterprises reduced their weight in the Italian economy, as a result of the privatization process of the 1990s. Finally, financial companies other than banks (mostly investment and mutual funds or private equity) increased their role but remained marginal.

The classification of controlling agents by Infocamere in 2016 is slightly different. In 2016, the predominant type is the family and individually owned business (36%), followed by private non-financial holdings (34%) which includes family groups, very common in Italy, and foreign companies, while state-controlled companies (3%) and financial companies (7%) have a lower incidence. The more recent classification introduces a new, residual type of ownership, the 'coalition' category, including companies in which a majority or controlling shareholder cannot be identified, and partially comparable to the previous 'holding' type. However, as pointed out by Baltrunaite et al. (2019), the family category underestimates the real incidence of family firms. First, it is based on a definition of family business which considers only close relatives, excluding other types of kinship relationship (such as the spouse). Second, it does not include family groups, where several members of the same family own a share of the company.

7.3.2.2 Control-Enhancing Mechanisms in Non-listed Companies

In non-listed companies, control is typically obtained via concentration of ownership. As shown in Table 7.3, the average stake of the largest shareholder never falls below 66% throughout the period. Nonetheless, many controlling shareholders in Italy typically rely on pyramidal groups (Barca et al., 1994; Bianchi et al., 2001). Given the high controlling stakes in these groups, the formation of pyramidal groups by non-listed firms is often an organizational strategy with the purpose of escaping employment law restrictions or eluding taxation rather than an instrument to reinforce control. In 1993, 56.5% of companies belonged to a pyramidal group, but in 2005, the last year for which a reconstruction of the pyramidal group is available, the percentage had decreased to 45.8 %, possibly as a result of the reforms in corporate governance practice and company law (Bianchi and Bianco, 2006).

In the absence of a direct majority stake, corporate control in Italy is preserved by relying on shareholders' agreements (i.e. formal agreements and voting pacts among shareholders, regulated by the law, with the aim of stabilizing control) and on clauses in companies' regulations that limit the transferability of shares (Gianfrate and Zanetti, 2007). In the year 2005, around 10% of non-listed companies adopted shareholder agreements and 46% had statutory clauses that limited share transfers, according to Bianchi and Bianco (2006). Implementation of these rules increased after the reform of company law, allowing companies greater freedom in drafting their by-laws.

7.3.3 Ownership Structure of Listed Firms (1993–2017)

In this section we analyse the evolution of the ownership structure of Italian listed companies, merging the data and the information provided by Consob's annual reports in order to cover the period of observation. Notably, the identity of listed companies' shareholders only became publicly available in 1994, and only for shareholders with at least 2% of the equity (voting rights), that is, the 'relevant shareholders', as defined by Consob.

7.3.3.1 Ownership and Control Structures

Figure 7.1 shows the evolution of ownership concentration of Italian listed companies, highlighting the share of the largest shareholder, the

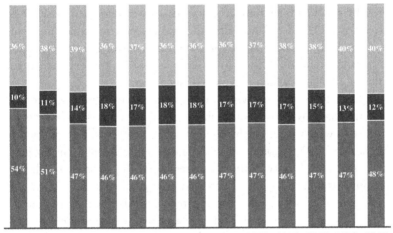

Figure 7.1 Ownership concentration of Italian listed companies in 1994–2017.
Note: The figure was built up by merging the time series and data presented in various reports, since the period under observation is long and no institutional report covers the whole period.
Source: Consob, various annual reports.

share of the other 'relevant' shareholders (i.e. the other shareholders with a stake of at least 2% of the equity who are required by Consob to disclose their identity) and the residual equity share floating on the market. The ownership pattern of Italian companies is highly stable over time, even when they are publicly traded. From 1998 to 2017, the average share of the largest shareholder remains almost constant at 47%, slightly increasing in the latest years. The aggregate stake of the other relevant shareholders kept growing from 1998 to 2011 (18%) but thereafter gradually declined, reaching 12% in 2017, whereas the share held by the market increased from 36% in 1994 to 40% at the end of the period.

The stability of the ownership structures of Italian listed companies reflects structural and cultural factors that are also present in other countries of Continental Europe, and ultimately can be connected to the owner's reluctance to release the firm's controlling stake. However, in Italy, there are two additional circumstances. First, the annual number of IPOs, typically reducing ownership concentration, is too small. Moreover, many new listings in the second half of the 1990s were by small and medium-sized companies that remained closely held after the IPO and did not alter the ownership concentration in the market. Second, the market for corporate control is not active and takeovers are rare. Hence listed companies do not experience the dilution of shares which is typical of such events.

Table 7.5 reports the evolution over time of ownership concentration weighted by market capitalization and shows a slightly different picture in which the growth of the market's share and the contraction of the largest shareholder stake are more pronounced. This suggests that ownership concentration has remained high within small and medium-sized firms but has decreased in large companies.

Turning to the events that formed this trend we note that, first, in the 1990s, ownership concentration decreased mainly due to the privatization of several large companies, though the trend was later reversed when a few individuals or groups acquired the privatized companies, e.g. Telecom, ENEL (electricity), Autostrade (motorways) and Ina (insurance). Second, in the early 2000s, the structure of some pyramidal groups was simplified (Bianchi and Bianco, 2006) by integrating companies situated at different levels of the control chain into one company with more dispersed shareholding. Third, several companies

Table 7.5 *Ownership concentration in Italian listed companies in 1990–2017 (weighted averages by market value; percentages on total capitalization by year)*

	Largest S/H	Other relevant S/H[a]	Market
1990	47.9	11.4	40.7
1998	33.8	9.7	56.5
2005	28.6	15.5	55.9
2010	34.0	13.5	52.5
2011	35.7	11.4	52.9
2012	34.8	9.4	55.8
2013	34.8	10.2	55
2014	34.5	9.2	56.3
2015	33.9	9.6	56.5
2016	34.0	7.2	58.8
2017	34.7	7.4	57.9

Note:
[a] Relevant shareholders are those with at least 2% of the equity, as defined by Consob.
Source: Consob, various annual reports. The table was built up by merging the time series and data presented in various reports, since the period under observation is long and no institutional report covers the whole period.

with very high ownership concentration were delisted and thus contributed to reducing the average market concentration. Fourth, the increasing use of coalitional control models based on shareholders' agreements led to an increase in the contestability of the control of listed companies. The year 2005 marks the further dilution of the average share of the largest shareholder as well as the increase of the 'other relevant shareholders', due to more corporate reorganizations and sales of more equity stakes held by the state. After 2010, ownership concentration stabilized around an average share of 34% (safely above the threshold of a mandatory takeover bid), and it has remained high to this day. Turning to the other 'relevant shareholders' (typically investment banks, mutual funds, insurance companies and banks), we find that their aggregate share increased before the financial crisis (15.5% in 2005), but then decreased to 11.4% in 2011 and to 7.4% in 2017, suggesting some caution by institutional investors in their interest in Italian companies.

7.3.3.2 Control Models of Italian Listed Companies

Table 7.6 shows the distribution of Italian listed companies by control model from 1996 to 2017. Consob classifies companies by types of control as follows: 'majority controlled', 'weakly controlled', (i.e. controlled through a minority controlling block), 'controlled through a shareholders' agreement' if a voting trust or a coalition among minority shareholders is in place, and 'non-controlled companies' if a controlling shareholder cannot be identified. If we compare the first and the last years in the table, 1996 and 2017, we note several differences. First, although the number of majority-controlled companies (i.e. mostly family firms) is stable, their share of total market capitalization has more than halved, from 66.8% to 29.8% in 2017, recouping from a low of 20.6% in 2010 (at the peak of the crisis). Second, weakly controlled companies have grown over the period, both in number and in market value, thus suggesting that some (large) companies are no longer controlled through a legal majority and that the majority type of control is becoming more

Table 7.6 *Control models of Italian listed companies (1996–2017)*

	Majority controlled		Weakly controlled		Controlled through a shareholder agreement		Non-controlled companies		Total	
	N	% cap	N	% cap	N	% cap	N	% cap	N	% cap
1996	130	66.8	26	12.2	26	4.8	26	16.2	208	100
1998	122	31.2	33	21.8	28	8.3	33	39	216	100
2005	124	22.8	28	30.6	24	16.5	44	30.1	220	100
2010	128	20.6	53	43.0	51	12.4	38	24	270	100
2015	115	28.1	52	34.8	30	6.0	37	31.1	234	100
2016	116	27.2	53	43.6	29	6.5	32	22.6	230	100
2017	120	29.8	57	39.8	22	5.3	32	25.1	231	100

Note: The table was built up by merging time series and data from various reports, since the period under observation is long and no institutional report covers the whole interval.

Source: Consob, Annual Reports and Reports on Corporate Governance of Italian Listed Companies (Statistics and Analyses).

typical for the smallest companies. Third, companies controlled through a shareholders' agreement first increase, especially in the years of the financial crisis, but thereafter they appear to have lost appeal and in 2017 their number was smaller than in 1996. Finally, 'non-controlled' companies (the category similar to 'public companies') appear to be slowly increasing both in number and in market capitalization.

To sum up, at the end of 2017, 52% of the listed companies were controlled by a shareholder with a legal majority while 86% of the companies were controlled by either a majority stake or a minority stake that ensures control (weakly controlled companies) or by a coalition.

7.3.3.3 Identity of the Ultimate Controlling Agent (Ultimate Ownership)

The ownership structure in listed companies is changing very slowly in Italy. Tables 7.7 and 7.8 illustrate the evolution of the identity of the controlling agent of Italian listed companies in two sub-periods, since Consob has adopted two slightly different classifications to identify the ultimate owners. The reconstruction of the control chain and the identification of the ultimate owners (Faccio and Lang, 2002) are difficult tasks in Italy due to the existence of pyramidal groups, some with the holding companies abroad, of multiple layers of parent companies, and of shareholder agreements.[10]

Table 7.7 reports the ownership types in listed companies over the period 1996–2002. We notice: (1) the dominant role of family firms, as identified by the 'individual' category, a role that is growing over time, (2) the relevance of the 'other company' category (grouping holding companies and parent companies of hierarchical and family groups and companies in which no single shareholder exercises control, hence widely held companies or firms controlled through a shareholders' agreement), which partially accounts for family firms that are organized as groups, (3) the slow decline of state ownership, in the decade characterized by privatizations and (4) the slight decline of financial

---

[10] Consob, among its market surveillance tasks, closely follows and monitors the evolution of the models of corporate governance and from 2012 has started to publish the Report on Corporate Governance of Italian Listed Companies, as an annex to the Annual Report. Unfortunately, no comparable information is available for the period 2003–2011.

Table 7.7 *Type of ownership in Italian listed companies in 1996–2002*

	Individual		Other company		Financial		State		Foreign		No UCA		Total	
	N	%	N	%	N	%	N	%	N	%	N	%	N	%
1996	45	21.63	54	25.96	19	9.13	21	10.10	17	8.17	52	25.00	208	100
2000	53	22.36	53	22.36	22	9.28	16	6.75	31	13.08	62	26.16	237	100
2002	64	27.71	49	21.21	18	7.79	18	7.79	24	10.39	58	25.11	231	100

Note: Financial includes banks, insurance companies and foundations. No UCA includes firms with no ultimate (identified) controlling agent, companies with no controlling shareholders, cooperatives or controlled by a company with no controlling shareholder.

Source: Our calculations on data from Consob annual report 2002.

Table 7.8 *Type of ownership in Italian listed companies in 2012–2017*

	Family		State		Financial		Mixed		No UCA		Total	
	N	%	N	%	N	%	N	%	N	%	N	%
2012	152	60.6	22	8.8	9	3.6	20	8.0	48	19	251	100
2015	143	61.1	19	8.1	10	4.3	14	6.0	48	20.5	234	100
2017	145	62.8	23	10.0	14	6.1	7	3.0	42	18.1	231	100

Note: Financial includes banks, insurance companies and foundations; mixed includes companies controlled through shareholder agreements and by foreign companies; no UCA includes firms with no ultimate (identified) controlling agent; companies with no controlling shareholders or controlled by a company with no controlling shareholder.
Source: Data sourced from Consob (2018).

institutions (banks, foundations and insurance companies). Finally, the residual type is the 'No UCA', No Ultimate Controlling Agent category, including a relatively large number of firms for which a controlling shareholder does not exist (like widely held firms or cooperatives) or cannot be identified, even by Consob. This category, possibly including some family firms with the holding company abroad, is quite large and stable over time.

Table 7.8 presents more recent trends. The data suggest that (1) family firms remain the prevailing control model, (2) state-controlled firms are slowly bouncing back (10% of total market capitalization in 2017) and (3) the number of financial companies with an identified controlling agent remain small. In contrast, as in the previous period, the 'no-UCA' category remains important for its share of total market capitalization (18.1%). This trend is in line with the findings in Table 7.6, showing the importance of companies that can ultimately be defined 'widely held' or at least not controlled by a majority share-holder. The black spot in this pattern remains the small and stable number of listed firms, which suggests a deep reluctance to go public felt by many successful medium-sized Italian companies[11].

7.4 The Determinants of Change in Corporate Ownership and Control

7.4.1 *Changes in the Institutional Context*

There were important transformations of the legal and institutional framework of Italian financial markets in the 1990s. Among the most influential changes were the privatization wave in the early 1990s and the reforms enacted as a response to the idea that slow economic growth and market inefficiencies were largely related to the small size of the equity market and to weak investor protection. Reforms most deeply affecting the financial markets were the new banking law in 1993, the privatization of the stock exchange in 1997, the new corporate law in 1998 (TUF), the issue of the Code of Corporate Governance in 1999 and the Consolidated Law on Savings Protection in 2005 (Law 62/2005, *Tutela del Risparmio*), the latter originating as a response to multiple fraudulent bankruptcies in the early 2000s (e.g. Parmalat and

---

[11] See Finaldi et al. (2020) for an updated review of the recent IPO trend in Italy and the EU.

Cirio). More recently, the adoption of a regulation of executive remunerations was issued in 2011 and a new law allowing firms to issue multiple voting shares and loyalty shares was passed in 2014, with the aim of encouraging small and medium-sized firms to go public (see subsequent discussion). All these changes contributed to bringing the Italian institutional framework closer to international best practice and standards. Overall, the purpose of these reforms is to reduce opportunities for conflicts of interest, to reduce (or make less attractive) the use of control-enhancing mechanisms (pyramids, cross-shareholdings and shareholder agreements) and to make the Italian capital market more attractive for international investors. In the following subsections, we examine whether the expected changes have materialized.

7.4.2 The Role of Institutional Investors

Consob defines 'institutional investors' as investment funds, banks and insurance companies with a shareholding stake in the listed firm lower than 10%. The presence, and the interest, of institutional investors in Italian listed companies are still low. In the period from 2010 to 2017, they invested in sixty to seventy-five companies (Consob, 2018), just about 30% of the total number of listed companies. This is not a good sign, since institutional investors are expected to play an important monitoring role within firms, thereby contributing to reducing agency costs.[12] However, their composition has changed over time, as foreign institutional investors have increased and Italian ones decreased in both number and market share. Moreover, the investment strategy of foreign and Italian funds differs. Italian institutional investors prefer investing in small companies in the industrial sector, whereas foreign banks and funds invest mostly in financial companies and in large firms. Within the group of Italian institutional investors, banks and insurance companies used to be the most important players at the beginning of the period but after 2015 their number has substantially declined and they were not replaced by domestic asset managers or private equity funds. Among foreign investors, assets managers are the dominant players and the category gathering private equity, venture capital and sovereign wealth funds is on the rise. This is good news for

---

[12] There is mixed evidence of the monitoring role of institutional investors. For recent evidence see Liu et al. (2020).

the (still) thin Italian financial market, as this class of investor can be viewed as the newest and more innovative source of funds for young, new technology firms that aim at entering the equity market.

7.4.3 *Change in the Use of Control-Enhancing Mechanisms*

7.4.3.1 Decline of Pyramidal Groups

One of the effects of regulatory reforms aimed at increasing protection for minority shareholders has been the decline in the importance of pyramidal groups (Bianchi et al., 2001; Bianchi and Bianco, 2006). Indeed, Consob (2018) reports that the percentage of companies belonging to pyramidal groups of the total listed companies has sharply decreased, from 44% in 1998 to 18.6% in 2017. Pyramidal groups, which are mainly composed of large companies, used to represent 75% of total market value in 1998, but just 36.9% in 2017. Moreover, the average number of firms belonging to a pyramidal group has remained stable (around three), but the 'leverage', the ratio between the units of equity capital controlled (on the basis of voting rights in ordinary shareholders' meetings) and the units of equity capital owned (on the basis of cash-flow rights pertaining to the controlling shareholder) has dropped over time, from 3.5 in 1998 to 1.6 in 2017. As a consequence, the 'wedge', the difference between the units of capital controlled and owned, has almost halved, from 24.2 to 12.3, confirming that hierarchical groups are becoming less popular as a means to achieve separation between ownership and control in Italy.

7.4.3.2 Rise and Decline of Shareholders' Agreements (Voting Pacts and Coalitions)

The rate of adoption of shareholders' agreements[13] by Italian listed companies increased especially in the period 1998–2010 (see Table 7.6). This increase is due partly to the privatization process, as the new private shareholders formed coalitions or signed voting pacts to enhance their control of the company. However, following the revision of the Corporate Governance Code, the number of shareholders' agreements in place has gradually declined. At the end of 2017 only twenty-two companies are controlled via a shareholders' agreement, corresponding

---

[13] The TUF regulates these agreements by mandating greater transparency through full public disclosure of the agreements and their renewals.

to 5.3% of market capitalization (Table 7.6). This decline may be attributed to the growing presence of institutional investors in listed companies. This trend may be reinforced by the increasing role of foreign institutional investors.

7.4.3.3 Changes in the Regulation of Shares' Voting Structure

The dominant voting structure of Italian stocks is 'one-share one-vote', though other classes of share with less or no voting rights are allowed. Moreover, in the past thirty years, as stocks with reduced voting rights were regarded with suspicion as a possible instrument of shareholders' expropriation (Zingales, 1994), the number of companies issuing non-voting shares has steadily declined (from 120 to 17 firms between 1992 and 2017, according to Consob, 2018). This decline is partly explained by mergers and delisting operations of companies with dual-class shares and partly by conversion of non-voting saving shares (i.e. *Azioni di Risparmio*) into ordinary voting shares to satisfy the preference of institutional investors for one-share one-vote.

However, in 2014, the Italian government enacted a new law (116/2014) allowing companies to issue shares with enhanced voting power, that is, multiple voting shares and loyalty shares. The purpose was to promote the development and liquidity of the stock market by incentivizing the owners of small and medium firms to go public by assuring them that they will not lose their company's control after the IPO. With multiple voting shares, newly listed companies may issue shares with up to three votes per share while with loyalty shares, companies may assign greater voting power, up to two votes per share, to shareholders who have held shares for at least two years. The former are expected to encourage firms to go public, the latter should foster long-term investments, stabilize investors with monitoring power and reduce the volatility of share prices. In the end, however, both instruments allow controlling shareholders to keep the firm's control tight even when they dilute their ownership. Not surprisingly, a lively debate in the financial press was sparked by the new law about the risks of encouraging the separation of control from ownership after the law was issued. Overall, at the end of June 2018, the numbers of companies whose by-laws provide for multiple voting shares and loyalty shares were 3 and 41, respectively (Consob, 2018).

7.5 Family Firms: Evolution of Control Structures and Determinants of Family Ownership

In this section, we focus on listed 'family firms', based on an original dataset with detailed, hand-collected variables for 155 non-financial listed firms from 2000 to 2017 (Abrardi and Rondi, 2020). To describe the company's ownership and governance structures, we collected data on the controlling share of the largest shareholders. To measure the controlling share, we identified the share of the largest relevant (as per Consob's definition) shareholder and, whenever two or more relevant shareholders could be associated by blood or marriage, we added up the respective stakes (thus identifying a 'family'). The dataset covers the majority of listed family firms in Italy. Family firms are relevant in other industrialized economies as well (Morck et al., 2005; Bertrand and Schoar, 2006), but in Italy they are also dominant in the public equity market, and this dominance is stable and long-lasting over time.

7.5.1 *The Role of Family Firms in the Public Equity Market*

In the year 2000, family firms represented 72% of total non-financial firms in our sample of listed firms (including state-controlled companies), 60% in 2010 and then 61% in 2017 (69.3% of all private firms). Looking at the percentage of family firms in the full sample of private-sector (i.e., non-state) firms in Figure 7.2, the data seem to suggest that the share of family firms is decreasing. Such a decrease, however, is not due to family firms exiting the equity market, but rather due to the entry of a larger number of private firms that cannot be classified as family firms.

7.5.2 *The Evolution of Ownership Structures: Controlling Shares and Institutional Investors*

Figure 7.3 shows the evolution of the controlling shares in family and (private) non-family firms, confirming the usual narrative about Italian firms that they are still controlled through very large equity stakes and the evidence provided in previous sections, but with greater detail. Within family firms, the (average) controlling share is never below 60%, but also in private non-family firms the largest shareholder owns

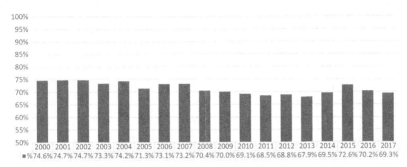

Figure 7.2 Share of family firms over the total of Italian private firms.
Source: own calculations.

Figure 7.3 Average controlling share of family and non-family Italian private firms.
Source: own calculations.

a substantial stake, greater than 30% (i.e. the mandatory threshold for takeovers) and increasing over time.

The evolution of institutional investors is also interesting to follow, because in most cases they represent the second-largest blockholder in a company, hence the only possible countervailing power vis-à-vis the majority shareholder. We can provide evidence for both the presence and the aggregate equity share of institutional investors in family firms. The overall trend for the aggregate equity share is on the rise but is weaker within family firms. Moreover, the proportion of firms with an institutional investor has decreased over time, which implies that institutional investors tend to be present in fewer companies, but with a larger equity share. This suggests that either institutional investors prefer to concentrate their investment in fewer companies, or they follow a herd behaviour strategy, looking at each other and choosing to invest in the same companies.

7.5.3 Control-enhancing Mechanisms in Family Firms vs Non-family Firms

The adoption of instruments that allow or reinforce the separation of ownership and control within family firms (vis-à-vis non-family firms) has changed since the early 2000s. In fact, within family firms, the fraction of companies with a dual-class share of votes has dropped from 40.4% in 2000 to 19.4% in 2017, and the percentage of firms with a shareholders' agreement decreased from 20.9% to 16.4%, thus indicating a better alignment between ownership and control. Contrary to family firms, the other listed companies slightly increased their adoption of voting pacts.

Another strategy that allows controlling shareholders to keep tight control of the firm is simply to run the company, or to have it run by a relative. The percentage of family firms with a family CEO is shown in Figure 7.4. In 2002, it was about 70%, but this important feature of family firms is changing over time. The trend is clearly decreasing and shows a marked drop after the 2008 crisis, but rose again, reaching 52.5% in 2017. Moreover, considering that the number of family firms with a family CEO is relatively stable over time, this evolution seems to

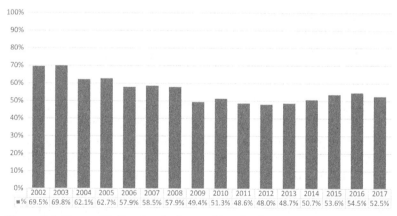

Figure 7.4 Share of Italian family firms with a family CEO.
Source: own calculations.

be explained by the entry of a new breed of family firm that opts for an external manager to run the company, not a relative of the controlling shareholder.

Finally, the grip of controlling shareholders on their companies is reinforced when the CEO holds the position of chair of the board of directors in the case of CEO–chair duality. Our data show that, despite the Corporate Governance Code's recommendation to keep the roles separated, the proportion of firms with CEO–chair duality is high (about 30%) – even higher in family firms (about 35% on average). This evidence is indicative of a situation of severe centralization of decision-making powers in family firms that already have the legal majority of voting rights.

7.6 Conclusion

In this chapter, we have sought to portray the evolution of the ownership and control structure of Italian firms over a long period – almost three decades from 1990 – in which many institutional changes and external shocks affected the industry, the financial system and the economy as a whole.

We have reviewed many reforms and institutional changes that occurred over the period, some promoted or enforced by the EU, such as the liberalization of capital markets and the privatization of the banking and public utility sectors, others introduced autonomously by the Italian government in response to financial or waves of company crises, or simply because they could be no longer postponed, such as the body of norms strengthening the legal protection of minority shareholders or the voluntary corporate governance code. We have provided a detailed account of the evolution and present status of the organizational forms of Italian companies, the control models of listed and unlisted firms, the concentration of their ownership, the identity of the largest shareholder, the control-enhancing mechanisms, the role of institutional investors and, last but not least, the control structure of family listed firms, which still represent the largest share in the private companies' segment of the stock exchange.

Despite many shocks and reforms, we have found that the main features of the ownership structure and of the control models are still in place. The Italian economy is, and remains, characterized by a predominance of manufacturing activity (the second in Europe by size, after Germany), of small and medium-sized firms that rely on banks for their external finance and are very reluctant to go public and release equity shares when they go. Hence, not surprisingly, the share of the controlling shareholder has remained very high, within listed firms, too, above 50–60% , even though, in the second half of the 1990s, several medium-sized firms were floated due to fiscal and regulatory reforms that reduced the cost of going public, and a few large former state monopolies were partially privatized. Both the small new entrants and the large network infrastructure companies remained tightly controlled by either their founders (with ownership stakes larger than 50%) or the state itself (with ownership stakes more than 30%). Despite a new law allowing firms to issue multiple voting and loyalties shares that help in keeping control separated from ownership, Italian firms' reluctance to go public still prevails. The effects of this new law have yet to be seen.

Equity finance, however, is important to ensure that companies can find the resources for new projects and investments, in short, to keep growing and expanding in the integrated market economy. The comparison of the top 20 companies' rankings in 1990 and in 2018 shows a slow decline of private manufacturing companies (both listed and not listed) from top positions and an advance of state-controlled public utilities and subsidiaries of foreign multinationals, mainly energy and service companies.

And yet the institutional reforms and the new laws have deeply changed the corporate governance, the transparency and the attitude towards investors of the relatively few listed companies. At the beginning of the period, Italy's stock market was well-known for its murky financial holdings (now illegal), vast pyramidal groups and inextricable cross-shareholdings. Over time, stronger pressure from the Consob, stricter rules by the stock exchange council, and the open dislike of foreign institutional investors led to a shortening of control chains and a dismantling of cross-shareholdings.

Another sign of modernization comes from foreign institutional investors. The change here has been dramatic, not so much for the size of their individual investment in each company, forcibly kept low by the extra-large stake of the controlling shareholder, but for the entry in the market of many new players which have replaced and almost dwarfed the few domestic investment banks. The interesting feature of the foreign investors' entry is that they initially spread their investment amongst many firms, but recently they have rearranged it in fewer companies but with larger stakes. Finally, our focus on listed family firms has revealed that more than 50% of them are still run by a 'family' CEO, though this share is slowly decreasing over time, and that they are steadily reducing dual-class shares and voting pacts, thus suggesting a willingness to reduce agency conflicts with minority shareholders. Of course, this descriptive evidence calls for a deeper analysis of the most important peculiarity of the Italian corporate governance system, family firms, and their 'un-diversification' mystery, that is, why their owners keep such large ownership stakes when they could control the company with a much lower personal investment.

PART V

European Transition Countries

8 | *Bulgaria*

EVGENI PEEV AND TODOR YALAMOV

8.1 Introduction

In Bulgaria and Slovenia – the two European transition countries included in this volume – the global corporate governance movement in the 1990s coincided with the radical societal change in Eastern Europe that began in 1989, known as the 'post-communist transition'.[1] In Bulgaria, the economic experiments during the 1960s and 1980s, intending to establish both effective mechanisms for control over managers and maintain the state ownership, had failed (Peev, 1995). These failures greatly fostered the public notion since 1989 of the necessity of abolishing socialist state ownership. At the same time, according to the dominant Washington Consensus policy of the early 1990s, privatization was the key pillar of the transition from socialism to capitalism (Williamson, 1993). Thus, in Bulgaria both public sentiment and policy prescriptions seemed to support the idea of the privatization of state ownership after the collapse of the planned economy.

The speed of ownership changes in large Bulgarian firms was different in the distinct transition stages. The Bulgarian transition might be divided into three stages: the first, lasting from the end of 1989 until the Bulgarian financial crisis of 1996–1997; the second – after the introduction of a currency board in July 1997 until 2007 when Bulgaria joined the EU; and the third – from 2007 to the present. During the first stage, the privatization process moved forward slowly because of fights for control of state-owned enterprises. Since 1997, a currency board arrangement and the start of negotiations for EU membership shaped a new framework of economic policy in Bulgaria. There was an acceleration of the privatization process and a few large Bulgarian firms were privatized. On 1 January 2007 Bulgaria joined the EU. In fact, this was the most important positive event in recent

---

[1] See for the driving forces of this change, e.g. Olson (2000).

Bulgarian history since the beginning of the transition. As a result, Bulgaria significantly reformed and aligned its commercial legislation with the EU legal framework both before and after joining the EU in 2007. On 10 July 2020, Bulgaria was allowed to join the Exchange Rate Mechanism II (ERM II). This was another positive step leading to a deeper European economic integration of the country.

In this chapter, we examine the change of ownership and control of large Bulgarian firms in the past few decades. The chapter is structured as follows. Section 8.2 discusses privatization and corporate governance and legal reforms in Bulgaria. Section 8.3 presents ownership data. Section 8.4 describes ownership structures in 1990 and 2018–2019, and the main patterns of ownership change. The determinants of ownership changes are discussed in Section 8.5. Conclusions are outlined in the last section.

8.2 Privatization, Corporate Governance and Legal Reforms

8.2.1 Organizational Forms

In Bulgaria, the prevailing legal forms of business organization are the joint-stock company (AD) and the limited liability company (OOD), accounting for 72% of all commercial entities in 2020.

8.2.1.1 Joint-Stock Company

The *Akcionerno druzestvo* (AD) is a joint-stock company comparable to both the public limited company in the United Kingdom and the Aktiengesellschaft in Germany. The AD issues shares which can be listed. Included in the definition AD is the *Ednolichno akcionerno druzestvo* (EAD), an AD that is 100% owned by a single entity. The minimal required capital for an AD is EUR25,565. The AD is required to prepare annual reports, which should also disclose self-owned and traded shares. Shareholders with at least 10% of capital can initiate claims for liability against the directors for company damages. There were 11,269 ADs in Bulgaria as of March 2020. Around 1,650 of them have a turnover of between EUR1 million and EUR10 million, and around 600 of them had a turnover higher than EUR10 million in 2018.

8.2.1.2 Limited Liability Company

The *Druzestvo s ogranichena otgovornost* (OOD) is a limited liability company comparable to both the private limited company in the

United Kingdom and the Gesellschaft mit beschränkter Haftung (GmbH) in Germany. The capital of the OOD is formed by the quotas of its members. Transferring (selling) quotas in OODs to third parties (i.e. not the current co-owners) is only possible after all due salaries and social security contributions are paid. The OOD does not usually issue shares. The OOD would also include the EOOD which is *Endolichno druzestvo s ogranichena otgovornost*, an OOD 100% owned by a single entity. The minimal required capital for an OOD is EUR1. There are around 700,000 registered OODs, but half of them are not operating at all. Slightly less than 12,000 have a turnover of over EUR1 million, and 1,100 of them have a turnover higher than EUR10 million.

8.2.1.3 Sole Proprietorship

There are also around 55,000 *Ednolichen turgovets* (ETs), which are sole proprietorships with at least one socially insured employee in 2018 and around twenty-five of them having a turnover exceeding EUR1 million in 2018.

8.2.2 Privatization

In the early 1990s, there were only a few scholars emphasizing the organic growth of the new private sector as a crucial factor for successful post-communist transition (see e.g. McKinnon, 1991). However, the dominant Washington Consensus policy emphasized the pivotal importance of privatization of state-owned enterprises at that time. The establishment of a private sector in Bulgaria was based on the Washington Consensus and EU Enlargement policies – both focusing on the key role of privatization in this process. The main difference between the various Bulgarian governments was the speed of privatization, not whether privatization was necessary or not.

In the early 1990s, Bulgarian privatization was governed by the Law on Transformation and Privatization of State and Municipal Owned Enterprises, adopted in 1992. Privatization made little progress and was applied mainly to small and medium-sized enterprises. Only 2,396 enterprises were privatized over the period 1992–1996, the major part of them being municipal property or parts of enterprises. The main reason for the slow progress in privatization was the continuing fight for corporate control between different interest groups (see e.g. Peev,

2003). Since 1996 there has been an acceleration of the privatization process. The applied basic methods were a Czech-like voucher privatization (named 'mass privatization' in Bulgaria) and management and employee buyout (MEBO).

Mass privatization was started by a socialist government (Prime Minister Videnov). Under the mass privatization scheme, privatization funds were specially designed domestic institutional investors regulated by the Securities and Stock Exchange Commission. The mass privatization programme envisaged that every citizen could buy vouchers at a cost of 5% of monthly income per capita at fifty times higher than nominal value of investment bonds. These bonds could be transferred to privatization funds (around 80% of citizens entrusted funds) or used directly in privatization auctions at the stock exchange. Privatization funds had to develop and publish their strategies similar to IPO prospects in order that citizens could make informed decisions on how to invest their privatization bonds. Funds had some important limitations on their investment activities as no more than 10% of their total bonds could be invested in one company and no more than 34% of shares of one company could be bought by a fund in initial auctions. However, after the completion of auctions, funds could trade with shares and expand their stake in privatized firms beyond the 34% threshold.

In 1996–1997, 1,050 enterprises were included in the mass privatization programme and about 15% of state assets were privatized. The emerging typical ownership structure was dispersed ownership with managerial or minority owner control exercised by privatization funds which were transformed into holding companies (Mueller, Dietl and Peev, 2003). A stage in the evolution of ownership structures that began in early 1998 was the fight between minority owners after mass privatization for the acquisition of effective control over the enterprises. This process had led to a concentration of corporate ownership. Because of the insufficient development of capital markets, the basic way to compete for corporate control was by proxy fights.

In 1998–1999, the 'reformist' government (Prime Minister Ivan Kostov) preferred management and employee buyout (MEBO) due to controversial close connections between policymakers and managers of state-owned enterprises. Privatization through MEBO envisaged the creation of a special company by employees, managers, managing and supervisory boards, and financial controllers, which could buy out the company. The government allowed newly appointed company directors to form such MEBO firms and to use mass privatization bonds (including bonds of relatives of management and employees) at a time when privatization funds were not allowed to attract more bonds. A further benefit was the possibility for deferred payment in cash for privatization deals. In 1998–1999, a large part of privatization deals were taken by MEBO schemes. In 1998 about 74.4% of the privatization deals were MEBO, in 1999 this share was 39%, and significantly dropped after criticism by the IMF and the World Bank.

In 2000, privatization of key companies in manufacturing had been completed. Some of the major privatized companies were Balkan Airlines, Neftochim, Petrol, Agropolichim, Himko, Antibiotic, Yambolen, OtK, Kremikovtzi, Promet, Asarel-Medet, DZU, Alumina, Arsenal and Beta. The privatization of energy utilities had barely started. In the financial sector, major privatization deals included the United Bulgarian Bank, the Bulgarian Post Bank, TB Express, Hebros Bank and Bulbank. As a result of the progress in privatization and with the establishment of new private companies, by 2001 the private sector accounted for 72% of GDP compared to only 26% in 1992.

In the 1990s, foreign participation in the privatization process was both modest and controversial. There were foreign investors with reputable business traditions such as Solvay (chemicals), Union Miniere Group (copper) and Brewinvest (brewing). However, there also existed another type of foreign investor whose capital had obscure origins (e.g. the case of Gad Zeevi (Israel), which privatized the Bulgarian national air carrier Balkan).

Until the adoption of the Law on Privatization and Post-Privatization Control in March 2002, a total of 7,002 deals had been contracted (until the end of 2001) resulting in income of EUR1,200 million. The average deal amounted to EUR168,000. One of the reasons for that is that 32% of the deals were for minority packages of shares and 31% were for separate parts/assets of the enterprises (PECA, 2021b). The new law changed the philosophy of privatization, focusing on larger companies and utilizing the stock exchange for privatization. Although the number of new deals was significantly less than the deals between 1993 and 2002, the average deal size was several times larger (PECA, 2021b).

As of 31 December 2018, all the assets subject to privatization had been privatized. They represent 66.31% of all state-owned assets

(PECA, 2021a).[2] Privatization since the beginning of 2002 has generated 71% of the total income from the privatization in Bulgaria (PECA, 2021b).

8.2.3 Corporate Governance and Legal Reforms

8.2.3.1 Shareholders' Protection

From 1996, the global corporate governance movement gradually entered Bulgaria. There was a remarkable new law 'production' and development of legal protection for shareholders. For example, the anti-self-dealing index (Djankov et al., 2008) showed that Bulgaria (0.66) scored higher than the United States (0.65) in 2003. Why was the investor protection score in Bulgaria so high? Comparative legal indexes like the anti-self-dealing index assessed the statute law, assuming strong law enforcement, and reflected only nominal legal change in Bulgaria. The Bulgarian legal reform following the foreign advisers copied 'best standards' easily into Bulgarian securities laws. However, in fact, the law enforcement has not proved so rigorous (Berglöf and Pajuste, 2005). More specifically, the inefficient court system was in reality responsible for bad shareholder protection in Bulgaria (Yalamov and Belev, 2002).

Since 2003, the Financial Supervision Commission has required all listed firms to have corporate governance programmes compliant with the OECD Principles of Corporate Governance and to report on their implementation annually. In October 2006, the Bulgarian Stock Exchange endorsed the Bulgarian Corporate Governance Code under a 'comply-or-explain' approach for listed companies on the stock exchange. Yet, at the end of 2016 only 56 companies out of the 397 listed had adopted the code (Nedelchev, 2017).

In 2006, there was a major change in companies' registration through the Law on Commercial Registry. The decentralized judicial procedure of company registration (entirely based on the submission of paper documents) was transformed into a centralized administrative one with the opportunity for entirely digital registration and subsequent digital operations. This legal change was a major step towards better transparency of all companies (including non-listed ones). Firms

---

[2] This statistic is based on the book value of assets of state-owned enterprises as of the end of 1995 using the World Bank criteria.

were required to submit financial reports, decisions of general meetings of shareholders, including company statutes and lists of shareholders presented at meetings, and this information was supposed to be accessible online free of charge.

Although there was always a requirement for maintaining a register of shareholders, it was only in 2010 that a unique company identifying number was issued, to be stated next to the company name. This has been a major improvement in terms of transparency as there were many cases of duplicate names of companies when the company registration was maintained by regional courts. The Commercial Law amendment in 2010 also introduced the requirement that when shares are used as a pledge, the company should be informed and this circumstance should also be stated in company books. The process of transferring company shares and real estate owned by the enterprise was streamlined to protect minority shareholder rights. In 2018, the Measures Against Money Laundering Act (MAMLA) was adopted, implementing the EU Fourth Anti-Money Laundering Directive (MLD4), which requires all firms in Bulgaria to collect and disclose information about their ultimate beneficial owners.

8.2.3.2 The Bulgarian Stock Exchange
The principal goals of mass privatization in Bulgaria were:

acceleration of privatization through attraction of local participants who have limited financial sources . . .; broadening the investment culture of many Bulgarian citizens who have the opportunity to take an investment decision . . .; development of the local capital market as the place where such shares could be sold or bought quickly and fairly. . . . (Prohaski, 1998)

The first trading session on the Bulgarian Stock Exchange – Sofia (BSE-Sofia) – took place on 21 October 1997. The stock exchange initially functioned under the Law on Securities, Stock Exchanges and Investment Companies (1995), which was replaced by the Law on Public Offering of Securities in late 1999 (enforced from 31 January 2000). With the start of EU accession negotiations in 1999, the Bulgarian company and securities laws were amended as part of broader legal reforms. In 2002 the Law on Public Offering of Securities was amended to institute the role of the independent director and the requirement of a minimum of a third of board members to be independent. There was still no requirement to have directors elected by minority shareholders. Since 2002, the

BSE has served primarily as an instrument for privatization. An overwhelming share of all privatization deals after the adoption of the Law on Privatization and Post-Privatization Control in 2002 was conducted through the BSE. For instance, according to the annual reports of the Public Enterprise and Control Agency, 88.7% of privatization deals in 2004 and 84.2% of deals in 2005 were conducted through the BSE (PECA, 2021c).

There has been a significant discrepancy between the remarkable corporate law 'production' and the resulting failing capital market development in Bulgaria. The striking features of the emerging Bulgarian securities market have been the low credibility of the market, low liquidity and a lack of efficient governance mechanisms (Peev, 2002). The capital market development was not sustainable. The market capitalization was scarcely 1% of GDP in 1997, in the first year of the existence of the BSE, and reached 4.4% of GDP in 2002. The total market capitalization of companies grew to 17% of GDP in 2005, reaching a peak of 49% of GDP in 2007 and an all-time maximum of the main index of the BSE (SOFIX) in January 2008 following the global market boom, but quickly lost ground in 2009 in the aftermath of the global financial crisis. In 2018, the total capital market capitalization of all segments of the BSE was just 8% of GDP, while the capitalization of non-financial firms at the BSE was only 5%. At the same time, 74% of the deals and 73% of the turnover were due to trade in securities issued by financial enterprises. Strikingly, the revenues of the BSE from selling information about the deals and issuers have been higher than the revenues from commissions for the deals themselves. Similarly, the revenues from registration taxes have been higher than the commissions. In 2018, the total turnover of the BSE was lower than that of any of the big retailers in Bulgaria (e.g. Kaufland, Lidl, Metro Cash and Carry, or Billa). In 2019, the turnover from non-financial issuers was less than that of the two metro lines in Sofia (around EUR50 million). All these facts suggest a lack of liquidity of the stock exchange. We discuss the potential determinants of the limited development of the BSE in Section 8.5.

8.2.3.3 Disclosure of Ownership

Article 65a of the Commercial Law stipulates that each company should collect, possess and disclose information on its ultimate beneficial owners. All data on physical and judicial persons, which directly or indirectly exercise control over the company, should be reported to the Commercial Register. The MAMLA stipulates additional measures applicable to the ultimate beneficial owners of clients and partners in commercial undertakings, including the definition of ultimate beneficial owners.

For listed companies, the shareholders are required to inform the Security and Stock Exchange Commission as well as the company itself any time they cross the thresholds of 5%, 10%, 15% and so on of ownership or voting rights. The requirement applies to physical and legal persons who have direct or indirect control of shares. The Bulgarian National Corporate Governance Code recommends companies listed on the BSE to disclose on their website their company by-laws, the ownership structure, the composition of the board of directors and board committees, financial reports for the last ten years and information for general meetings of shareholders – past decisions and future agendas, auditors, shares, bonds and other financial instruments issued by the company.

8.3 The Data

Our analysis is based on ownership data drawn from the Bureau van Dijk (BvD) Amadeus and Orbis databases, the APIS web service (a basic provider of legal and business information in Bulgaria), the Commercial Register in Bulgaria and other sources. We have collected four basic datasets.

(1) Sample 'Top 100 in T0'. This sample includes the top 100 non-financial firms (listed and unlisted) measured by total assets in the initial period of the 1990s. The size of the companies is determined by total assets between 1993 and 1998. When information on ownership was not available, data was gathered through the APIS web service.

(2) Sample 'Listed in T0'. This includes all listed non-financial firms in Bulgaria in the initial period (before August 1998). The sample represents firms in the first year of existence of the BSE, all of which were state-owned enterprises at the beginning of the transition. Some of them have already been subject to privatization and the remaining state-owned shares were later privatized through the stock exchange.

(3) Sample 'Top 100 in T1'. This includes the top 100 non-financial firms (listed and unlisted) measured by total assets in 2018 with ownership information in 2019.
(4) Sample 'Listed in T1'. This includes all the listed non-financial companies (as of November 2019) with ownership data for 2018–2019.

The datasets' construction is described in the introductory chapter of this volume.

8.4 The Ownership Structures

8.4.1 *Patterns of Ownership Change (mid-1990s to late 2010s)*

We document a few patterns tracing the ownership and control structure of Bulgarian companies in the mid-1990s and in 2018–2019. Table 8.1 reports ownership concentration in the initial period (the mid-1990s). It focuses on samples of the top 20 and the top 100 non-financial firms and listed non-financial companies on the BSE. In the top 20 firms, ownership concentration was very high. The prevailing largest shareholder (in fourteen of twenty cases) owned 100% of the total shares outstanding. In the sample of the top 100 firms, on average, the largest shareholder owned about 78% of outstanding shares and the average total share of all shareholders having 10% or more of shares in a company was about 90%.

In the sample of 672 listed companies in the initial period, ownership concentration was relatively low. The largest shareholder at the median held 33% of outstanding shares. This might be explained by several factors: (1) all companies, which appeared listed on the stock exchange, were privatized at least partially through privatization funds, (2) privatization funds were not allowed to considerably invest in large companies – they had a maximum threshold of 10% of their own capital for investment in a single company, (3) privatization funds were not allowed to gain a considerable share of any company – the maximum threshold was 34% of the privatized enterprise and (4) as funds' strategies included acquiring minority shareholdings in different companies for subsequent block-trading, they had lots of ownership stakes below 10%. The average ownership stake of a privatization fund in a company after the first wave of mass privatization was 17% (Miller and Petranov, 2000).

Table 8.1 *Ownership concentration in the 1990s in Bulgaria*

	Number of firms	Largest shareholder (C1)[a]				Second-largest shareholder (C2)[a]				Third-largest shareholder (C3)[a]				All largest shareholders (Largest SH)[b]			
		Min.	Med.	Mean	Max.	Min.	Med.	Mean	Max.	Min.	Med.	Mean	Max.	Min.	Med.	Mean	Max.
Top 100[c]	100	0.01	93.35	77.92	100	0.1	20	19.23	50	1.7	10	10.39	20	13.2	100	90.03	100
Top 20[d]	20	25.3	100	89.98	100	3.2	11.2	15.9	38	1.7	8.35	8.35	15	25.3	100	94.13	100
Listed[e]	672	1.4	33	37.63	100	0.6	15	16.65	44.4	0.1	8	9.5	22	10	33	45.48	100

Notes:

[a] The table shows results for the first year with available ownership data in the 1990s. C1, C2 and C3 are the shareholdings in % of the largest, second- and third-largest shareholders in a company.

[b] Largest SH is the total share of all shareholders having 10% or more of outstanding shares in a company.

[c] Top 100 are the largest 100 firms (both listed and unlisted) in Bulgaria.

[d] Top 20 are the largest 20 firms (both listed and unlisted) in Bulgaria.

[e] Listed are listed firms in Bulgaria.

Source: Bureau van Dijk (1999), Amadeus database, own calculations.

Table 8.2 presents the largest shareholders by ownership categories in the initial period. As we have already mentioned in Section 8.2, the delay of privatization was a distinctive feature of the Bulgarian post-communist transition. Thus, it was not surprising that the state was still the largest owner in 75% of the top 20 firms and 42% of the top 100 firms in the mid-1990s. Furthermore, one of the top 20 and ten of the top 100 firms were indirectly controlled by the state (not reported in Table 8.2). The median direct ownership stake of the state in state-owned companies both in the top 20 and the top 100 was 100%.

Who de facto controlled the state-owned companies with 100% state participation? This question may seem trivial but the Bulgarian early transition has produced bizarre types of control. Contrary to the conventional view that 100% state ownership also means strong government control, studies in 1992–1994 documented that these companies were actually under managerial control or interest group control (Peev, 1995). These types of control were based on unestablished property rights or on the influence by interest groups. First, unestablished property rights were property rights structures which failed to determine clearly who owns company assets, who is a bearer of residual risk, who is a decision-maker and who nominates the members of the board of directors (Shleifer, 1994). Second, interest group control was based on the influence of newly established private firms affiliated to interest groups with close political connections. In the early transition period (1989–1996), these firms were affiliated to interest groups belonging to former communist circles (e.g. Multigroup, TRON, Orion, the coalition of interest groups G13 etc.). Since 1997, the 'crony' firms have been affiliated to both the newly emerged interest groups (e.g. Olympus) and coalitions close to the existing interest groups (e.g. the Business Club Vazrazdane). Bulgarian interest group control followed the Russian model (Boycko et al., 1993) despite its delay in privatization.

Privatization has been seen as a natural solution to the agency problems of state-owned companies with 100% state participation. Interestingly, since the privatization wave of 1996 the state has remained an important major shareholder in privatized public companies. In our sample of listed companies, Table 8.2 shows that the state was the largest shareholder in about 47% of listed firms with a median 33% ownership stake. This happened on purpose – to preserve political control over the economy. Studies report that only

Table 8.2 *Largest shareholders by ownership categories in the 1990s in Bulgaria*

Ownership categories[a]	Top 100 (percentage of firms)[b]	Min.[c]	Med.	Mean	Max.	Top 20 (percentage of firms)[b]	Min.[c]	Med.	Mean	Max.	Listed (percentage of firms)[b]	Min.[c]	Med.	Mean	Max.
Families/individuals	3	30	60	60.33	91						0.6	33.8	62.7	64.35	98.2
State	42	25.3	100	91.17	100	75	25.3	100	93.22	100	46.88	20	33	42.88	100
Non-financial	14	25	61	68.69	100	5	100	100	100	100	15.62	20	40	44.53	100
Financial	1	75	75	75	75						0.3	25	37.55	37.55	50.1
Holdings	5	75.5	85.5	86.82	99.9						6.1	20	60	59.8	86.6
Others											0.3	29.8	34.4	34.4	39
Foreign	31	23.9	72.2	73.83	100	20	49.5	75.9	75.33	100	6.25	22	59	61.06	97.4
Dispersed	4	0.01	4.7	5.7	13.2						23.95	1.4	10	10.49	19.9
Total	100					100					100				
Number of firms	100					20					672				

Notes:

[a] The table shows results for the first year with available ownership data in the 1990s. We identify the company's direct controlling owner as the largest shareholder holding 20% or more of outstanding shares. When no single entity owned at least 20%, a company was categorized as having dispersed ownership. Ownership categories: Families/individuals, state, non-financial firms, financial (banks, other financial institutions) and holdings are domestic shareholders. Foreign are all foreign shareholders (physical and legal persons).

[b] Percentage of firms: Percentage of firms controlled by each ownership category or with dispersed ownership.

[c] Descriptive statistics (min., med., mean and max.) are the percentage of ownership stake of the ownership category in firms controlled by this ownership category.

Source: Bureau van Dijk (1999), Amadeus database, own calculations.

295 of 1,006 enterprises in the first wave of mass privatization had more than 70% of their capital privatized. Even in this segment, the state maintained an average stake of 17.1%. In 488 enterprises with privatized capital between 50% and 70%, the state preserved on average a 38.3% share of the capital (Miller and Petranov, 2000). Our estimate of the average state-owned stake (42.88%) in the sample of listed companies is similar (see Table 8.2).

Foreign investors were the second most important ownership category in the initial period. They were the largest owners in 20% of the top 20 firms and 31% of top 100 firms. However, the presence of foreign owners among Bulgarian listed firms was rather modest (only 6.25% of listed companies). This was due to the dominant methods of privatization (voucher privatization and MEBO). Successive Bulgarian governments have preferred local investors and corporate insiders over foreign investors (see the discussion in Section 8.2.2).

Dispersed ownership was not typical among the top 100 or top 20 firms. In the sample of listed companies, about 24% of firms had dispersed ownership. In fact, companies with dispersed ownership were a product of the mass privatization when (1) there was no strategic interest by privatization funds at the time of the auctions, (2) the companies were too large to have more than 20% of their shares privatized by a single fund right away and (3) there was no interest or agreement between shareholders for quick block-trading and ownership aggregation. Three out of the four companies with dispersed ownership among the top 100 firms in the initial period did not survive until 2018–2019 and 32% of listed companies with dispersed ownership in the initial period had also disappeared as companies by 2018–2019.

Table 8.3 reports the ownership concentration in 2018–2019. Among the top 20 and top 100 firms, there was no change in ownership concentration compared to the late 1990s. It remained very high. However, ownership concentration has remarkably increased in listed companies. The largest shareholder at the median held 51.58% of outstanding shares and the median total ownership stake of all shareholders having 10% or more of outstanding shares was 90.19%. The increase in ownership concentration seems at odds with the fundamental goals of privatization heralded by the proponents of mass privatization in Bulgaria in the 1990s. For example, among the main privatization goals was the development of Bulgarian financial markets, including the

Table 8.3 *Ownership concentration in 2018–2019 in Bulgaria*

	Number of firms	Largest shareholder (C1)[a]				2nd-largest shareholder (C2)[a]				3rd-largest shareholder (C3)[a]				All largest shareholders (Largest SH)[b]			
		Min.	Med.	Mean	Max.	Min.	Med.	Mean	Max.	Min.	Med.	Mean	Max.	Min.	Med.	Mean	Max.
Top 100[c]	100	13.35	100	87.08	100	0.02	12.22	17.3	50	0.06	5.02	6.1	19.95	13.35	100	95.12	100
Top 20[d]	20	25.38	100	93.46	100	0.14	12.3	11.36	20.68	6.59	9.43	9.43	12.27	46.06	100	95.84	100
Listed[e]	171	8.2	51.58	57.29	100	0.06	17.83	19.75	47.91	0.01	7.94	10.62	32.98	13.35	90.19	83.16	100

Notes:

[a] C1, C2 and C3 are the shareholdings in % of the largest, second- and third-largest shareholders in a company.

[b] Largest SH is the total share of all shareholders having 10% or more of outstanding shares in a company.

[c] Top 100 are the largest 100 firms (both listed and unlisted) in Bulgaria.

[d] Top 20 are the largest 20 firms (both listed and unlisted) in Bulgaria.

[e] Listed are listed firms in Bulgaria.

Source: Bureau van Dijk (2020), Orbis database, own calculations.

market for corporate control (see e.g. OECD, 1997). How might one explain the increasing ownership concentration of Bulgarian listed companies? According to the law and finance literature, ownership concentration would be a substitute for weak shareholders' legal protection typical in the civil law countries in Continental Europe, and Bulgaria in particular. However, as we discussed in Subsection 8.2.3, *nominal* shareholders' protection in Bulgaria has become strong but law enforcement has remained weak. Thus, the increase in ownership concentration might be seen as a response to the danger of expropriation under the conditions of weak law enforcement. Property rights protection and the rule of law appear more appropriate variables explaining shareholders' protection (see also e.g. Mahoney, 2001).

Table 8.4 presents the largest shareholders by ownership categories in 2018–2019. A few patterns of ownership change may be outlined. First, there was a sharp decrease in the role of the state in all the samples. The state was the largest shareholder in 25% of the top 20 firms (down from 75% in the mid-1990s) and only 9% of the top 100 firms (down from 42% in the mid-1990s). The state had virtually disappeared as a direct largest shareholder of listed firms. Nevertheless, the state still remained among the key *ultimate* owners among the top 20 firms (not reported in Table 8.4). Eleven of the top 20 firms were ultimately controlled by the state, accounting for 68% of assets of the top 20 firms. The ongoing importance of ultimate state ownership in the largest twenty firms in Bulgaria has also been documented in other studies (see on state-controlled firms in 2008, e.g. Gugler et al., 2013; see on state-controlled firms in 2015, e.g. Peev and Yalamov, 2020). Second, there was an increase in the role of multinational companies in all the samples. Foreign investors had become the largest owners in 35% of the top 20 firms (20% in the mid-1990s) and 46% of the top 100 firms (31% in the mid-1990s). The presence of foreign owners among Bulgarian listed companies has doubled (from only 6.25% in the mid-1990s to 11.7% in 2018–2019). Third, the increase in ownership concentration, which was documented on Table 8.3, is also confirmed examining firms with initially dispersed ownership. The percentage of listed companies with dispersed ownership has declined from 24% to only 4.69% in 2018–2019. Strikingly, the median largest shareholder by any ownership category had a majority ownership stake ranging from a 50.5% stake of financial owners to a 75% stake of the state in 2018–2019.

Table 8.4 Largest shareholders by ownership categories in 2018–2019 in Bulgaria

Ownership categories[a]	Top 100 (percentage of firms)[b]	Min.[c]	Med.	Mean	Max.	Top 20 (percentage of firms)[b]	Min.[c]	Med.	Mean	Max.	Listed (percentage of firms)[b]	Min.[c]	Med.	Mean	Max.
Families/individuals	8	45.31	50	61.91	100						16.37	25.02	52.65	59.84	99.78
State	9	50	100	94.44	100	25	100	100	100	100	0.58	75	75	75	75
Non-financial	22	41.91	96.44	84.63	100	5	100	100	100	100	42.11	24.28	51.62	57.81	100
Financial	3	25.38	100	75.13	100	5	25.38	25.38	25.38	25.38	19.88	20.54	50.5	56.28	99.99
Holdings	10	100	100	100	100	30	100	100	100	100	4.09	54.36	66.23	70.53	87.22
Others											0.58	53.2	53.2	53.2	53.2
Foreign	46	51.27	100	92.26	100	35	53.91	100	91.96	100	11.7	29.49	66.49	65.83	100
Dispersed	2	13.35	15.725	15.725	18.1						4.69	8.2	13.63	13.35	18.1
Total	100					100					100				
Number of firms	100					20					171				

Notes:

[a] We identify the company's direct controlling owner as the largest shareholder holding 20% or more of outstanding shares. When no single entity owned at least 20%, a company was categorized as having dispersed ownership. Ownership categories: Families/individuals, state, non-financial firms, financial (banks, other financial institutions) and holdings are domestic shareholders. Foreign are all foreign shareholders (physical and legal persons).

[b] Percentage of firms: Percentage of firms controlled by each ownership category or with dispersed ownership.

[c] Descriptive statistics (min., med., mean and max.) are the percentage of ownership stake of the ownership category in firms controlled by this ownership category.

Source: Bureau van Dijk (2020), Orbis database, own calculations.

8.4.2 *The Declining Number of Listed Companies*

In the initial period, there were four listed companies in the top 20 and thirty-one listed companies in the top 100. Of these thirty-one companies, in 2019 only ten have remained listed and only two of them have remained in the top 100. In 2019 among the top 20, only one company was listed (Sopharma) and among the top 100 only eleven companies were listed. Only two of these listed companies were widely held and in the remaining nine companies the largest shareholder held on average 55% of outstanding shares. Strikingly, out of 672 listed companies in 1998 only 70 (or 10.4%) remained listed in 2018–2019.

The key factors for the fall of the number of listed companies are the lack of IPOs and delisting. From the establishment of the BSE in 1997 until the end of 2018 only fifteen of successfully listed IPOs were able to raise more than EUR5 million. Some of them (i.e. Corporate Commercial Bank and Enemona) have already been insolvent. The future delisting of the companies listed in 1998 was predictable at the start of mass privatization, as there were not enough guarantees that the privatization funds and listed companies would not dilute small shareholders' value and rights. There were a number of cases where shareholders (even the state) were not properly informed and were not able or were even not allowed to attend general meetings of shareholders and as a result they lost even their controlling stakes (Yalamov and Belev, 2002).[3]

8.4.3 *Ownership Evolution*

Table 8.5 reports the evolution of the largest shareholder in the top 100 companies over the decades studied. First, while in the initial period the dominant shareholder was the state, in 2019 the dominant shareholder was a foreign entity. Second, twenty-seven out of the thirty-two state-owned enterprises (SOEs) in the mid-1990s were transformed into private companies. The most common change was

---

[3] A notably bad example was the AKB Fores Sozialen Privatization Fund (later transformed into AKF Fores Holding), which gained control over a company Polimeri. The company was closed for production in 2000 and its assets were stripped until its insolvency in 2010 and bankruptcy in 2012. The family owners of AKB Fores have been prosecuted in criminal proceedings.

Table 8.5 *Matrix of ownership change of the top 100 firms (type of largest shareholder) in Bulgaria*

	Dispersed	Family	Financial	Foreign	Holding	Non-financial	State	Total (1990s)[a]
Financial				1				1
Foreign		1		8		3		12
Holding						1		1
Non-financial					1	2		3
State	2			10	8	7	5	32
Not in the top 100 in the 1990s		8	2	27	1	9	4	51
Total (2019)	2	8	3	46	10	22	9	100

Notes:

[a] We identify the company's direct controlling owner as the largest shareholder holding 20% or more of outstanding shares. When no single entity owned at least 20%, a company was categorized as having dispersed ownership. The table shows results for the first year with available ownership data in the 1990s and ownership data in 2019.

Source: Bureau van Dijk (1999), Amadeus database, own calculations; Bureau van Dijk (2020), Orbis database, own calculations.

privatization (nineteen out of thirty-two SOEs) and restructuring of direct government ownership to a holding intermediary (eight out of thirty-two SOEs). About half of the privatized companies were sold to foreign investors. Third, more than half of the companies in the top 100 in 2019 that did not have a direct or indirect ancestor from the top 100 in the mid-1990s were foreign-owned companies. Some companies owned by foreign companies in the top 100 in the initial period still existed in 2019, but did not rank in the top 100 firms (e.g. DEU Bulgaria owned by DEU Korea, which was sold to Impexstroy, Russia). Another interesting trend is the sale of ownership stakes by some foreign investors and their replacement by local or other foreign investors.

To summarize, a massive ownership transformation has been observed in major Bulgarian businesses since the 1990s. Of the top 100 firms in the mid-1990s, 38% were no longer in the top 100 in 2019 due to various reasons (e.g. liquidation) and the bulk of the rest have experienced a major ownership transformation (e.g. privatization, sale of assets). Major trends are the decrease in state ownership and an increase in foreign ownership (46% of the top 100 in 2019). Following the predictions of literature on 'economic entrenchment' (see e.g. Morck et al., 2000, 2005) one might speculate that the remarkable ownership change in Bulgarian big business has decreased 'economic entrenchment' of corporate insiders and had positive effects on economic performance. In a similar vein, one might expect that privatization in general (see e.g. Estrin et al., 2009) and privatization to foreign investors in particular (see e.g. EBRD, 1995) would improve long-term performance. We leave the questions about the lasting effects of these ownership changes for future research.

8.4.4 The Destruction of Large Firms and the Entry of Newly Established Private Firms in Bulgarian Big Business

Joseph Schumpeter (1942) wrote: 'Situations emerge in the process of creative destruction in which many firms may have to perish that nevertheless would be able to live on vigorously and usefully if they could weather a particular storm' (p. 90). What was the effect of the post-communist transition 'storm' on large Bulgarian firms? There has been substantial change in the landscape of large Bulgarian companies since then. First, 10% of the top 20 and 29% of the top 100 firms in the mid-1990s failed to survive into 2018–2019. Some of the well-known epic corporate governance failures include Kremikovtzi (ranked 5th) and Polimeri (ranked 24th), which were listed on the stock exchange, and Plama (ranked 11th) and Balkan Airlines (ranked 27th), privatized to foreign investors. Second, 10% of the top 20 and 29% of the top 100 firms survived but did not preserve their position among the top 100 firms in 2018–2019. Third, two-thirds of surviving companies from the top 20 and half of those that survived from the top 100 went through significant restructuring (splits, mergers, privatization or change of majority owner from foreign to domestic or vice versa). Fourth, there were significant ownership changes of the large companies that have been in the top 100 in the initial period and in 2018–2019. Almost 70% of them had not only a new majority shareholder but its type was different.

There has been a substantial process of destruction in the Bulgarian economy, proxied by the exit of large firms, since the 1990s. How important, then, was the entry of newly established private firms into the cohort of the top 100 Bulgarian firms in this process of big business transformation? First, in the initial period 74% of the top 100 companies were mature, having existed for more than twenty years, 8% were of an intermediate age (between ten and twenty years) and just 18% were new companies; having existed for less than ten years. Around twenty-five years later, 55% of the top 100 companies were mature, 34% were of an intermediate age and only 11% were new companies. It appears that only a few newly established firms have had a significant growth rate over the past decades and have entered the list of the top 100 firms. Second, among the top 20 companies in 2019, there were no new companies and just 25% of the top 20 were companies of an intermediate age. Third, among listed companies in 2019, 5.85% were new companies, 17.54% were of an intermediate age and 76.61% were mature companies. Among the new listed companies, only one company was included in the SOFIX, BGTR30 and BGBX40, the three indexes of BSE. In sum, the destruction of large Bulgarian firms, proxied by their exit rate, was not coupled with an entry of newly established private firms into the cohort of the top 100 firms. It appears that this destruction has not been so 'creative'.

8.5 The Determinants of Ownership Change

What have been the determinants of the ownership patterns of large Bulgarian companies in the past decades? In what follows, we focus on (1) the political determinants, (2) the path-dependence factors, (3) the EU accession and the rise of foreign ownership and (4) Bulgarian capital market development and the insignificant role of institutional investors.

8.5.1 The Political Determinants

Ownership transformation in Bulgaria since 1989 has been a key part of the process of abolishment of Soviet-type socialism and the establishment of a market economy. What were the driving forces of this process? The transition to a market economy is not an ordinary economic transformation, based on Hayek's notion of spontaneous order. There was a wealth of anecdotal evidence that the major driving forces of the collapse of communism in Bulgaria and post-communist transition were the communist circles themselves (see e.g. *Financial Times*, 1994). Mancur Olson argued that in transition countries, the driving forces of the post-communist transition were not the entrepreneurial and business part of society but the 'parasitic circles' of the communist regime (Olson, 2000). The disproportionate power for collective action of these small groups with narrow parasitic interests has been an 'internal contradiction' in the societies in transition from communism to democracy. These forces were expected to design an efficient corporate governance system but they merely preserved the status quo, i.e. their power.

Mark Roe (1991, 1994) argues that the political ideology (e.g. the social democratic tradition in Western Europe) determines the ownership concentration in large firms (e.g. the high ownership concentration observed in Western Europe). This is one of the key hypotheses explaining the ownership structure of large firms. What has been the political ideology explaining ownership change in large firms in Bulgaria? The common answer usually focuses on the powerful role of neoliberalism in reshaping the policies in both Western and Eastern Europe since the beginning of the 1990s (Birch and Mykhnenko, 2009). The major debate arises about markets against the state and the increase in the role of the markets through liberalization, deregulation and privatization. Thus, neoliberalism can be seen as an important factor in shaping Washington Consensus policy and privatization in Bulgaria in particular.

Studies of corporate law and governance in Western Europe also show that economic nationalism appears as an important variable explaining the resistance of the EU member states regarding various initiatives of the European Commission for corporate law harmonization (see e.g. Gordon, 2003, 2018). Economic nationalism refers to 'the preference for natives over foreigners in economic activities' (see e.g. Dinc and Erel, 2013). Is economic nationalism important for explaining ownership change patterns in Bulgaria? The question about the role of economic nationalism in the post-communist ownership transformation does not seem trivial. The privatization experience of countries in Western Europe such as in the United Kingdom and France in the 1980s appeared not to be that relevant. In Bulgaria in 1989, all the non-financial enterprises and banks were state-owned and domestic private companies had to be created from scratch. In the early Bulgarian transition period, many formal and informal channels were used to transfer capital from state sources to 'crony' private firms mostly belonging to former communist circles (see OECD, 1997; Koford, 2000). This process was not just a Bulgarian trademark and was also observed in other transition countries labelled with various terms such as asset stripping, looting, tunnelling (for the transfers after voucher privatization in the Czech Republic), *prihvatizaziya* (for the privatization in Russia), spontaneous privatization (for the early privatization in Hungary), collusion privatization or mass fraud (for mass privatization) and hijackers-swindlers privatization (for MEBO privatization) in Bulgaria. Firms affiliated to interest groups with political connections were major actors in this process.[4] Under these conditions, the economic nationalism of Bulgarian corporate insiders had a bizarre form. On the one hand, the

---

[4] In Bulgaria, for example, Multigroup Holding was a typical actor in this process of privatization and siphoning off funds of the privatized enterprises. By 2002 the Multigroup Holding controlled more than 100 privatized companies from different sectors and had established a network of international companies, which controlled Bulgarian subsidiaries. It had investments in the top 100 companies in the initial period such as Topenerdji AD (8.25%) and Barteks (subsidiary of Multigroup). The Multigroup network vanished after the killing of Mr Ilia Pavlov (the founder of the group) in 2003. The company Plama AD and Evroenerdji AD (the majority owner of Plama) also disappeared after the company assets were stripped. The situation after the privatization of the national carrier Balkan Air was similar. Kremikovtzi AD, a large black metallurgy company, was another typical case of how an enterprise could be used to siphon off the government budget (through not paying electricity and rail fright) even when it was privatized. More about Multigroup can be found in Ganev (2007).

policies in the early 1990s favoured Bulgarian insiders over outsiders by both opposing privatization to foreigners and privatization at all, and supporting the establishment of domestic big business. The intertwining between the state and business shaped the reality of post-communist transition. The state maintained its nominal ownership in large Bulgarian firms in the 1990s and the presence of foreign investors was negligible. However, on the other hand, emerging major Bulgarian businesses were involved in capital flight, rent-seeking and looting. The uncertainty surrounding the future of SOEs, including uncertainty about who would own and control them, may partly explain this behaviour. This uncertainty has created an environment resembling the situation described by Mansur Olson as:

> when an autocrat has no reason to consider the future output of the society at all, his incentives are those of a roving bandit and that is what he becomes ... In a world of roving bandits some individuals may have possessions, but no one has a claim to private property that is enforced by the society. There is typically no reliable contract enforcement.... (Olson, 1993)

One might speculate that the marriage of economic nationalism with 'roving banditry' was not an easy business strategy but it appeared an essential part of the paradoxical 'economic nationalism' of Bulgarian corporate insiders in the early 1990s promoting national capital development, delaying privatization and constraining foreign investors' entry as well as looting Bulgarian firms and exporting capital abroad through capital flight.

8.5.2 *The Path-Dependence Factors*

Are the initial conditions important? The striking features of the initial conditions for property rights transformation in Bulgaria were the *nominal* state ownership of enterprises and an informal *de facto* total control by former communist circles over SOEs and state institutions as well as substantial uncertainty due to the volatile political environment, narrow-interest fighting groups and consequent short-time business horizons.

Corporatization (conversion of SOEs into joint-stock or limited liability companies, wholly owned by the state) began in 1989 when Decree No. 56 on Business Activity came into effect. Corporatization of large enterprises in the early 1990s created confusion over property rights assignment. At the beginning of this process there was a shift of control rights to enterprise insiders, mainly managers. Decree No. 56 and subsequent practice reflected the enhanced power of managers.[5]

The first Bulgarian government not directly connected to the former communist circles came to power in 1991. It tried to reassert state ownership of the enterprises and to overcome the vagueness of the property rights created under communist rule. New top managers were appointed in some enterprises. Typically, competition for managers' posts was strongest in the largest companies. A study at the end of 1993 showed that, of seventy companies, only nineteen managing directors – just over 25% – remained from the former communist regime. In the same sample, there were eighteen largest companies with a workforce of over 500 people, of which only one kept the same director (Peev, 1995). However, contrary to optimistic expectations, the behaviour of the new top managers, unconnected to the former communist regime, was quite ambivalent. On the one hand, the state appointed the new managers to keep companies in operation and pre-pare them for efficient structural adjustment, including eventual privatization. On the other hand, the new directors operated in unchanged conditions of power and without accountability.

Strikingly, a number of interest groups and affiliated firms, directly or indirectly connected to the former communist circles, emerged as important economic actors in the 1990s. However, as the evidence presented in the previous section has shown, the persistence of domestic private owners in large Bulgarian firms over the last decades was fairly weak. The rise of a few oligarchs and the subsequent fall of most of them was a typical feature of the Bulgarian post-communist transition.[6]

Indeed, the initial corrupt conditions of ownership transformation in the 1990s have partly determined the transition to a less-developed market economy. (For early studies on the transition to 'crony' capit-alism, see e.g. Peev, 2002.) Contrary to the optimistic expectations that

---

[5] Studies of early post-communist transition have documented inefficient behaviour of managers in Eastern Europe (see e.g. Voszka, 1992; Frydman and Rapaczynski, 1993). For the corporatized SOEs, private firms, and SOEs, see e.g. Peev (1999).

[6] Comprehensive analysis of the nexus between organized crime, oligarchs and the state, and its roots in the former communist party and security services was presented by Bezlov and Tsenkov (2007). The study also suggested that state-owned firms and management buyout privatization have been used to fuel oligarchs and also launder some organized crime money.

EU accession would radically improve the quality of the governmental institutions in Bulgaria, it appears that for the time being the process of eroding 'state capture' (Hellman and Schankerman, 2000) and the rise of an independent judiciary is moving quite slowly. This unstable institutional environment has been prone to political uncertainty and has been hostile to the sustainable development of big domestic businesses in Bulgaria.

8.5.3 *The EU Accession and the Rise of Foreign Ownership*

We have presented evidence on the rise of foreign ownership in large Bulgarian firms over the last few decades. The key driving factor was the start of the EU accession talks in Bulgaria, which have led to dramatic corporate governance and legal changes. These changes have created a significant improvement in the institutional environment for foreign investors in Bulgaria. Before the accession on 1 January 2007, the legal and institutional environment had been radically transformed in compliance with the *acquis communautaire*. Since 2007, further converging regulation and self-regulation have been developed (e.g. from the Bulgarian National Corporate Governance Code in 2007 and Conflict of Interest Prevention and Ascertainment Act in 2008 to the Markets in Financial Instruments Act in 2018, Anti-Money Laundering Measures Act in 2018 and The Law on Public Enterprises in 2019). Thus, while in the first transition period (1990–1996) the average net FDI inflows (in current USD) in Bulgaria was USD64 million, in the second period (1997–2006) it dramatically increased to USD2.2 billion and after the EU accession it continued to grow to USD3.7 billion (2007–2018) (World Bank, 2021).

8.5.4 *The Capital Market and the Insignificant Role of Institutional Investors*

We have documented the limited development of the Bulgarian capital market over the past few decades. Empirical studies of stock market prices confirm capital market inefficiency (e.g. Bogdanova and Ivanov, 2014). This appears at odds with one of the mainstream hypotheses about financial development. This hypothesis predicts that a country's trade and financial openness will constrain the rent-seeking behaviour of domestic interest groups and lead to strong financial development proxied by the country's capital market capitalization and number of listed companies (Rajan and Zingales, 2003). In Bulgaria, there has been a high level of trade and capital liberalization over the years. The Index of Economic Freedom for 2021 shows that Bulgaria was ranked twentieth among forty-five countries in Europe, and the Bulgarian overall economic freedom score was above the regional and world averages (Miller, Kim and Roberts, 2021). Yet the BSE has remained dysfunctional. Why do we observe weak development of the capital market in Bulgaria? We may speculate about a few potential factors.

After the collapse of communism in 1989, Bulgaria was at a stage which required it to 'catch up' with other advanced EU market economies. The experience of developed countries showed that specific institutions emerged to accumulate capital, which enabled economic 'catch-up' growth. For example, Japan and other East Asian countries developed concentrated banking systems and active government industrial policies. The 'developmental state' has been a crucial common factor in this process. In the early 1990s, post-communist studies have rarely examined the interactions between the building of state institutions and privatization. Among a few exceptions, see e.g. McKinnon (1991) who discussed the importance of institutions building *before* privatization of large firms. A number of recent a cross-country studies on Eastern Europe showed the crucial importance of the quality of country institutions and ownership types on company performance. See e.g. Mueller and Peev (2007) and Gugler and Peev (2010) on investment performance, and Peev and Yurtoglu (2008) on leverage. However, in Bulgaria the organic development of the private sector and state building were not important pillars of the Washington Consensus policy in the 1990s. The privatization of SOEs was the key policy for private-sector establishment and capital market development.

The main factor for the establishment of Bulgarian public companies on the BSE was mass privatization. In fact, in the 1990s all the companies on the stock exchange were listed through a mass privatization process and the main capital market activity of privatization funds was the redistribution of shares through private placement not mediated by the price mechanism. The basic tool used for this redistribution was block trades of shares (trade involving more than 200,000 shares) and the major economic goals were the private benefits of fund managers, directors and controlling shareholders. The stock exchange was used only to register already conducted trade. The trading led to ownership concentration and a dilution of minority stakes. Delisting became a key trend. The lack of development of the secondary market for shares of privatized companies led to a lack of capital needed for their restructuring. Moreover, diversifying risk through portfolio investment in domestic companies appeared nearly impossible. Among external factors, international corporate scandals as well as the global financial crisis in 2008–2009 were additional forces decreasing the popularity of stock investment in Bulgaria. Thus, the Bulgarian capital market remained underdeveloped and the presence of institutional investors was negligible mostly due to the low quality of country institutions and the establishment of Bulgarian public companies through mass privatization.

8.6 Recent Developments and Conclusion

Despite the substantial scale of privatization since the 1990s, SOEs still hold an important position in the Bulgarian economy (both in terms of assets and employed people). In 2019, there were around 1,000 SOEs (930 majority controlled and 41 with 10%–50% state ownership, OECD, 2019). Although there have been considerable improvements since the mid-1990s, important corporate governance vulnerabilities of Bulgarian SOEs still existed in 2019. The problems include a lack of independent directors, board selection procedures not being clear and transparent, no formal requirements for board membership, a lack of clear boundaries between the roles of the boards in individual SOEs and the ministries, which essentially allow the government to expand the ownership rights to SOEs without limitation, and the seldom use of specialized board committees by Bulgarian SOEs (OECD, 2019). It is still too early to say if there will be enough checks and balances to guarantee the improvement in the quality of corporate governance of SOEs in Bulgaria.

9 | *Slovenia*

JOŽE P. DAMIJAN, ANAMARIJA CIJAN AND
JAKOB STEMBERGER

9.1 Introduction

Slovenia has not only gone through the global corporate governance
developments of the 1990s, but has also faced major changes in its
socio-economic system. Since 1989, Slovenia has started to shift its
economy from socialism to capitalism. The most significant part of this
post-communist transition is based on privatization. Additionally,
Prašnikar and Gregorič (2002) state that one of the most crucial
aspects of the transition is management's ability to utilize privatized
firms to carry out their restructuring.

Slovenia's transition from a socialist state to a market economy can
be divided into two major periods. The first was the building of the
new independent state (since June 1991), while the second was driven
by the aspiration to join the European Union (applying for membership in June 1996). Slovenia's reform activities were formed on two
policy sets. The first involves policies directed to achieving macroeconomic stabilization and both internal and external liberalization. The
second is focused on structural and institutional reforms, including
the building of institutions, privatizating state-owned assets, reforming
the enterprise and financial sectors, reforming public utilities, the pension, social welfare and tax systems, and public administration (Mrak,
Rojec and Silva-Jáuregui, 2004).

The country's reform strategy has been developed in multiple key
documents. The most important, from the reform process point of view
and its policy impact, has been the Strategy of the Republic of Slovenia
for the Accession to the European Union: Economic and Social Part,
adopted in January 1998. The document defines a consistent set of
medium-term economic and social policy measures needed to complete
the country's economic transformation into a market economy and to
prepare it for accession to the EU. The EU and major international
financial institutions have fully endorsed the contents of this document.

The reform activities presented in Slovenia's accession strategy have been successfully implemented (Mrak et al., 2004).

However, as Mrak et al. (2004) point out, there have been three key features distinguishing the transition process in Slovenia from other post-communist countries. First, Slovenia implemented a gradualist approach to transition (the Mencinger model), rather than opting for the 'big bang' approach to transition. Second, Slovenia's transition from a planned to a market economy was paired with a transition from a regional component of a federal economy to a national economy. The parting from the ex-Yugoslavia and the introduction of high tariffs on trade between newly established independent countries meant that Slovenian companies effectively lost one-third of their market. This forced companies to adapt quickly in terms of efficiency and technical standards in order to serve the more demanding export markets of the then European Community. Third, Slovenia inherited from the former Socialist Federal Republic of Yugoslavia a unique enterprise ownership framework based on self-management and a unique institutional setting (social ownership), allowing for a relatively independent (from the state institutions) enterprise management structure. In contrast, most of the other transition countries started their transitions with an ownership structure dominated by the state.

In this chapter, we study the ownership transformation of the Slovenian economy after 1991. Though initially the Slovenian ownership structure was not formally dominated by the state (due to so-called social ownership), it became so due to the applied distribution formula in the process of privatization. Starting with a 20% ownership share in all privatized companies, the state was able to expand the control in all strategic sectors via investment strategies of the two state funds – Capital Fund for Pension and Disability Insurance (the so-called KAD) and the Restitution Fund (the so-called SOD). By 2008, Slovenia was perceived by the OECD, EBRD and European Commission as a new EU member state with the largest state-owned holdings and the lowest share of foreign ownership. However, due to exuberances prior to the global financial crisis of 2009 in the form of numerous management buyouts and ownership consolidations within and across industries backed by the then government, the landscape of the Slovenian corporate ownership structure was changed dramatically in the decade after the financial crisis. The major reason was that companies involved in management buyouts, mergers and acquisitions or pure irrational investments took on too much financial leverage, making them unable to service their increased debt levels. This led to a full-blown financial crisis lasting for five years and characterized by banks with heavily impaired balance sheets and with most indebted companies on the verge of or filed for bankruptcy.

After late 2013 when the government decided to bail out the banks, the process of radical ownership changes and privatization started. The first channel was a series of foreign acquisitions of troubled companies. The second channel was the commitment of the then government to the European Commission to privatize fifteen state-owned companies and to privatize all banks receiving state aid as part of the bank rehabilitation programme. By early 2020, this process was finished. The third channel was the process of selling off large or medium-sized companies privatized to managers in the period 2005–2008 that fell victim to the banks due to their excess leverage. While some of the biggest insolvent companies were sold individually by the consortiums of banks, the bulk of the insolvent companies were sold by the Bank Assets Management Company (BAMC), the Slovenian 'bad bank', which started operating in 2014. In the period 2014–2019, most of the companies in the BAMC portfolio were sold to foreign investors or holding companies. This explains the radical increase in ownership concentration in the top 100 Slovenian companies over the three decades studied and the rise of holdings and foreign strategic investors as the main owners of the top Slovenian companies at the end of the 2010s.

This chapter is organized in the following order. Section 9.2 presents privatization and corporate governance reforms in Slovenia after independence. Section 9.3 outlines Slovenia's legal framework of corporate governance. Section 9.4 presents how state-owned enterprises (SOEs) are regulated. The main pattern of ownership changes since 1990 are presented in Section 9.5. The political economy of corporate governance and ownership changes in Slovenia is discussed in Section 9.6.

9.2 Privatization and Corporate Governance Reforms

9.2.1 *Privatization and Corporate Governance*

The restructuring of Slovenia's enterprise sector dates to the late 1980s. In the early stages, most of the focus was on the three aspects of reform. First, an appropriate legal and institutional framework for enterprise creation and the promotion of entrepreneurial initiative needed to be established. Second, the enterprise sector had to be rehabilitated. In order to achieve that goal various programmes of enterprise rehabilitation were launched. Third, the privatization of SOEs began. Due to political reasons, the actual start of the privatization process had not followed immediately after the passage of the Ownership Transformation Act in 1992. Slovenia's approach towards privatization has been a combination of free distribution of shares (mass or voucher privatization), internal buyouts at a discount (insiders privatization) and commercial privatization. The emphasis on internal buyouts was the major characteristic of Slovenian privatization and assisted the status quo by circumventing larger layoffs but at a cost of firm underperformance (Mrak et al., 2004).

Mechanisms of privatization determined the corporate governance structure in Slovenia after independence. These privatization mechanisms were established by the Slovenian Privatization Law of 1992, based on the formula of '20% + 20% + 20% + 40%': (1) 20% of shares were transferred to two state funds – the first 10% was allocated to the Capital Fund for Pension and Disability Insurance (KAD) and the second 10% to the Restitution Fund (SOD); (2) 20% of shares were assigned to authorized investment companies; (3) 20% of shares were allotted to employees, former employees and retired workers of those enterprises in exchange for certificates; (4) the last 40% of shares could have either been privatized externally by a public offering of shares and listing on the stock exchange, or alternatively they could be privatized internally, through buyouts from management, current and former employees or close family members and retired workers.

By allowing firms to choose how 40% of shares were distributed, the privatization law enabled either internal or external ways of ownership change. This resulted in the 'clash for control' among both inside and outside owners, such as state-controlled funds, privatization investment funds and other physical or institutional outside owners (Damijan and Damijan, 2019). These methods of privatization affected the ownership and control structures of Slovenian enterprises after privatization, and impacted Slovenian firms' performance. According to Damijan, Gregorič and Prašnikar (2004), dominant insider owners and domestic non-financial firms have a more positive effect on financial performance of privatized firms compared to state-controlled funds. Moreover, Simoneti et al. (2005) discovered that mass privatization agents were more efficient owners compared to the government in a regulated and transparent legal and economic system.

9.2.2 Corporate Governance Reforms

The mentioned 'clash for control' of privatized firms continued after privatization as well. Three significant and competing groups of owners attempting to obtain control of those companies emerged. The first were managers, buying out shares of employees and other external owners through management and employee buyouts (MEBOs). The second were foreign strategic investors and the third was the state. Contrary to other ex-socialist states in Central and Eastern Europe, the state persisted as a significantly more dominant owner in Slovenia (OECD, 2011a, 2011b). Consequently, the foreign investors' role was considerably more restricted. In Slovenia, the state has kept large direct ownership or indirect control with the help of state-controlled funds (KAD and SOD) in the energy sector, telecommunications, financial sector and transportation (Damijan and Damijan, 2019).

Both funds have slowly condensed ownership in several strategic firms, where the state's strategy was to limit foreign strategic investors. These significant direct and indirect asset holdings of the state forced Slovenia's corporate governance to be a profound concern. The state's direct and indirect possessions of assets gave any political coalition in office a mechanism to have control over several enterprises and to take part in an adverse selection of candidates for firms' supervisory boards. Changing both supervisory boards and boards of directors of companies as well as boards of state-controlled funds (KAD and SOD) after each election became the political norm. The degree of direct and indirect state ownership has offered the government a mechanism to have an active role in nominating politically connected people into supervisory boards and boards of directors. As the government failed to be an efficient shareholder, state-owned and state-controlled firms' performance was suppressed, due to the absence of best practices in selecting high-quality members of boards of directors and, as a result, due to the lack of implemented high-quality business practices (Damijan and Damijan, 2019).

The state's involvement resulted in poor management practices and an absence of stability in state-owned and state-controlled firms.

During the moderation stage between 1992 and 2004 with stable political coalitions, the corporate governance of most of the largest companies remained stable with rare changes in supervisory boards and boards of directors. However, after the EU accession in 2004, changes in the structure of political coalitions became more common. Thus, each coalition in power used the mechanism of direct and indirect ownership to influence the structures of supervisory boards with the paramount objective of replacing the boards of directors (Damijan and Damijan, 2019).

The key milestone for improvements in the quality of corporate governance practices in Slovenia was the start of accession negotiations with the OECD in 2007. As part of those discussions, the OECD Council chose to review corporate governance practices in Slovenia. The Review of Corporate Governance in Slovenia (hereafter: Review) highlighted some of the most significant corporate governance challenges for Slovenia before it could become a full member of the OECD, which materialized in July 2010. The Review stated that the major factor of Slovenia's corporate governance outline as of 2009 was the:

importance of managing State-Owned Enterprises (SOEs) to ensure that there is a consistent and transparent ownership policy; that the state acts as an informed and responsible shareholder; and that SOE boards are appropriately composed to ensure that they have the skills and authority to exercise their functions. (OECD, 2011b)

State-owned enterprises were recognized as a major part of both listed and non-listed firms. The Review revealed that the government had considerable control over numerous firms in the domestic market. The Review emphasized that direct holdings are concentrated mostly in the financial (banking and insurance), infrastructure and energy sectors. Moreover, indirect holdings were most often carried out with the help of two state-controlled funds established as a part of the privatization process – the pension fund (KAD) and the restitution fund (SOD). Finally, the Review suggested numerous reforms in corporate governance practices and the legal framework to be implemented by the Slovenian government (Damijan and Damijan, 2019).

After the OECD Review, Slovenia made major strides to improve its corporate governance quality, particularly focusing on regulating SOEs. In 2010, the Slovenian government founded a new central ownership agency named AUKN (State Assets Management Agency).

That agency was replaced by the Slovenian Sovereign Holding (SSH) in late 2012, managing SOD and partly of KAD. In 2015, the government implemented a State Assets Management Strategy, and three particular corporate governance codes for state-owned, listed and non-listed firms were adopted by the respective major stakeholders (Damijan and Damijan, 2019).

Predicting these alterations and advancements, the OECD finished its Review in 2011 on a vastly positive note, applauding the Slovenian government's endeavours to improve both the quality of corporate governance of SOEs and the treatment of minority shareholders and limiting the possibility for 'share-parking' practices. Arguably, the last decade has become a success in terms of Slovenia formally establishing a modern framework of transparent corporate governance, regulating both listed and non-listed private companies and SOEs. Nevertheless, even with all these legal and institutional advancements, the practices used by both private dominant owners and especially by political coalitions in power regarding the management of direct and indirect state ownership have not changed fundamentally.

9.3 Legal Framework of Corporate Governance in Slovenia

9.3.1 Overall Legal Framework of Corporate Governance

The corporate governance legislation framework in Slovenia consists of the Companies Act, the Banking Act, the Market in Financial Instruments Act and the Auditing Act. Moreover, both the Bank of Slovenia and the Ljubljana Stock Exchange have issued frameworks, containing provisions applicable to corporate governance. The former institution offers the groundwork relevant for banks and the latter provides the foundation for listed companies. Examination and compliance with three voluntary corporate governance codes promote transparency and credibility in listed and unlisted companies or SOEs. As mentioned, one of the key drivers for the improved quality of corporate government practices in Slovenia during the last decade stems from the pre-accession discussion with OECD together with the OECD Review of Corporate Governance practices in Slovenia.

Besides the earlier outlined Acts, there are three sets of voluntary codes that grant supplementary groundwork on rules and practices for different types of firm with regard to their ownership structure (Damijan and

Damijan, 2019): the Slovenian Corporate Governance Code for Listed Companies, the Corporate Governance Code for Unlisted Companies, and the Corporate Governance Code for State-Owned Enterprises.

Both the pre-accession dialogue between Slovenia and OECD, and the OECD Review of Corporate Governance practices in Slovenia represent pivotal factors for improved quality in the Slovenian corporate governance practices during the last decade. The Review highlighted weaknesses of regulation practices in both the private sector and SOEs. The main issue within SOEs was the allowance of government interference with the private firms' management, more precisely, the nominations of supervisory boards by government in the two state-controlled funds (KAD and SOD) and in direct state holdings. Thus, past governments had a chance to significantly affect the working of large sectors of Slovenian commercial companies and corporate control (Damijan and Damijan, 2019).

The OECD Review offered various proposals to improve the quality of corporate governance practices, among them: (1) transformation of the pension and restitution funds – KAD and SOD respectively; (2) formation of a new central ownership agency to establish a vigorous Code of Corporate Governance, a detailed capital investment strategy, classification of assets between strategic and portfolio investments together with clear government objectives for asset groups; (3) revision of the Companies Act with a focus on prompter management of minority shareholders; (4) strengthening operational and financial independence of the Securities Market Agency; and (5) continuing to oversee any share-parking activities and aiming to prevent them (Damijan and Damijan, 2019).

It appears natural to assess the effectiveness of the changed corporate governance legal and institutional framework in Slovenia. Correspondingly, one can examine the survey results among company managers offered by a report of EBRD in 2017. The latter labelled the overall Slovenian corporate governance framework as moderate, with legal and voluntary frameworks (disclosure and transparency, institutions and stakeholders) marked as moderately strong. Similarly, rights of minority shareholders were classified as fair to moderately strong, yet internal controls and structure together with boards' functioning were assessed as fair (EBRD, 2017).

Nevertheless, various challenges are still observed when analysing corporate governance practices in Slovenia. One must acknowledge that corporate governance compliance with the code increased over time, as highlighted by the raised number of companies that affirm full compliance. Yet the unrealistic information provided by firms stands out (EBRD, 2017). As an illustration, failures of both large companies (e.g. Istrabenz, Pivovarna Laško, Merkur, SCT) and mid-size companies due to the global financial crisis together, with several financial difficulties observed within companies, revealed inefficient corporate governance practices among Slovenian enterprises. From the mass privatization in the early 1990s, several problems were inherited such as conflicts of interest between the management and supervisory boards, questionable share-parking practices, inefficient management and operational practices of supervisory boards as well as an absence of regulatory intervention. Notably, the global financial crisis unravelled these inefficiencies and inadequate practices through the disappearance or sell-off of particular firms, thereby strengthening the corporate governance system. Initially, that could not be resolved by either legal and voluntary corporate governance framework changes or regulatory intervention. However, after the crisis firms learned from that experience and regulators have become more active players in monitoring legislation compliance (EBRD, 2017).

9.3.2 Voluntary Corporate Governance Code

The previously mentioned four principal corporate governance Acts together with the voluntary codes, characterizing the three distinctive ownership structures outlined later, represent the Slovenian corporate governance framework. All three Codes were amended and modified in 2016, mainly due to the international alterations in regulation of corporate governance within the Companies Act (ZGD-1) amendments, the G20/OECD Principles of Corporate Governance and OECD Guidelines on Corporate Governance of SOEs. Moreover, domestic initiatives improved corporate governance practices and guidelines as well (Damijan and Damijan, 2019). Additionally, the Code for SOEs was updated in 2019.

The Slovenian Corporate Governance Code for Listed Companies (hereafter: CG Code for LCs), adopted by The Ljubljana Stock Exchange Inc. and by the Slovenian Directors' Association in October 2016, amended the code of 2009 that had been in force since the beginning of 2010. The CG Code for LCs outlines the governance, management and leadership fundamentals built on the 'comply-or-explain' approach intended for both listed companies on the Slovenian market and for other companies. Even though changes in the 2016 version are mostly editorial and nomotechnical, one must examine some important alterations. First, a new provision (Diversity Policy) provides improved diversity and gender balance within supervisory and management bodies. Second, the equal shareholders treatment is refined (Ljubljana Stock Exchange Inc. and Slovenian Directors' Association, 2016).

The Corporate Governance Code for Unlisted Companies (hereafter: CG Code for UCs) was adopted by the Chamber of Commerce and Industry of Slovenia, the Ministry of Economic Development and Technology, and the Slovenian Directors' Association in May 2016. The code can be applied to all companies with the exception of listed companies. The CG Code for UCs is a response to the requirements of Article 59 of the Companies Act (ZGD-1) for companies that are subject to audit procedures. According to Article 59, these companies need to include a corporate governance statement as a distinctive section of their firm's financial reports. Even though the CG Code for UCs is voluntary, a firm that is subject to audit needs to provide explanations in cases where any divergence from the code recommendations is observed. Compliance with both the Code for UCs and Code for LCs brings a more transparent and credible governance system, thereby boosting domestic and foreign investor confidence in the system as well as strengthening stakeholders' and staff confidence (Damijan and Damijan, 2019).

The Corporate Governance Code for State-Owned Enterprises (hereafter: CG Code for SOEs) – a successor of the Corporate Governance Code for Companies with Capital Assets of the State introduced in 2014 – was adopted by the SSH in March 2016 and was revised in 2017 and 2019 (Slovenian Sovereign Holding, 2016 and 2019). The CG Code for SOEs lays out the foundations for both SOEs and subsidiary companies in the group where the controlling company is state-owned. It characterizes government principles and supervision of SOEs in order to deliver a more transparent and credible corporate governance system within SOEs, thereby increasing the quality of corporate governance and improving performance. The revision in 2019 introduced new recommendations regarding the following: (1) diversity and succession policy; (2) the acceptance of an annual work plan; (3) external reporting quality; (4) amendments to the Code of Ethics and Corporate Integrity; and (5) some changes in the treatment of relationships between stakeholders and shareholders.

9.4 Regulation of State-Owned Enterprises

As presented in Section 9.1, Slovenia used to be an outlier in terms of the ownership structure among the EU new member states (EU-NMS). This was traditionally characterized by the lowest share of foreign-investment enterprises (FIEs) and by the largest share of SOEs. While in most EU-NMS the share of FIEs used to be between 40% and 80%, in Slovenia it was below 20%. Similarly, in other EU-NMS the share of SOEs in the business sector was far below 10% (except Poland), while in Slovenia it exceeded 35% in 1999. While the share of FIEs in Slovenia increased and the share of SOEs decreased between 1999 and 2007, the overall picture in 2007 was still preserved (OECD, 2011c).

Ever since the OECD's Review, the Slovenian state has made notable steps in order to enhance the quality of corporate governance of SOEs. In 2009, the government designed swiftly the Policy on Corporate Governance of State-Owned Enterprises. With that, the government committed to form an independent central ownership agency in order to harmonize government ownership's actions. The Law on the Corporate Governance of State Capital Investments – which stipulated the formation of the central ownership agency – took effect in April 2010. Furthermore, the policy also requested better-defined and more transparent relations between the government, KAD and SOD (Damijan and Damijan, 2019).

In 2010, the Slovenian government formed a central ownership agency called AUKN (State Assets Management Agency). Its paramount intention was to centrally manage capital assets owned by the state. However, the AUKN took part in multiple suspicious acts, such as forcing the management boards of selected SOEs to cooperate in recapitalization of certain banks owned by the state. Consequently, it was relinquished in late 2012. Its replacement was the Slovenian Sovereign Holding (SSH), which took the portfolio and part of SOD, but was also designated to the management of the portfolio of all other state funds. Therefore, the SSH is the main manager of state-owned assets.

In 2015, the State Assets Management Strategy (hereafter: Strategy) was adopted by the government. It was based on the OECD Guidelines on Corporate Governance of State-Owned Enterprises. According to this Strategy, SSH's portfolio is divided into 'strategic' investments with a required state majority (two-thirds of the portfolio), important investments with a required state holding of more than 25% (nearly a fifth of the portfolio) and portfolio investment that can be fully privatized (15% of the portfolio). However, as noted by the OECD (2017b), this classification is not explicitly linked to any economic, security or financial framework.

Another matter is whether and to what extent this Strategy has altered the prevailing past corporate governance practices in SOEs. According to the EBRD (2017), practices, pursued by the leading political coalitions, regarding the managing of both direct and indirect state holdings have not significantly improved over time. As a rule, after a change in political regime following parliamentary elections, the government still replaces the supervisory boards of the SSH followed by the appointment of a new board of SSH directors. Consequently, the SSH starts with a process of replacements of supervisory boards in companies in the SSH portfolio, leading to comprehensive changes in the management boards as well.

Due to the frequent changes in management and supervisory boards, and as appointed managers are selected exclusively according to the political constellation of the governing coalition, both the stability and quality of management within SOEs are constantly undermined. As a consequence, SOEs are found to be less productive than their private-sector counterparts (Domadenik, Prašnikar and Svejnar, 2016). An important recommendation by the OECD (2017b) was to strengthen SOEs' corporate governance by installing more professional supervisory boards of the SSH that could boost SOEs' performance.

9.5 Main Patterns of Ownership Change since 1990

9.5.1 The Data

This section is based on two datasets provided by the Agency of the Republic of Slovenia for Public Legal Records and Related Services (AJPES). We combine data on corporate annual reports (financial statements and balance sheets) with data from the Business Registry, which provides data on ownership structures of companies. The dataset consists of all firms registered in Slovenia.

According to the common methodology of this volume, the data is classified into several samples as follows:

(1) Sample 'Top 100 in T0'. This sample includes the top 100 non-financial firms (measured by total assets) in the initial period between 1994 and 1997. The earliest annual data available was taken.
(2) Sample 'Listed in T0'. This includes all listed non-financial firms in Slovenia in the initial period between 1994 and 1997. The earliest annual data available was taken.
(3) Sample 'Top 100 in T1'. This includes the top 100 non-financial firms (measured by total assets) in the final period between 2015 and 2018. The latest annual data available was taken.
(4) Sample 'Listed in T1'. This includes all listed non-financial companies in Slovenia in the final period between 2015 and 2018. The latest annual data available was taken.

9.5.2 Evolution of Ownership Structure

Using our unique datasets tracing ownership changes in Slovenia over the period from the mid-1990s to the late 2010s, we have documented a few key patterns of ownership transformation as outlined below.

9.5.2.1 Overall Changes

Major changes regarding the concentration of ownership are depicted in Table 9.1 and Figure 9.1. The median values of the cumulative share of the largest shareholders (i.e. those exceeding 10% each of outstanding shares in a company) indicate that there was a significant increase in ownership concentration in the largest Slovenian companies over the decades studied. The median total share of the largest shareholders in the 100 largest companies increased on average by forty percentage points (an increase from 56.5% to 94.8%). A similar increase in ownership concentration is recorded among the twenty largest firms. This indicates a significant ownership consolidation in the largest Slovenian firms since the start of privatization. The main reason for this is the acquisition of the largest firms by foreign strategic owners. For obvious reasons, in listed companies ownership concentration is significantly lower. It has not changed much over the past decades.

Table 9.1 *Changes in concentration of ownership in Slovenia by largest shareholders, mid-1990s to mid-2010s (%)*

| Initial period | Number of firms | All largest shareholders[a] | | | |
		Min.	Med.	Mean	Max.
Top 100[b]	100	12.7	56.5	58.0	100
Top 20[c]	20	12.7	69.0	63.0	100
Listed[d]	86	12.7	57.1	58.3	100
Final period	Number of firms	Min.	Med.	Mean	Max.
Top 100[b]	100	15.0	94.8	80.9	100
Top 20[c]	20	15.0	95.9	73.6	100
Listed[d]	12	15.0	61.5	67.1	68.7

Notes:
[a] The figure for the largest shareholders is defined as the total share of all shareholders having 10% or more of outstanding shares in a company.
[b] Top 100 are the largest 100 firms (both listed and unlisted) in Slovenia.
[c] Top 20 are the largest 20 firms (both listed and unlisted) in Slovenia.
[d] Listed are listed firms in Slovenia.
Source: AJPES (1995–2020); own calculations.

Figure 9.1 Change in median ownership share in Slovenian companies by largest shareholders, mid-1990s to mid-2010s (%).
Note: The figure for the largest shareholders is defined as the total share of all shareholders having 10% or more of outstanding shares in a company.
Source: AJPES (1995–2020); own calculations.

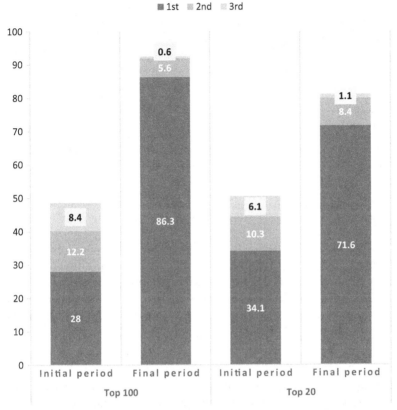

Figure 9.2 Change in composition of ownership shares among the three largest shareholders in Slovenian companies, mid-1990s to mid-2010s (%).
Note: Median values are used.
Source: AJPES (1995–2020); own calculations.

As shown in Figure 9.2, the ownership consolidation over the past decades happened mainly due to the strengthening of the share of the largest owner at the expense of all the other owners. Among the top 20 firms, in half of them the largest shareholder at least doubled its share (an increase in the median share from 34.1% to 71.6%). Among the top 100 firms, the largest shareholder increased its share even more – by at least threefold in half of the companies (i.e. an increase in median share from 28% to 86.3%).

However, one has to be aware that this finding is in large part driven by the change in the composition of companies in the top 20 and top

Table 9.2 *Changes in composition of companies in the top 20 and top 100 group in Slovenia between the mid-1990s and mid-2010s*

	Number of firms remaining in top group	Per cent (%)	Number of firms with same largest shareholder	Of which: state owned
Top 20[a]	16	80	10	9
Top 100[b]	52	52	23	15

Notes: Figure for largest shareholders is defined as the total share of all shareholders having 10% or more of outstanding shares in a company.
[a] Top 20 are the largest 20 firms (both listed and unlisted) in Slovenia.
[b] Top 100 are the largest 100 firms (both listed and unlisted) in Slovenia.
Source: AJPES (1995–2020); own calculations.

100 group in Slovenia between the mid-1990s and late 2010s. Table 9.2 shows that in the top 20 companies the composition remained quite stable with only 20% of companies dropping out of the group by the final period of our sample (the mid-2010s). Only 52% of companies that were in the top 100 companies in the initial period remained in this group until the final period of our sample. There are three main reasons for dropping out of the top rankings. The first reason is a merger with another company in the industry. In particular, the retail sector was subject to industry consolidation as there were fourteen retail companies in the top 100 that have been merged with another company – mainly to the retailer Mercator. There were also a number of mergers in the manufacturing sector, in particular in the food and beverages industry. Another reason is bankruptcy, in particular after the financial crisis starting in 2008, with eight construction companies and two retailers going bankrupt. The third reason is obviously a comparatively poor performance of the ex-top firms and a rise of better performing firms. This effect accounts for about 20% of the changes in composition of the samples of the largest firms.

Only half of the top 20 companies preserved their major shareholder until the late 2010s, while among the top 100 firms there are only twenty-three such cases (see Table 9.2). This indicates a vast ownership change among the Slovenian largest companies since the start of privatization.

Interestingly, state ownership has appeared as the most resilient factor for survival of companies in the sample and the most resilient type of ownership. Table 9.2 also reports that out of ten companies among the twenty largest companies that remained in the group and that persisted with the same initial largest shareholder until the late 2010s, nine are state-owned. In the group of the top 100 companies, there were fifteen such cases out of twenty-three companies that both survived in the sample and remained with their initial largest shareholder. State ownership is associated with industry sectors such as infrastructure (e.g. Port of Koper, the state highway company DARS) or utilities (e.g. energy production and distribution).

9.5.2.2 Changes by Type of Ownership

In addition to the rise of ownership concentration since the start of privatization, there was also a change in the type of owner. Figure 9.3 presents the percentage of firms with majority shareholders by ownership type in the top 100 firms in the mid-1990s and mid-2010s. Among the top 100 companies, one can observe three major patterns. First, the most notable trend is a decline of the share of state-owned companies (from 32% to 20%) and companies owned by financial institutions (from 16% to 4%). The government mostly pursued privatization in

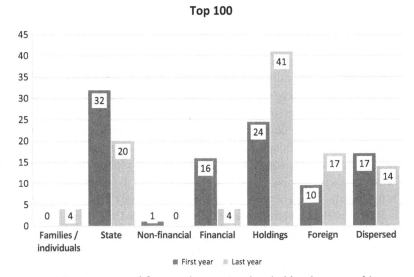

Figure 9.3 Percentage of firms with majority shareholders by ownership type in the top 100 Slovenian firms in the first and the last year of the sample.
Source: AJPES (1995–2020); own calculations.

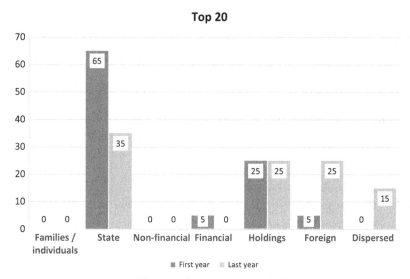

Figure 9.4 Percentage of firms with majority shareholders by ownership type in the top 20 Slovenian firms in the first and the last year of the sample (%).
Source: AJPES (1995–2020); own calculations.

the period 2004–2008 and also after resolving the banking sector crisis after 2013. Financial institutions sold most of their non-financial holdings right after the start of privatization in the mid-1990s. Government and financial institutions have mostly sold companies to either company management via their holding companies or to foreign investors.

Second, in this process, with a 41% stake (up from 24% in mid-1990s) holding companies became the most significant majority owner of the largest Slovenian firms. Those holding companies are mainly management companies formed and owned by a particular group of managers to acquire the majority share of the company they manage. Later on these holding companies are used as a vehicle to expand through acquisitions of other companies in the same or other industries.

Third, foreign investors increased their overall share from 10% to 17% of all top 100 companies (see Figure 9.3).

Figure 9.4 shows the percentage of firms with majority shareholders by ownership type in the top 20 firms in the mid-1990s and mid-2010s. Among the top 20 firms, privatization of state-owned companies was even more pronounced as the share of majority state-owned companies decreased from 65% to only 35%. For example, the government

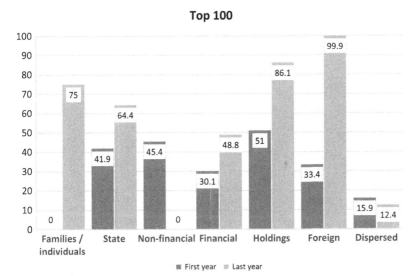

Figure 9.5 Ownership share of the largest shareholder by ownership categories in the top 100 Slovenian firms in the first and the last year of the sample (%). *Source:* AJPES (1995–2020); own calculations.

decreased its holdings in the pharmaceutical firms Lek and Krka and the biggest oil company Petrol. Major beneficiaries in this process were foreign investors, increasing their share to 25%, while for managers organized in holdings these companies were too large to be acquired. Dispersed ownership has also increased among the top 20 largest firms, which is due to IPOs of some companies, such as Telekom Slovenije.

Figure 9.5 presents the ownership share of the largest shareholder by ownership type in the top 100 firms in the mid-1990s and mid-2010s. Another trend clearly visible is the increase in ownership concentration within each ownership category among the top 100 companies. Most of the largest owners have strengthened their ownership share to more than 60%. Most concentrated ownership is in companies controlled by holding companies and foreign investors. This is due to the fact that holding companies are controlled by one owner (consisting of one or a group of managers), while in the case of foreign investors these are mainly strategic investors.

This trend is even more pronounced among the top 20 firms, where holding companies and foreign investors maximized their holdings to

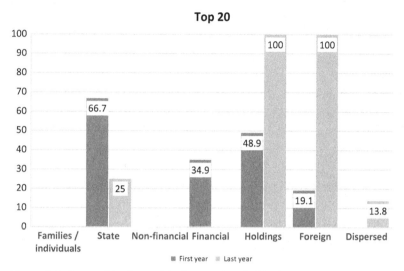

Figure 9.6 Ownership share of the largest shareholder by ownership categories in the top 20 Slovenian firms in the first and the last year of the sample (%).
Source: AJPES (1995–2020); own calculations.

100% (see Figure 9.6). The exception are the largest companies controlled by the state as the state decreased its holding to 25% on average.

Figure 9.7 presents the ownership share of the largest shareholder by ownership type in listed companies in the mid-1990s and mid-2010s. According to the data in the last year of the sample, financial companies were not involved in listed companies with ownership stakes bigger than 10%. They usually divested after the global financial crisis in the period 2009–2013. The importance of foreign companies declined because after a takeover they typically bought out all the remaining shares outstanding and delisted. On the other hand, companies controlled by holdings strengthened their positions. While the government decreased its holdings in some of the biggest companies, it still retained a minority controlling share (25%) or blocking share in some of the companies (such as Petrol and the pharmaceutical company Krka).

While this section has depicted major trends in ownership change since the early transition, a lot of action and battle for control is missing in this picture, partly due to the fact that we were analysing only the largest 100 firms and partly because the trend of privatization

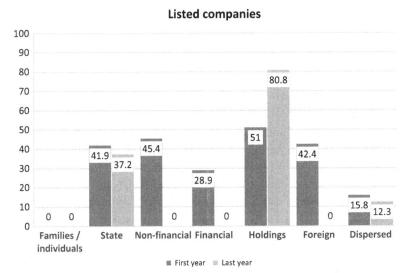

Figure 9.7 Ownership share of the largest shareholder by ownership categories in listed Slovenian companies in the first and the last year of the sample (%).
Source: AJPES (1995–2020); own calculations.

and the significant increase in foreign ownership do not reveal the underlying processes and why this happened. This is the story of the last section.

9.6 Political Economy of Corporate Governance and Ownership Changes in Slovenia

The previous section has demonstrated substantial changes of both the composition of the group of 100 largest companies in Slovenia and the ownership structure of the largest Slovenian companies since the start of privatization. Out of the top 100 companies in the initial group, only half of them (fifty-two) remained in the group in the final period, while only a quarter of them (twenty-three) remained with the initial major owner. Moreover, the most notable trend observed in the period since the start of privatization was a decline of the share of state-owned companies and companies owned by financial institutions, while major beneficiaries of this sell-off were holding companies and foreign investors.

A large part of these changes in the composition and of the turn-around in ownership structure of the top 100 Slovenian companies is associated with the pre-2008 boom and subsequent financial crisis. It was the financial crisis that led to the forced privatization of state-owned firms and the forced sell-off of overleveraged companies.

The global financial crisis hit the Slovenian economy hard. The downturn was dramatic: from 7% economic growth in 2007 to a 7.8% decline in 2009, from 22% public debt as a percentage of GDP in 2007 to 52% in 2012 and to 80% in 2014. In only a few years Slovenia made 'progress' from the best pupil in the class of EU new member states to a country on the verge of bankruptcy. At the same time, while the government was on the brink of asking the European Commission for financial assistance similar to that experienced by Greece, Cyprus, Spain and Portugal, overleveraged companies fell victim to the banks and those avoiding bankruptcy were subject to a massive sell-off. The financial crisis changed the landscape of the Slovenian corporate ownership structure to a similar extent as the transition from the semi-planned socialist system to the market economy.[1]

The most apparent reasons for the downturn, of course, were the financial extravagances and skyrocketing corporate debts in the run-up to the crisis. In the booming years between 2005 and 2008, stock values more than tripled and the construction sector doubled as a percentage of GDP. A number of irrational real estate projects and a number of corporate acquisitions and management buyouts, attempting to swelled stock prices, failed dismally. After the outbreak of the financial crisis, all the failed projects ended up in banks' troubled balance sheets with non-performing loans amounting to more than 20% of GDP at the end of November 2013.

The severity of the downturn was enhanced by the bad management of the crisis by the political class. A number of fatal policy mistakes were made, such as increases in wages in the public sector by 10% and the minimum wage by 25% at the onset of the crisis in 2009. As pensions and social transfers are indexed to wages, both of them also increased by the same percentage. As a consequence of these policy mistakes, public expenditure increased roughly by 10%, while crisis-ridden fiscal revenues decreased by the same percentage. The budget deficit surged to annual levels exceeding 6% of GDP and public debt as

---

[1] Damijan (2012) argues that a substantial part of the economic decline and corporate sell-off can be attributed to the legacy of the corporate governance system in Slovenia.

a percentage of GDP increased from 22% in 2007 to 80% of GDP in 2014. However, the worst policy mistake was not to engage in resolving the problem of the troubled banks, but waiting for almost five years, until the end of 2013 before rehabilitating them. While irrationality, greed and incompetence of the political class can well explain 'how' the crises unfolded, they fall short of understanding 'why' it happened on such a big scale and 'why' the political class was so reluctant to start resolving the problem.

As we explain subsequently, the fundamentals of the crisis-to-come were built into the system long ago. And there were the same systemic reasons that prevented the policymakers from acting accordingly when the crisis unfolded. A useful tool for thinking about what went so wrong in Slovenia is institutional analysis. It helps to understand the roots of the crisis by taking into account the set of politically induced economic and corporate governance rules that shaped the motives and behaviour of the two major groups of agents.

It is a common notion that under communism before 1990, the incentives to work and to conduct a business were distorted. The key condition for engaging in business activities was to be part of or at least being approved by the political elite. This system was not only less efficient in terms of economic development, it also created a lot of frustration for the majority of the less privileged, in particular for those not able to enter the elite. When the system collapsed in 1990, the incentives and rules were gradually changed. However, there were three crucial remnants of the old system that determined the economic evolution of the newly established democratic country.

First, despite the democratic changes, the old institutional system remained well preserved. Market regulation remained poor and market entrants or foreign companies found it hard to fight against the domestic firms run by insiders such as well-connected managers or by state-appointed managers. The judicial system remained extremely slow and inefficient in resolving the business disputes where domestic firms were involved. Many foreign companies or new entrants were scared off or driven out of the local market.

Second, the previous economic system was based on legally undefined corporate property, called 'social ownership'. In a process of privatization, this socially owned corporate property was not privatized but rather distributed. In this vein, the Act passed by parliament was not titled a privatization act, but rather the Act on

Ownership Transformation. This means that the firms could not be privatized to foreign bidders but were simply redistributed to domestic agents. The bulk of ownership was intended to be redistributed to employees, former employees and retired workers, but mostly to the acting managers, who had the right and access to bank loans to buy larger stakes in the companies (see the privatization formula discussed in Subsection 9.2.1). The remainder of the property value, 20% of each firm's shares, was simply transferred to two state-owned funds (KAD and SOD). Some of the firms, such as big banks and firms in the energy sector, were defined as being 'national strategic assets' and remained in state ownership. This was the way the old political elite could either transfer the ownership to their members (existing managers and their families) or keep it under state control. In 1995, when the first wave of privatization ended, about half of total company assets were still under state control, while a quarter of the assets were controlled by the managers via their holding companies.

Third, after the political upheaval of the 1990, groups of frustrated individuals from the previous system organized into political parties. A coalition of newly established political parties, called Demos, eventually won the first free elections and formed the first democratically elected government in 1990. However, the coalition lost power only two years later due to internal fighting and a lack of political skill. The old political elite, formed under the liberal democrat and social democrat parties, came back to power and stayed there for an additional twelve years. Its main focus was on protecting the economic interests of the elite centred around newly privatized or state-owned companies and to extract the rents from the companies controlled directly or indirectly by the state. The long-lasting frustrations among the members of the new political parties relegated from power, and most notably concentrated around Mr Janez Janša, were deepened further.

Though the system was in a sense rigid, it was a stable one. The symbiosis between the old political elite, the new capital owners' class and the managers in state-controlled firms managed to produce a high and stable economic growth with very little volatility, which was not typical of the other European transition countries. Slovenia was running ahead of other European transition countries mainly due to its political stability and the inherited solid export-based industrial structure.

Things changed dramatically in 2004 when Janez Janša, the symbolic figure of historical frustration, came to power. After taking power, the main goal of Mr Janša and a circle of cronies tied to his political party was primarily to make up for what they felt they had been historically deprived of. It appears that their goal was not to change the institutional system, neither to improve the incentives nor to lift regulations or privatize the companies to foreigners. Instead, they took on the Spanish colonization strategy as described by Daron Acemoglu and James A. Robinson in the introductory chapter to *Why Nations Fail* (2012). By winning power, they took control of the economy. This was made possible due to the existing ownership structure, with all large firms from retail to the finance and energy sectors being controlled by the governmentand the corporate governance system in place. Within one year, most of the large companies controlled by the state saw newly appointed supervisory boards and management boards. The positions were filled by individuals close to the coalition political parties, but mostly lacking the skills and experience in managing companies. The main focus was on extracting rents by using the established channels of selected suppliers now controlled by the circle of Janša's cronies.[2]

The strategy of the new government also involved taking control of national TV and radio broadcasting as well as the major newspapers. This period also saw many suspicious semi-privatizations and exchanges of stakes in companies. A prime example is the deal involving the biggest retailer Mercator. In a chain of deals, the government, using the stakes controlled by both state-owned funds KAD and SOD, engaged in 'swapping' the stakes in Mercator for the stakes in the two largest newspapers that were controlled by a brewery company. In this way, the government gained control over the two biggest newspapers and thus the main media in the country.

However, it appears that the main focus of the government was building a new capitalist elite by concentrating ownership by both the state and the circle of cronies close to Janez Janša. The period of global economic boom during 2004–2007 and Slovenia's entry into the EU made the strategy seem feasible. After joining the EU, the country risk premia for Slovenia declined to the level of its advanced neighbouring countries, Austria and Italy. Borrowing became extremely cheap. Firms

---

[2] Several managers belonging to the circle of the then prime minister Janez Janša who were appointed to the boards of the state-controlled companies during Janša's term in the government were later prosecuted on charges of misconduct.

started to invest in risky businesses. At the same time, managers – either politically sponsored or with the consent of the new government – started to take on loans for takeovers both within and across industries as well as for management buyouts. This was possible as the major banks were owned by the state and controlled by government-appointed managers and supervisory board members.

However, managers in companies with a state-controlled block share, perceived to be close to the old political elite, got nervous of being replaced or deprived. To secure their privileges they attempted a parallel process of privatization by buying out the state's shares at high market values. Interestingly, the government accepted this strategy and was willing to approve the privatizations of state-owned minority or controlling shares to the managers perceived close to the old political elite. Surprisingly, the acting government and some members of the old political elite were able to cooperate on single privatization cases. There were speculations in the media about possible corruption related to those privatization cases. Banks, most of them either majority state-owned or controlled by the state, assisted in supplying huge amounts of loans under extremely favourable conditions and by taking the over-valued acquired shares as collateral. During the 2004–2007 period, Slovenian banks took on EUR10 billion (30% of GDP) of short-term loans abroad and lent it to the risky investors at home. Roughly one-third of it was spent on acquisitions and management buyouts.

The strategy, however, did not work out as envisaged. When the crisis hit in the second half of 2008, the firms and their new owners were left with big short-term debt that they were unable to refinance, while banks were left with collateral consisting of shares worth only a fraction of their pre-crisis value. Moreover, the highly indebted firms were extremely vulnerable and unable to respond to the sudden dramatic decrease in aggregate demand. The economy collapsed in 2009 with GDP declining by 7.8%.

Due to the combination of inappropriate domestic economic policies and the prevailing austerity course imposed by the European Commission in 2010, the downturn of 2009 evolved into a full-blown financial crisis and protracted economic depression lasting until 2014. The Slovenian government only decided to bail out the banking sector in 2013. In the meantime, due to a depressed economy and public debt increasing to 70% of GDP by the end of 2013, Slovenia fell victim to the pressures of the international financial markets. The latter were also pricing the information of the unresolved banking sector into the lending rate to the Slovenian government. The pressure was mounting during 2013. At the same time, some EU governments unofficially made approval of the bail-out programme by the European Commission (EC) conditional upon the privatization of some state-owned companies. Hence, in the middle of 2013 the Slovenian government came up with a list of fifteen companies to be privatized. The list was approved by Parliament in June 2013.[3] Most of the companies on the list were subsequently privatized. In addition, back in 2013 the then government had committed to the EC to privatize all banks receiving state aid through the bank rehabilitation programme. The EC was very strict on this commitment, forcing the government to privatize all bailed-out banks. By early 2020, all bailed-out state-owned banks were privatized (NKBM, NLB, Abanka, Banka Celje).

Most large or medium-sized companies privatized to managers in the period 2005–2008 fell victim to the banks due to their excess leverage and those avoiding bankruptcy were subject to a massive sell-off. While some of the biggest insolvent companies – such as the retailers Mercator and Merkur, Brewery Laško, Cimos, Helios and the like – were sold individually by the consortiums of banks, the bulk of the insolvent companies were sold by the Bank Assets Management Company (BAMC), the Slovenian 'bad bank', which was established in 2012 and started operating in 2014. In the period 2014–2019, most of the companies in the BAMC portfolio were sold to foreign investors or holding companies that were able to acquire the troubled companies at very affordable prices.

Hence, the financial crisis after 2008 managed to change the landscape of the Slovenian corporate ownership structure. Paradoxically, three decades after the privatization was enacted, the financial crisis brought about an ownership structure similar to other European transition countries. In other words, the financial crisis did the job that the old political elite was trying to prevent when it legislated the 'ownership transformation' law.

---

[3] The list involved Adria Airways, Aero, Elan, Fotona, Helios, Aerodrom Ljubljana, Adria Airways Tehnika, NKBM, Telekom Slovenije, Cinkarna Celje, Gospodarsko razstavišče, Paloma, Terme Olimia Bazeni, Unior and Žito.

References

Abdelal, R. (2009). *Capital Rules: The Construction of Global Finance.* Cambridge, MA: Harvard University Press.

Abrardi, L. and L. Rondi (2020). Ownership and Performance in the Italian Stock Exchange: The Puzzle of Family Firms. *Journal of Industrial and Business Economics*, 47(4): 613–643.

Acemoglu, D. and J. A. Robinson (2012). *Why Nations Fail: The Origins of Power, Prosperity, and Poverty.* New York: Crown Publishers.

Agell, J., P. Englund and J. Södersten (1998). *Incentives and Redistribution in the Welfare State: The Swedish Tax Reform.* London: Macmillan.

Aggarwal, R., I. Erel, M. Ferreira and P. Matos (2011). Does Governance Travel Around the World? Evidence from Institutional Investors. *Journal of Financial Economics*, 100(1): 154–181.

Agnblad, J., E. Berglof, P. Hogfeldt and H. Svancar (2001). Ownership and Control in Sweden: Strong Owners, Weak Minorities, and Social Control, in F. Barca and M. Becht (eds.), *The Control of Corporate Europe.* Oxford: Oxford University Press, 228–258.

Aguilera, R. and G. Jackson (2010). Comparative and International Corporate Governance. *Academy of Management Annals*, 4(1): 485–556.

AJPES (1995–2020). Agency of the Republic of Slovenia for Public Legal Records and Related Services, Financial Data. Available at: www.ajpes.si/

Aminadav, G. and E. Papaioannou (2020). Corporate Control around the World. *Journal of Finance*, 75(3): 1191–1246.

Appel, I. R., T. A. Gormley and D. B. Keim (2016). Passive Investors, Not Passive Owners. *Journal of Financial Economics*, 121(1): 111–141.

Armour, J. and D. A. Skeel (2007). Who Writes the Rules for Hostile Takeovers, and Why: The Peculiar Divergence of US and UK Takeover Regulation. *Georgetown Law Journal*, 95: 1727–1794.

Baltrunaite, A., E. Brodi and S. Mocetti (2019). Assetti proprietari e di governance delle imprese italiane: Nuove evidenze e effetti sulla performance delle imprese. *Questioni di Economia e Finanza*, Occasional Paper no. 514, Banca d'Italia.

Bank, S. A. and B. R. Cheffins (2008). Tax and the Separation of Ownership and Control, in W. Schoen (ed.), *Tax and Corporate Governance*. Berlin, Heidelberg: Springer.

Barca, F. and M. Becht (2001). *The Control of Corporate Europe*. Oxford: Oxford University Press.

Barca, F., M. Bianchi, F. Brioschi et al. (1994). Assetti proprietari e mercato delle imprese. Vol. II: *Gruppo, proprietà e controllo nelle imprese italiane medio-grandi*. Bologna: Il Mulino.

Barko, T., M. Cremers and L. Renneboog (2017). Activism on Corporate Social Responsibility. European Corporate Governance Institute Working Paper.

Bates, S. (2010). How Polly Peck Went from Hero to Villain in the City. *The Guardian*, 26 August.

BBC (2012). Businessman Asil Nadir Stole Nearly £150m, Court Hears. Available at: www.bbc.com/news/uk-16686197

Bebchuk, L. A. and A. Hamdani (2009). The Elusive Quest for Global Governance Standards. *University of Pennsylvania Law Review*, 157 (5): 1263–1317.

Bebchuk, L. A. and S. Hirst (2019). Index Funds and the Future of Corporate Governance: Theory, Evidence, and Policy. National Bureau of Economic Research Working Paper.

Bebchuk, L. A. and M. J. Roe (1999). A Theory of Path Dependence in Corporate Ownership and Governance. *Stanford Law Review*, 52(1): 127–170.

Becht, M. and E. Boehmer (2001). Ownership and Voting Power in Germany, in F. Barca and M. Becht (eds.), *The Control of Corporate Europe*. Oxford: Oxford University Press.

Becht, M., J. Franks, J. Grant and H. F. Wagner (2017). Returns to Hedge Fund Activism: An International Study. *Review of Financial Studies*, 30(9): 2933–2971.

Berglöf, E. and A. Pajuste (2005). What Do Firms Disclose and Why? Enforcing Corporate Governance and Transparency in Central and Eastern Europe. *Oxford Review of Economic Policy*, 21(2): 178–197.

Bertrand, M. and A. Schoar (2006). The Role of Family in Family Firms. *Journal of Economic Perspectives*, 20: 73–96

Bessler, W., J. Beyenbach, M. S. Rapp and M. Vendrasco (2021). The Global Financial Crisis and Stock Market Migrations: An Analysis of Family and Non-family Firms in Germany. *International Review of Financial Analysis*, 74: 101692.

Bessler W. and T. Book (September 2021). Deutsche Börse Group, Strategien zur nachhaltigen Finanzierung der Zukunft Deutschlands.

Bessler, W., W. Drobetz and J. Holler (2015). The Returns to Hedge Fund Activism in Germany. *European Financial Management*, 21(1): 106–147.

Bessler, W. and M. Vendrasco (October 2019). Corporate Governance and the Relevance of Shares with Unequal Voting Rights in Europe, working paper.

Bezlov, T. and E. Tsenkov (2007). *Organized Crime in Bulgaria: Markets and Trends*. Sofia: Center for the Study of Democracy.

Bianchi, M. and M. Bianco (2006). Italian Corporate Governance in the Last 15 Years: From Pyramids to Coalitions? ECGI: Finance Working Paper No. 144/2006.

Bianchi, M., M. Bianco and L. Enriques (2001). Pyramidal Groups and the Separation Between Ownership and Control in Italy, in F. Barca and M. Becht (eds.), *The Control of Corporate Europe*. Oxford: Oxford University Press.

Bianchi M., M. Bianco, S. Giacomelli, A. Pacces and S. Trento (2005). *Proprietà e controllo delle imprese italiane*. Bologna: Il Mulino.

Birch, K. and V. Mykhnenko (2009). Varieties of Neoliberalism? Restructuring in Large Industrially Dependent Regions across Western and Eastern Europe. *Journal of Economic Geography*, 9(3): 355–380.

Bloom, N., P. Bunn, S. Chen et al. (2019). The Impact of Brexit on UK Firms. NBER Working Paper No. w26218. Available at: https://ssrn.com/abstract=3450244

Bogdanova, B. and I. Ivanov (2014). Adaptive and Relative Efficiency of Stock Markets from Southeastern Europe: A Wavelet Approach. *Applied Financial Economics*, 24(10): 705–722.

Bond, S. R., M. P. Devereux and A. Klemm (2007). The Effects of Dividend Taxes on Equity Prices: A Re-examination of the 1997 U.K. Tax Reform. IMF Working Paper. Available at: https://ssrn.com/abstract=1033204

Bowen, D. (1993). Rolling over the Past. *The Independent*, 21 November.

Boycko, M., A. Shleifer, R. W. Vishny, S. Fischer and J. D. Sachs (1993). Privatizing Russia. *Brookings Papers on Economic Activity*, 2: 139–192.

Branson, D. (2012). Global Convergence in Corporate Governance? What a Difference 10 Years Make, in T. Clarke and D. Branson (eds.), *The SAGE Handbook of Corporate Governance*. London and New Delhi: SAGE Publications Ltd.

Breinlich, H., E. Leromain, D. Novy and T. Sampson (2019). Voting with Their Money: Brexit and Outward Investment by UK Firms. CESifo Working Paper No. 7751. Available at: https://ssrn.com/abstract=3426939

BT Group (2002). Annual Report and Form 20-F 2002. Available at: www .btplc.com/report/pdf02/Annualreport/FullReport.pdf

Bundesministerium der Finanzen (2001, 2020). Beteiligungsbericht des Bundes (Federal Participation Report).

Bureau van Dijk (1999). Amadeus Database.

(2020). Orbis Database.

Cadbury Committee (1992). *The Financial Aspects of Corporate Governance.* London: The Committee on the Financial Aspects of Corporate Governance and Gee and Co. Ltd.

Calligaris, S., M. Del Gatto, F. Hassan, G. I. P. Ottaviano and F. Schivardi (2016). Italy's Productivity Conundrum. A Study on Resource Misallocation in Italy. *European Economy*: Discussion Papers 2015 –030 (DG ECFIN), European Commission.

Carlsson, R. H. (2007). Swedish Corporate Governance and Value Creation: Owners Still in the Driver's Seat. *Corporate Governance: An International Review*, 15(6): 1038–1055.

Carney, R. W. and T. B. Child (2013). Changes to the Ownership and Control of East Asian Corporations between 1996 and 2008: The Primacy of Politics. *Journal of Financial Economics*, 107: 494–513.

Carpenter, R. E. and L. Rondi (2000). Italian Corporate Governance, Investment and Finance. *Empirica*, 27: 365–388.

(2006). Going Public to Grow? Evidence from a Panel of Italian Firms. *Small Business Economics*, 27: 387–407.

Chandler A. D., Jr (1990). *Scale and Scope. The Dynamics of Industrial Capitalism.* Cambridge, MA; London, UK: The Belknap Press of Harvard University Press.

Cheffins, B. (2001). History and the Global Corporate Governance Revolution: The UK Perspective. *Business History*, 43(4): 87–118, DOI: 10.1080/ 713999243

Cheffins, B, (2018). The Rise and Fall of Berle-Means Corporation, University of Cambridge, Faculty of Law, Legal Studies Research Paper No. 50/ 2018.

Chhaochharia, V. and Y. Grindstein (2007). The Changing Structure of US Corporate Boards: 1997–2003. *Corporate Governance: An International Review*, 15: 1215–1223.

Consob (2018). Report on Corporate Governance of Italian Listed Companies. Available at: www.consob.it/web/consob-and-its-activities/ rcg2018

Coval, J. D. and T. J. Moskowitz (1999). Home Bias at Home: Local Equity Preference in Domestic Portfolios. *The Journal of Finance*, 54(6): 2045–2073.

Dahya, J., J. J. McConnell and N. G. Travlos (2002). The Cadbury Committee, Corporate Performance, and Top Management Turnover. *Journal of Finance*, 57: 461–483.

Damijan, J. P. (2012). Sloweniens Krise, ein Erbe unbewältigter Geschichte. Die Presse, 08.09.2012. Available at: www.diepresse.com/1288096/slo weniens-krise-ein-erbe-unbewaltigter-geschichte

Damijan, S. and J. P. Damijan (2019). Corporate Governance in Slovenia: Working at Last? *Corporate Governance and Organizational Behavior Review*, 3(2). Available at: http://doi.org/10.22495/cgobr_v3_i2_p4

Damijan, J. P., A. Gregorič and J. Prašnikar (2004). Ownership Concentration and Firm Performance in Slovenia. LICOS Discussion Paper No. 142. Available at: www.econstor.eu/bitstream/10419/74972/1/dp142.pdf

Davies, P. and K. J. Hopt (2013). Corporate Boards in Europe: Accountability and Convergence. *The American Journal of Comparative Law*, 61: 301–375.

Deakin, S., P. Sarkar and M. Siems (2018). Is There a Relationship Between Shareholder Protection and Stock Market Development? *Journal of Law, Finance, and Accounting*, 3(1): 115–146.

de la Cruz, A., A. Medina and Y. Tang (2019). Owners of the World's Listed Companies. OECD Capital Market Series, Paris.

Demirguc-Kunt, A. and R. Levine (eds.) (2001). *Financial Structure and Economic Growth. A Cross-Country Comparison of Banks, Markets, and Development*. Cambridge, MA: MIT Press.

Deutsche Bundesbank (2014). Monthly Report, September, 19–32.

Dimson, E., O. Karakaş and X. Li (2015). Active Ownership. *Review of Financial Studies*, 28(12): 3225–3268.

Dinc Serdar, I. and I. Erel (2013). Economic Nationalism in Mergers and Acquisitions. *The Journal of Finance*, 68(6): 2471–2514.

Djankov, S., R. La Porta, F. Lopez-de-Silanes and A. Shleifer (2008). The Law and Economics of Self-Dealing. *Journal of Financial Economics*, 88: 430–465.

Doidge, C., G. A. Karolyi and R. M. Stulz (2017), The U.S. Listing Gap. *Journal of Financial Economics*, 123(3): 464–487.

Domadenik, P., J. Prašnikar and J. Svejnar (2016). Political Connectedness, Corporate Governance, and Firm Performance. *Journal of Business Ethics*, 139: 411–428.

Duru, A., D. Wang and Y. Zhao (2013). Staggered Boards, Corporate Opacity and Firm Value. *Journal of Banking and Finance*, 37: 341–360.

EBRD (1995). *Annual Transition Report*. London: EBRD.

(2017). Corporate Governance in Transition Economies: Slovenia Country Report. Available at: www.ebrd.com/what-we-do/sectors/legal-reform/cor porate-governance/sector-assessment.html

Edmans, A, and C. G. Holderness (2017). Blockholders: A Survey of Theory and Evidence, in B. E. Hermalin and M. S. Weisbach (eds.), *The Handbook of the Economics of Corporate Governance*. Vol. I. North Holland: Elsevier, 541–636.

Enrique, L. (2006). EC Company Law Directives and Regulations: How Trivial Are They? *University of Pennsylvania, Journal of International Economic Law*, 27(1): 1–76.

Espenlaub, S., A. Khurshed and A. Mohamed (2012). IPO Survival in a Reputational Market. *Journal of Business Finance and Accounting*, 39: 427–463.

Estrin, S., J. Hanousek, E. Kocenda and J. Svejnar (2009). Effects of Privatization and Ownership in Transition Economies. *Journal of Economic Literature*, 47(3): 699–728.

European Commission (2016). European Economy Institutional Paper 031, July: State-Owned Enterprises in the EU. Luxembourg: Publications Office of the European Union.

Eurosif, European SRI Study (2018). Available at: www.eurosif.org/wp-content/uploads/2018/11/European-SRI-2018-Study.pdf

Faccio, M. and L. H. Lang, (2002). The Ultimate Ownership of Western European Corporations. *Journal of Financial Economics*, 65(3): 365–395.

Fahlenbrach, R. and C. Schmidt (2017). Do Exogenous Changes in Passive Institutional Ownership Affect Corporate Governance and Firm Value? *Journal of Financial Economics*, 124(2): 285–306.

Federal Statistical Office (2019). Unternehmensdemographie. Data as of 28 November. Available at: www.bfs.admin.ch/bfs/de/home/statisti ken/industrie-dienstleistungen/unternehmen-beschaeftigte/unternehmen sdemografie.html

Ferreira, M. (2018). Risk Seeker or Risk Averse? Cross-Country Differences in Risk Attitudes Towards Financial Investment, in A. Samson (ed.), *The Behavioral Economics Guide 2018*, 86–95. Available at: www .behavioraleconomics.com

Finaldi Russo, P., F. Parlapiano, D. Pianeselli and I. Supino (2020). Firms' Listings: What Is New? Italy versus the Main European Stock Exchanges. *Questioni di Economia e Finanza*, no. 555. Rome: Banca d'Italia.

Financial Times (1994). Ex-Communists Embrace a Half-Capitalist Bulgaria, 10 May.

Franks, J. and C. Mayer (2001). Ownership and Control of German Corporations. *Review of Financial Studies*, 14: 943–977.

(2017). Evolution of Ownership and Control Around the World: The Changing Face of Capitalism. European Corporate Governance Institute (ECGI): Finance Working Paper No. 503.

Franks, J., C. Mayer, P. Volpin and H. F. Wagner (2012). The Life Cycle of Family Ownership: International Evidence. *Review of Financial Studies*, 25(6): 1675–1712.

Franks, J., C. Mayer and H. F. Wagner (2015). The Survival of the Weakest: Flourishing Family Firms in Germany. *Journal of Applied Corporate Finance*, 27(4): 27–35.

FRC (2010). *The UK Stewardship Code*. London: The Financial Reporting Council.

Frydman, R. and A. Rapaczynski (1993). Insiders and the State: Overview of Responses to Agency Problems in East European Privatizations. *Economics of Transition*, 1(1): 39–53.

Fukuyama, F. (1989). The End of History? *The National Interest*, 16: 3–18.

Ganev, V. (2007) *Preying on State: The Transformation of Bulgaria after 1989*. Ithaca, NY: Cornell University Press.

Gelter, M. (2017). Comparative Corporate Governance: Old and New, in B. Choudhury and M. Petrin (eds.), *Understanding the Company: Corporate Governance and Theory*. Cambridge: Cambridge University Press, 37–59.

Gianfrate, G. and L. Zanetti (2007). Shareholders' Coalitions and Control Contestability: The Case of Italian Voting Trust Agreements. *Corporate Ownership & Control*, 4(4): 30–35.

Gilson, R. J. (2005). Controlling Shareholders and Corporate Governance: Complicating the Comparative Taxonomy. *Harvard Law Review*, V119(6): 1641–1679.

Gilson, R. J. and J. N. Gordon (2013). The Agency Costs of Agency Capitalism: Activist Investors and the Revaluation of Governance Rights. *Columbia Law Review*, 113(4): 863–927.

Glete, J. (1994). *Nätverk i näringslivet*. Stockholm: SNS Förlag.

Goergen, M. (2018). *Corporate Governance. A Global Perspective*. Andover: Cengage Learning, EMEA.

Goergen, Marc, M. C. Manjon and L. Renneboog (2008). Recent Developments in German Corporate Governance. *International Review of Law and Economics*, 28(3): 175–193.

Goergen, M. and L. Renneboog (2001). Strong Managers and Passive Institutional Investors in the UK, in M. Barca and M. Becht (eds.), *The Control of Corporate Europe*. Oxford: Oxford University Press, 258–284.

Gordon, J. N., 2003. An International Relations Perspective on the Convergence of Corporate Governance: German Shareholder Capitalism and the European Union, 1990–2000. Harvard Law School, The Center for Law, Economics, and Business, Discussion Paper No. 406.

(2018). Convergence and Persistence in Corporate Law and Governance, in J. N. Gordon and W.-G. Ringe (eds.), *The Oxford Handbook of Corporate Law and Governance*. Oxford: Oxford University Press, 28–55.

Gordon J. N. and W.-G. Ringe (eds.), (2018). *The Oxford Handbook of Corporate Law and Governance*. Oxford: Oxford University Press.

Gordon J. N. and M. J. Roe (eds.) (2004). *Convergence and Persistence in Corporate Governance*. Cambridge: Cambridge University Press.

Grossman, S. J. and O. D. Hart (1988). One Share-One Vote and the Market for Corporate Control. *Journal of Financial Economics*, 20: 175–202.

The Guardian (2020). Creeping NHS Privatization Is Hampering Our Covid-19 Response. 8 May. Available at: www.theguardian.com/soci ety/2020/may/08/creeping-privatisation-of-nhs-is-hampering-our-covid-19-response

Gugler, K. (2001). *Corporate Governance and Economic Performance*. Oxford: Oxford University Press.

Gugler, K., D. C. Mueller and E. Peev (2013) Determinants of Ultimate Control of Large Firms in Transition Countries: Empirical Evidence. *Journal of Institutional and Theoretical Economics*, 169(2): 275–303.

Gugler, K. and E. Peev (2010). Institutional Determinants of Investment-Cash Flow Sensitivities in Transition Economies. *Comparative Economic Studies*, 52: 62–81.

(2018). The Persistence of Profits in Banking: An International Comparison. *Applied Economics*, 50(55): 5996–6009.

Guiso, L., P. Sapienza and L. Zingales (2004). Does Local Financial Development Matter? *The Quarterly Journal of Economics*, 119(3): 929–969.

Hackethal, A., R. H. Schmidt and M. Tyrell (2005). Banks and German Corporate Governance: On the Way to a Capital Market-Based System? *Corporate Governance: An International Review*, 13(3): 397–407.

Hall, P. A. and D. Soskice (eds.) (2001). *Varieties of Capitalism. The Institutional Foundations of Comparative Advantage*. Oxford: Oxford University Press.

Hansmann, H. and R. Kraakman (2001). The End of History for Corporate Law. *The Georgetown Law Journal*, 89: 439.

Hellman, J. and M. Schankerman (2000). Intervention, Corruption and Capture: The Nexus Between Enterprises and the State. *Economics of Transition*, 8(3): 545–576.

Hellwig, M. (2000). Corporate Governance and the Financing of Investment for Structural Change, No. 00-32, Sonderforschungsbereich 504 Publications, University of Mannheim.

Helwege, J., C. Pirinsky and R. Stulz (2007). Why Do Firms Become Widely Held? An Analysis of the Dynamics of Corporate Ownership. *Journal of Finance*, 62: 995–1028.

Henrekson, M. and U. Jakobsson (2001). Where Schumpeter Was Nearly Right: the Swedish Model and Capitalism, Socialism and Democracy. *Journal of Evolutionary Economics*, 11(3): 331–358.

(2003). The Transformation of Ownership Policy and Structure in Sweden: Convergence towards the Anglo-Saxon Model? *New Political Economy*, 8(1):73–102.

(2005). The Swedish Model of Corporate Ownership and Control in Transition, in H. Huizinga and L. Jonung (eds.), *The Internationalization of Asset Ownership in Europe*. New York: Cambridge University Press, 207–246.

(2012). The Swedish Corporate Control Model: Convergence, Persistence or Decline? *Corporate Governance: An International Review*, 20(2): 212–227.

Henrekson, M., U. Jakobsson and M. Stenkula (2020). The Rise and Decline of Industrial Foundations as Controlling Owners of Swedish Listed Firms: The Role of Tax Incentives. *Scandinavian Economic History Review*, 68(2): 170–191.

Hogfeldt, P. (2005). The History and Politics of Corporate Ownership in Sweden, in R. K. Morck (ed.), *A History of Corporate Governance around the World: Family Business Groups to Professional Managers*. National Bureau of Economic Research Conference Report. Chicago and London: University of Chicago Press, 517–580.

Höpner, M. (2007). Corporate Governance Reform and the German Party Paradox. *Comparative Politics*, 39(4): 401–420.

Höpner, M. and L. Krempel (2004). The Politics of the German Company Network. *Competition and Change*, 8(4): 339–356.

Hopt K. J. (2015a). Corporate Governance in Europe. A Critical Review of the European Commission's Initiatives on Corporate Law and Corporate Governance, ECGI Law Working Paper No. 296/2015.

(2015b). Law and Corporate Governance: Germany within Europe. *Journal of Applied Corporate Finance*, 27(4): 8–15.

IHS Markit and DIRK (June 2021). Who Owns the German DAX? The Ownership Structure of the German DAX 30 in 2020: A Joint Study of IHS Markit and DIRK. Available at: https://cdn.ihsmarkit.com/www/pdf/ 0621/DAX-Study-2020—DIRK-Conference-June-2021_IHS-Markit.pdf

The Independent (2004). Lord Hanson: Archetype of the Thatcherite Tycoon. 3 November. Available at: www.independent.co.uk/news/obituaries/lord-hanson-531819.html

Investment & Pensions Europe (2019). Top 400 Asset Managers 2019. Available at: www.ipe.com/top-400-asset-managers-aum-grows-1-amid-market-volatility/10031518.article

Investors AB (1999) Annual Report.

Ipreo und DIRK (2015). Investoren der Deutschland AG 2.0 Die Aktionärsstruktur des deutschen Leitindex DAX, June.

Ivanova, M. R. (2017). Institutional Investors as Stewards of the Corporation: Exploring the Challenges to the Monitoring Hypothesis. *Business Ethics: A European Review*, 26: 175–188.

Jirjahn, U. (2011). Ökonomische Wirkungen der Mitbestimmung in Deutschland: Ein Update. *Schmollers Jahrbuch*, 131: 3–57.

Kandel, E., K. Kosenko, R. Morck and Y. Yafeh (2019). The Great Pyramids of America: A Revised History of U.S. Business Groups, Corporate Ownership, and Regulation, 1926–1950. *Strategic Management Journal*, 40(5): 781–808.

Koford, K. (2000). Citizen Restraints on 'Leviathan' Government: Transition Politics in Bulgaria. *European Journal of Political Economy*, 16: 307–338.

Kraakman, R., J. Armour, P. Davies et al. (2017). *The Anatomy of Corporate Law: A Comparative and Functional Approach*. Oxford: Oxford University Press.

La Porta, R., F. Lopez-de-Silanes and A. Shleifer (1999). Corporate Ownership Around the World. *The Journal of Finance*, 54(2): 471–517.

La Porta, R., F. Lopez-de-Silanes, A. Shleifer and R. Vishny (1997). Legal Determinants of External Finance. *Journal of Finance*, 52: 1131–1150. (1998). Law and Finance. *Journal of Political Economy*, 106: 1113–1155.

Liu, C., A. Low, R. W. Masulis and L. Zhang (2020). Monitoring the Monitor: Distracted Institutional Investors and Board Governance. *The Review of Financial Studies*, 33(10): 4489–4531.

Ljubljana Stock Exchange Inc. and Slovenian Directors' Association (2016). *Slovenian Corporate Governance Code for Listed Companies*. Available at: www.zdruzenje-ns.si/english/cg-resources/corporate-governance/

Lloyd-Jones, R. and M. J. Lewis (1994). Personal Capitalism and British Industrial Decline: The Personally Managed Firm and Business Strategy in Sheffield, 1880–1920. *Business History Review*, 68(3): 364–411.

Loderer, C. and U. Waelchli (2010). Protecting Minority Shareholders: Listed Versus Unlisted Firms. *Financial Management*, 39(1): 33–57.

Loughran, T. and J. R. Ritter (1995). The New Issues Puzzle. *The Journal of Finance*, 50(1): 23–51.

Mahoney, P. G. (2001). The Common Law and Economic Growth: Hayek Might Be Right. *Journal of Legal Studies*, 30(2): 503–525.

Mayer, C. (2018). *Prosperity: Better Business Makes the Greater Good*. Oxford: Oxford University Press.

Mayson, S., D. French and C. Ryan (1996). *Mayson, French & Ryan on Company Law*, 13th ed. London: Blackstone Press Limited.

McCahery, J. A., Z. Sautner and L. T. Starks (2016). Behind the Scenes: The Corporate Governance Preferences of Institutional Investors. *Journal of Finance*, 71(6): 2905–2932.

McKinnon, R. (1991). *The Order of Economic Liberalisation: Financial Control in the Transition to a Market Economy*. London: The Johns Hopkins University Press.

Mediobanca (1990 and 2018). Le principali società italiane. Milan: Ufficio Studi. Available at: www.mbres.it

Megginson, W. and J. Netter (2001). From State to Market: A Survey of Empirical Studies on Privatization. *Journal of Economic Literature*, 39 (2): 321–389.

Meyer, R. E. and M. A. Höllerer (2010). Meaning Structures in a Contested Issue Field: A Topographic Map of Shareholder Value in Austria. *Academy of Management Journal*, 53(6): 1241–1262.

Miller, J. B. and S. Petranov (2000). The First Wave of Mass Privatization in Bulgaria and Its Immediate Aftermath. *Economics of Transition*, 8(1): 225–250.

Miller, T., A. B. Kim and J. M. Roberts (2021). *Index of Economic Freedom*. Washington, DC: The Heritage Foundation. Available at: www.heritage .org/index/pdf/2021/book/index_2021.pdf

Mira, S., M. Goergen and N. O'Sullivan (2019). The Market for Non-executives: Takeover Performance and the Subsequent Holding of Directorships. *British Journal of Management*, 30: 415–436.

Morck, R., D. Stangeland and B. Yeung (2000). Inherited Wealth, Corporate Control, and Economic Growth: The Canadian Disease? in R. Morck (ed.), *Concentrated Corporate Ownership*. Chicago and London: The University of Chicago Press, 319–372.

Morck, R., D. Wolfenzon and B. Yeung (2005). Corporate Governance, Economic Entrenchment, and Growth. *Journal of Economic Literature*, 43(3): 655–720.

Mrak, M., M. Rojec and C. Silva-Jáuregui (2004). *Slovenia: From Yugoslavia to the European Union*. Washington, DC: The World Bank.

Mueller, D. C. (1983). *The Political Economy of Growth*. New Haven, CT: Yale University Press.

(2003). *Public Choice*. Cambridge: Cambridge University Press.

Mueller, D. C., H. Dietl and E. Peev (2003). Ownership, Control and Performance in Large Bulgarian Firms. *Journal of Institutional Innovation, Development and Transition*, 7: 71–88.

Mueller, D. C. and E. Peev (2007). Corporate Governance and Investment in Central and Eastern Europe. *Journal of Comparative Economics*, 35: 414–437.

Mukwiri, J. (2020). The End of History for the Board Neutrality Rule in the EU. *European Business Organization Law Review*, 21(2): 253–277.

Nachemson-Ekwall, S. (2017). Swedish Institutional Investors as Large Stake Owners: Enhancing Sustainable Stakeholder Capitalism, in M. Kallifatides and L. Lerpold (eds.), *Sustainable Development and Business*. Stockholm: SSE Institute for Research (SIR), 255–276.

Nedelchev, M. (2017). Overview of Corporate Governance in Bulgaria. *Entrepreneurship*, 5(2): 70–76.

Nenova, T. (2003). The Value of Corporate Voting Rights and Control: A Cross-Country Analysis. *Journal of Financial Economics*, 68(3): 325–351.

North, D. C. (1990). *Institutions, Institutional Change and Economic Performance*. Cambridge: Cambridge University Press.

OECD (1997). *OECD Economic Surveys: Bulgaria 1997*. Paris: OECD Publishing.

(2011a). *Board Practices: Incentives and Governing Risks, Corporate Governance*. OECD Publishing. Available at: http://dx.doi.org/10.1787/9789264113534-en

(2011b). *Corporate Governance in Slovenia 2011*. Paris: OECD Publishing.

(2011c). *OECD Economic Surveys: Slovenia 2011*. Paris: OECD Publishing.

(2017a). *Economic Surveys: Austria*. Paris: OECD Publishing.

(2017b). *OECD Economic Surveys: Slovenia 2017*. Paris: OECD Publishing.

(2019). *OECD Review of Corporate Governance of State-Owned Enterprises: Bulgaria*. Available at: www.oecd.org/corporate/ca/Corporate-Governance-of-SOEs-in-Bulgaria.pdf

Office for National Statistics (2018). Ownership of UK Quoted Shares: 2018. Available at: www.ons.gov.uk/economy/investmentspensionsand trusts/bulletins/ownershipofukquotedshares/2018

Olson, M.(1982). *The Rise and Decline of Nations*. New Haven, CT and London: Yale University Press.

Olson, M. (1993). Dictatorship, Democracy, and Development. *American Political Science Review*, 87(3): 567–576.

(2000). *Power and Prosperity. Outgrowing Communist and Capitalist Dictatorships.* New York: Basic Books.

ONS (2020). *Ownership of UK Quoted Shares: 2018.* London: Office for National Statistics. Available at: www.ons.gov.uk/economy/investment spensionsandtrusts/bulletins/ownershipofukquotedshares/2018

Pacces, A. M. (2007). *Featuring Control Power: Corporate Law and Economics Revisited.* Rotterdam: Rotterdam Institute of Law and Economics, Erasmus University.

Pargendler, M. (2019). The Grip of Nationalism on Corporate Law. European Corporate Governance Institute (ECGI): Law Working Paper No. 437/2019.

PECA (2021a). Privatizirani aktivi kym 580 mln.lv. Available at: www.appk .government.bg/upload/92/aktivi580_BG_2019.pdf

(2021b). Prihodi ot privatizacia. Available at: www.appk.government.bg/ upload/95/Prix.1993-2019+.pdf

(2021c). Annual Report. Available at: www.appk.government.bg/bg/69

Peev, E. (1995). Separation of Ownership and Control in South-Eastern Europe: The Case of Bulgaria. *Europe-Asia Studies*, 47(5): 859–875.

(1999). *Separation of Ownership from Control in Southeast Europe: A Comparison of Bulgaria, Romania and Albania 1990–96.* Sofia: Kota.

(2002). Ownership and Control Structures in Transition to 'Crony' Capitalism: The Case of Bulgaria. *Eastern European Economics*, 40(5): 73–91.

(2003). Corruption in Transition: Firms' Political Strategies and Corporate Governance in Bulgaria, in Center for the Study of Democracy (ed.), *Corruption and Anticorruption.* Sofia: Center for the Study of Democracy, 138–148.

(2015). Institutions, Economic Liberalization and Firm Growth: Evidence from European Transition Economies. *European Journal of Law and Economics*, 40(1): 149–174.

Peev, E. and D. Mueller (August 2012). Democracy, Economic Freedom and Growth in Transition Economies. *Kyklos*, 65(3): 371–407.

Peev, E. and T. Yalamov (2020). New Evidence on the Ultimate Ownership of Large Firms: A Comparative Analysis of Eastern and Western Europe. Working paper.

Peev, E. and B. Yurtoglu (2008). Corporate Financing in the New Member States: Firm-Level Evidence for Convergence and Divergence Trends. *European Business Organization Law Review*, 9(3): 337–383.

Piore, M. and C. Sabel (1984). *The Second Industrial Divide.* New York: Basic Books.

Prašnikar, J. and A. Gregorič (2002). The Influence of Workers' Participation on the Power of Management in Transitional Countries: The Case of Slovenia. *Annals of Public and Cooperative Economies*, 73(2): 269–297. Available at: https://doi.org/10.1111/1467-8292.00194

Prohaski, G. (1998). *A Review of Bulgarian Privatization*, 23–24 November. Paris: OECD.

Puca, M. and M. Vatiero (2017). Ownership and Innovation: Evidence from Switzerland. Working paper. Available at: https://ssrn.com/abstract=2739880 or http://dx.doi.org/10.2139/ssrn.2739880

Putnam, R. (1993). *Making Democracy Work: Civic Traditions in Modern Italy*. Princeton: Princeton University Press.

Rajan, R. G. and L. Zingales (2003). The Great Reversals: The Politics of Financial Development in the Twentieth Century. *Journal of Financial Economics*, 69: 5–50.

Rapp, M.-S. and C. Strenger (2015). Corporate Governance in Germany: Recent Developments and Challenges. *Journal of Applied Corporate Finance*, 27(4): 16–34.

Ringe, G. (2015). Changing Law and Ownership Patterns in Germany: Corporate Governance and the Erosion of Deutschland AG. *The American Journal of Comparative Law*, 63: 493–538.

Rodrik, D. (2006). Goodbye Washington Consensus, Hello Washington Confusion? A Review of the World Bank's Economic Growth in the 1990s: Learning from a Decade of Reform. *Journal of Economic Literature*, XLIV: 973–987.

Roe, M. J. (1991). A Political Theory of American Corporate Finance. *Columbia Law Review*, 91: 10, 11.

(1994). *Strong Managers, Weak Owners: The Political Roots of American Corporate Finance*. Princeton: Princeton University Press.

(2000). Political Preconditions to Separating Ownership from Corporate Control. *Stanford Law Review*, 53: 539–606.

(2003). *Political Determinants of Corporate Governance: Political Context, Corporate Impact*. Oxford and New York: Oxford University Press.

(2006). Legal Origins, Politics, and Modern Stock Markets. *Harvard Law Review*, 120: 460–527.

Roe, M. J. and T. G. Coan (2017). Financial Markets and the Political Center of Gravity. *Journal of Law, Finance, and Accounting*, 2(1): 125–171.

Royal Bank of Scotland (2019). The Royal Bank of Scotland Group plc Annual Report and Accounts 2019. Available at: www.investors.rbs.com/~/media/Files/R/RBS-IR-V2/results-center/14feb2020/rbs-plc-annual-report.pdf

Rydqvist, K., J. Spizman and I. Strebulaev (2014). Government Policy and Ownership of Equity Securities. *Journal of Financial Economics*, 111: 70–85.

Schmidt, C. and R. Fahlenbrach (2017). Do Exogenous Changes in Passive Institutional Ownership Affect Corporate Governance and Firm Value? *Journal of Financial Economics*, 124(2): 285–306.

Schneider, R., A. Wagner and C. W. Bernasconi (2016). Der Verwaltungsrat zwischen Regulierung und Marktdisziplin. *Expert Focus*, 9: 670–676.

Schönfelder, B. (2020). *Ein Luhmann-Leitfaden für Ökonomen*. Berlin: Berliner Wissenschafts-Verlag.

Schumpeter, J. (1942). *Capitalism, Socialism and Democracy*. This edition 2003. London and New York: Routledge.

Shleifer, A. (1994). Establishing Property Rights. Proceedings of the Annual Conference on Development Economics. World Bank.

Siems, M. (ed.) (2016). *CBR Extended Shareholder Protection Index*. Cambridge: Centre for Business Research, University of Cambridge. Available at: www.repository.cam.ac.uk/bitstream/handle/1810/256566/ cbr-spi-30-countries-codebook-and-methodology.pdf?sequence=9&isAll owed=y

Simoneti, M., J. P. Damijan, B. Majcen and M. Rojec (2005). Case-by-Case versus Mass Privatization in Transition Economies: Owner and Seller Effects on Performance of Firms in Slovenia. *World Development*, 33 (10): 1603–1625.

Slovenian Sovereign Holding (2016). *Corporate Governance Code for State-Owned Enterprises*. Available at: www.zdruzenje-ns.si/english/cg-resources/corporate-governance/

  (2019). *Corporate Governance Code for State-Owned Enterprises*. Available at: www.sdh.si/en-gb/news/1782/slovenian-sovereign-holding-revises-corporate-governance-code-for-soes-and-introduces-several-new-cases-of-good-practice

Stiefel, D. (2000). Fifty Years of State-Owned Industry in Austria, in P. Toninelli (ed.), *The Rise and Fall of State-Owned Enterprise in the Western World (Comparative Perspectives in Business History)*. Cambridge: Cambridge University Press, 237–252.

Stiftung Familienunternehmen (2009). *Borsennotierte Familienunternehmen in Deutschland*. Munich: Center for Entrepreneurial and Financial Studies (CEFS) of the Technical University of Munich (TUM).

  (2019). *Borsennotierte Familienunternehmen in Deutschland: Bedeutung, Merkmale, Performance*. Munich: Center for Entrepreneurial and Financial Studies (CEFS) of the Technical University of Munich (TUM).

Svensson, T. (2002). Globalisation, Marketisation and Power: The Swedish Case of Institutional Change. *Scandinavian Political Studies*, 25(3): 197–229.

SWIPRA Surveys (2013–2019). Corporate Governance Developments in Switzerland. Available at: www.swipra.ch/

Thomson, S. (2006). The Hidden Meaning of the Codes: Corporate Governance and Investor Rent Seeking. *European Business Organization Law Review*, 7(4): 845–861.

Tielmann A. and D. Schiereck (2017). Arising Borders and the Value of Logistic Companies: Evidence from the Brexit Referendum in Great Britain. *Finance Research Letters*, 20: 22–28.

Trapp, R. (1997). Budget '97: Pension Funds in Uproar Over Abolition of Tax Credit. *The Independent*, 3 July.

Traù F. (ed.) (1999). *La 'questione dimensionale' nell'industria italiana*. Bologna: Il Mulino.

Trend. (n.d.) Available at: www.trend.at/

Trif, D. (2020). German Corporate Governance Standards Overhauled. *Sustainalytics*, 16 March.

Vatiero, M. (2017). Learning from the Swiss Corporate Governance Exception. *Kyklos*, 70(2): 330–343.

Vitols, S. (2001). Varieties of Corporate Governance: Comparing Germany and the UK, in P. Hall and D. Soskice (eds.), *Varieties of Capitalism: The Institutional Foundations of Comparative Advantage*. Oxford: Oxford University Press, 337–360.

Voszka, E. (1992). Spontaneous Privatization in Hungary, in J. Earle, R. Frydman and A. Rapaczynski (eds.), *Privatisation in the Transition to a Market Economy: Studies of Preconditions and Policies in Eastern Europe*. London: Pinter Publishers and New York: St Martin's Press, 89–107.

Wagner, A. F. and C. Wenk (2022). Say-on-Pay and Shareholder Value: The Tension between Agency and Hold-up. European Corporate Governance Institute (ECGI): Finance Working Paper No. 500/2017. Available at: https://ssrn.com/abstract=1793089

Warburton, J. A. (2012). Competition in Financial Services: Evidence from British Mutual Funds. *Journal of Empirical Legal Studies*, 9: 827–858.

Weber, A. (2009). An Empirical Analysis of the 2000 Corporate Tax Reform in Germany: Effects on Ownership and Control in Listed Companies. *International Review of Law and Economics*, 29: 57–66.

Wiberg D. (2008). Institutional Ownership: The Anonymous Capital. Corporate Governance and Investment Performance, Jonkoping International Business School, Jonkoping University.

Williams, A. (2020). Why a Sensible Deadline for US–UK Trade Talks Is Next April. *Financial Times*, 13 May. Available at: www.ft.com/con tent/81f43006-3c1e-4147-a1bf-affd33ccd0e4

Williamson, J. (1993). Democracy and the 'Washington Consensus'. *World Development*, 21(8): 1329–1336.

World Bank (2021), Foreign Direct Investment, Net Inflows, BoP Current USD. Available at: https://data.worldbank.org/indicator/BX.KLT.DINV .CD.WD?locations=BG

Yalamov, T. and B. Belev (2002). Corporate Governance: An Antidote to Corruption. Examples/Lessons Learned in Bulgaria and Transition Countries, in A. Shkolnikov (ed.), *Corporate Governance: An Antidote to Corruption*. Washington, DC: CIPE, 33–36.

Zattoni, A. and A. Minichilli, (2009), The Diffusion of Equity Incentive Plans in Italian Listed Companies: What Is the Trigger? *Corporate Governance: An International Review*, 17: 224–237.

Zehnder Egon (2018). Global Board Diversity Tracker. Available at: www .egonzehnder.com/global-board-diversity-tracker/

Zingales, L. (1994). The Value of the Voting Right: A Study of the Milan Stock Exchange Experience. *Review of Financial Studies*, 7(1): 125–148.

Index

Abanka, 263
Accounting Control Act (Austria), 58
Acemoglu Daron and James Robinson, 261
acquis communautaire, 234
active share ownership, 147
agency capitalism, 6
AJPES, 16, 248
Aktiengesellschaft (AG), Austria, 56
Alternative Investment Market (AIM), 48
Anglo-American model, 13, 56, 76, 93, 96, 99–100, 104, 170. *See also* Anglo-Saxon model
Anglo-Saxon model, 6, 8–10, 24, 100, 138, 151, 168
Annual Accounts Act (Sweden), 157
Anti-Money Laundering Measures Act (Bulgaria), 234
anti-self-dealing index, 214
APIS, 16, 217
asset managers, 125, 137–138, 141, 197
asset owners, 125
assets under management, 138
Auditing Act (Slovenia), 243
AUKN (State Assets Management Agency) (Slovenia), 242, 247
Austria, 2, 19, 24–25, 27, 55–83, 102, 261
Austrian Commercial Register (*Firmenbuch*), 58
Austrian Financial Market Authority, 58
Austrian Ministry of Finance, 61

Banca Commerciale, 183
Banca Commerciale Italiana, 179
Banco di Roma, 179

Bank Assets Management Company (BAMC), 239, 263
Bank of Italy, 16, 176, 182
Bank of Slovenia, 243
Banka Celje, 263
bank-based financial system. *See also* insider system
Banking Act (Slovenia), 243
banks, 2, 19–20, 24, 36, 50, 70, 72, 84, 93, 96–97, 103–104, 122, 162, 176, 180, 197, 259–260, 262–263
Barca, Fabrizio and Marco Becht, 1
Bebchuk, Lucian and Mark J. Roe, 2, 11
Beneficial Owners Register Act (Austria), 60
Benetton family, 184
Bennet, Carl, 167
Berle–Means corporation, 3, 6
BGBX40, 229
BGTR30, 229
Big 3, 138
BlackRock, 138
board of directors, 35, 38, 111–112, 114–115, 138, 141, 146, 170, 178, 181, 203, 215, 236, 241, 248
Brexit, 51
British disease, 12, 14
Bulbank, 213
Bulgaria, 2, 24, 26–27, 209–236
Bulgarian Post Bank, 213
Bulgarian Stock Exchange, 215–216, 226
Bureau van Dijk, 16, 40, 217

Canada, 11–12
Canadian disease, 11
capital control, 10, 26, 170
CEO, 156, 170, 181
CEO duality, 35

Chamber of Commerce and Industry of
    Slovenia, 246
Chandler, Alfred D., 14, 104
Cheffins, Brian, 1, 6, 75
China, 14
closed-end investment funds, 25,
    151–152, 162
co-determination, 27, 86, 99
Co-Determination Act (Germany), 87
Cohen committee, 38
collapse of communism, 99
Commercial Code (Austria), 58
Commercial Code (Germany), 87
Commercial Law (Bulgaria), 215–216
Commercial Register (Bulgaria), 16,
    217
Companies Act (Slovenia), 243
Companies Act (Sweden), 155–156
Companies Act (UK), 33, 38
Companies Act (ZGD-1) (Slovenia),
    245–246
Companies House, 16, 41
compensation, 115, 181
complementary institutions, 11, 19, 25,
    27, 56, 77, 79, 83
concentration of ownership, 6, 13,
    20–22, 24, 41, 43, 55, 64–65, 68,
    82, 84, 90, 93, 97, 104–105, 108,
    116, 128, 132–133, 138, 156, 158,
    163, 177, 186–189, 204, 218, 222,
    224, 230, 239, 249, 255
Conflict of Interest Prevention and
    Ascertainment Act (Bulgaria), 234
Consob (The National Commission for
    Companies and the Stock
    Exchange) (Italy), 16, 176, 179,
    182, 189, 193, 197, 204
Consolidated Finance Act (*Testo Unico
    della Finanza* – TUF) (Italy), 180
Consolidated Law on Savings
    Protection (Italy), 196
control, 6, 77, 162, 192–193, 212
    clash for control, 240
    concentration of corporate control, 6,
        152, 170
    contestability, 5
    control-enhancing mechanisms, 197
    distribution of corporate control, 12
    insider control, 14
    interest group control, 220

majority control, 55, 65, 93, 96, 159
managerial control, 170
private benefits of control, 98, 235
relative control, 97
in state-owned companies with
    100% state participation, 220
supermajority control, 82
ultimate control, 72, 75
convergence, 2, 5, 9, 19, 21, 23, 27, 29,
    56, 83, 99, 104, 143, 166,
    169–170
coordinated market economy, 20, 25,
    80–81, 99, 104
Corporate Commercial Bank, 226
Corporate Governance and
    Transparency Act (Germany), 103
corporate governance code
    Austrian Corporate Governance
        Code, 58
    Bulgarian National Corporate
        Governance Code, 214, 217, 234
    Cadbury Report, 34, 36
    Combined Code (UK), 36
    Corporate Governance Code (Italy),
        177, 181, 196, 198, 203
    Corporate Governance Code for
        Listed Companies (Slovenia),
        244–245
    Corporate Governance Code for
        State-Owned Enterprises
        (Slovenia), 244
    Corporate Governance Code for
        Unlisted Companies (Slovenia),
        244
    German Corporate Governance Code
        (Kodex), 87
    Greenbury Report, 36
    Higgs Report, 35
    Myners Report, 36
    Swedish Corporate Governance
        Code, 155–157
    Swiss Code of Best Practice for
        Corporate Governance,
        115
Corporate Governance Directive (DCG)
    (Switzerland), 115
corporate insiders, 2–3, 10–13, 20–21,
    24–25, 84, 101, 105–106, 145,
    167, 169, 171, 222, 231, 233
Corporate Law (Italy), 177

corporate scandals, 6, 27, 34–35, 100, 181
corporate social responsibility, 144
corporatization, 232
Council for Swedish Financial Reporting Supervision, 156
creative destruction, 228
Credito Italiano, 179
Croatia, 79
cross-shareholding, 12, 146, 179, 204
Cyprus, 79, 258
Czech Republic, 231

DAX-30 companies, 84–85, 96, 104
Decree No. 56 on Business Activity (Bulgaria), 232
delisting, 199, 226, 236, 256
Deutsche Bank, 104
Deutsche Börse AG, 86
Deutschland AG, 1, 20, 84–85
dichotomous structure, 25
diffused ownership, 10, 100, 170. *See also* dispersed ownership
Directive on Financial Reporting (Switzerland), 114
Directive on Information Relating to Corporate Governance (Switzerland), 114
Directive on Regular Disclosure Obligations (DRDO) (Switzerland), 114
dispersed ownership, 20, 22, 26, 68, 96, 98, 100–101, 122, 151, 166, 222, 224
Dodd–Frank Act, 38

EBRD, 238, 244
EC, *See* European Commission
eclectic theory of corporate ownership, 28
economic entrenchment, 7, 12, 101, 117, 169, 228
economic nationalism, 5, 79, 231
Economiesuisse, 115
EEA, 157
Employee Retirement Income Security Act (ERISA) (UK), 36
English disease, 12
entrepreneurial company (Germany), 86

entrepreneurs, 21, 171
ESG (Environmental, Social and Governance), 144–145
EU (European Union), 1, 63, 79, 81, 140, 143, 153, 203, 209, 237, 261
EU 5th Anti-Money Laundering Directive, 60
EU accession, 75, 215, 234, 242
EU Enlargement, 211
EU Fourth Anti-Money Laundering Directive (MLD4), 215
EU Market Abuse Directive (MAD), 87
EU Market Abuse Regulation (MAR), 60, 87
EU Transparency Directive (2013/50/ EU), 39
European Commission, 1, 79, 231, 238, 258, 262
European Community, 238, *See* European Union
European Council, 88
European integration, 4, 10, 26, 81
European Monetary Union, 175, 178
European Parliament, 88
European Union. *See* EU
Eurosif, 144
Exchange Rate Mechanism II (ERM II), 210
exchange trade funds, 96
exit strategy, 137

families, 2, 12–13, 19–20, 24–25, 76, 80, 82, 85, 93, 96, 99, 102, 104, 106, 117, 128, 132, 146, 151, 162–163, 166, 168, 177, 187
family CEO, 201–202, 204
family-controlled firms and holdings, 168
family-controlled groups, 176
family firms, 132, 163, 188, 193, 196, 200, 202
heir–family controlled firms, 11
family ownership, 8, 25, 85, 100, 117, 153
Federal Act on Stock Exchanges and Securities Trading (Switzerland), 111
Federal Gazette (Germany), 89
Federal Ministry of Finance (Austria), 60

Federal Ministry of Finance (Germany),
    102
Federal Ministry of Justice and
    Consumer Protection (Germany),
    89
fiduciary duties, 137
Financial Conduct Authority (FCA)
    (UK), 38
financial development, 12, 14, 132, 234
financial firms, 39, 60, 62, 163, 166,
    196, 253, 257. *See also*
    institutional investors
Financial Instruments Trading Act
    (Sweden), 157
financial liberalization, 1, 13, 153, 170
Financial Market Infrastructure Act
    (FMIA) (Switzerland), 112
Financial Market Infrastructure
    Ordinance (FMIO) (Switzerland),
    111
Financial Reporting Council (FRC)
    (UK), 34
Financial Supervision Commission
    (Bulgaria), 214
Financial Supervisory Authority
    (Finansinspektionen) (Sweden),
    157
firms
    A2A, 185
    Agropolichim, 213
    Alitalia, 183
    Alumina, 213
    Amazon, 6
    Antibiotic, 213
    Arsenal, 213
    Asarel-Medet, 213
    ASPI (Autostrade per l'Italia), 184,
        190
    Astrazeneca AB, 163
    B.A.T. Industries Plc, 46
    Balkan Airlines, 213, 229
    Barilla, 185
    Beta, 213
    Billa, 216
    Brewery Laško, 263
    Brewinvest, 213
    British American Tobacco Plc, 46
    British Telecommunications Plc, 48
    BT Group Investments Limited, 46
    BT Group Plc, 46, 48

Cartiere Burgo, 185
Cimos, 263
Cirio, 181, 197
Coloroll, 34
DARS, 253
Dell International Holdings Limited,
    46
DEU Bulgaria, 228
DEU Korea, 228
Deutsche Post, 102
Deutsche Telecom, 102
Diageo Plc, 46
DZU, 213
Edison, 185
Edizione, 184
EFIM, 185
Electrolux, 169
Electricité de France, 185
ENEL, 185, 190
Enemona, 226
Eni, 179, 185
Enron, 6, 38, 181
Ericsson, 169
ESSO Italiana, 185
Facebook, 6
Falck, 185
Ferrovie dello Stato, 185
Ferruzzi, 185
Fincantieri, 183
Finmeccanica, 184
GFT, 185
GlaxoSmithKline Holdings Limited,
    48
GlaxoSmithKline Plc, 48
Google, 6
Grandmetropolitan Plc, 46
GSE, 185
H&M, 168
Hanson Plc, 46
Hanson Trust, 46
HeidelbergCement AG, 46
Helios, 263
Himko, 213
IKEA, 168
Impexstroy, 228
Ina, 179, 190
Investor AB, 162
IRI (Istituto per la Ricostruzione
    Industriale), 183, 185
Istrabenz, 245

Kaufland, 216
Kremikovtzi, 213, 229
Krka, 255–256
Kuwait Petroleum Italia, 185
Lek, 255
Leonardo, 184
Lidl, 216
Luxottica Group, 185
Marzotto, 185
Mercator, 261, 263
Merkur, 245, 263
Metro Cash and Carry, 216
Mondadori, 185
Neftochim, 213
OtK, 213
Parmalat, 181, 196
Petrol, 213, 256
Pirelli, 185
Pivovarna Laško, 245
Plama, 229
Polimeri, 229
Polly Peck International (PPI), 34
Port of Koper, 253
Poste Italiane, 185
Promet, 213
Prysmian, 185
RCS, 185
SARAS, 185
SCT, 245
SMI, 185
Solvay, 213
Sopharma, 226
STET telecommunications, 184
Stockholms Stadshus AB, 163
Telecom (Italy), 190
Telekom Slovenije, 255
Union Miniere Group, 213
Vattenfall AB, 163
Volkswagen, 102
Volvo Car AB, 163
WorldCom, 6, 181
Yambolen, 213
foreign investors, 19–20, 22, 39, 46, 50,
   72, 76, 82, 84, 93, 96–98, 100,
   104–105, 122, 153, 163, 170, 187,
   204, 213, 222, 224, 228, 232, 234,
   238–239, 241, 247, 254–255, 257,
   263
foreign ownership, 2, 25–26
France, 77, 79–80, 102, 128, 231

Franks, Julian, 19, 21, 56, 72, 76, 78,
   80, 83–84, 89–90, 100, 103, 132,
   145
FTSE 100 index, 34
FTSE 500, 35

G20/OECD Principles of Corporate
   Governance and OECD Guidelines
   on Corporate Governance of
   SOEs, 245
General Standard, Deutsche Börse,
   98
German Commercial Register, 88
German company network, 15,
   103–104
German competition law, 88
German Federal Financial Supervisory
   Agency, 88
German left-wing government, 103
German Stock Corporation Act (AktG),
   86, 88
German Transparency Register, 88
Germany, 2, 12, 14–15, 20, 24–27, 68,
   77–78, 80, 84–107, 128, 159
Gesellschaft mit beschränkter Haftung
   (GmbH), Austria, 57
Gilson, Ronald J., 6, 13, 26
global corporate governance
   revolution, 1, 4, 23, 25, 29, 75, 85,
   100, 171
global financial crisis, 6, 36, 50, 78,
   88–89, 100, 216, 236, 238, 252,
   256, 258, 263
global market, 9, 15, 97–98, 103,
   168
globalization, 4, 26, 81, 99–101, 105,
   122, 146, 152, 168, 170
Gordon, Jeffrey N., 1–3, 5–6, 9, 11,
   21, 23, 26, 79, 99, 140, 143, 168,
   231
Great Depression, 183
Greece, 258
Guidelines for Good Board Practice
   (Sweden), 155
Guidelines on Corporate Governance of
   State-Owned Enterprises, 248

Hansmann, 4–5, 19, 23, 28, 56, 76, 83
Hausbank system, 56, 79
Hebros Bank, 213

hedge funds, 97
Henry and Reinier Kraakman, 4–5, 19,
    23, 28, 56, 76, 83
Her Majesty's (HM) Treasury, 50
Herfindahl index, 128, 134
hierarchical governance structure, 27
holding companies, 20, 46, 75, 93, 96,
    102, 151, 159, 166, 187, 212,
    254–255, 257, 260, 263
hybrid ownership landscape, 20, 26,
    28, 107

identity of owners, 16, 55, 65, 68, 70,
    82, 93, 188
  employee ownership, 49
  hedge funds, 84
  individuals, 19, 36, 39, 49, 76, 85,
    128, 132, 162, 187
  industrial foundations, 153
  insurance companies, 20, 39, 49, 96,
    197
  mutual funds, 39, 162, 187
  non-financial firms, 20, 40, 46, 72,
    75, 93, 96, 99, 102, 105–106, 159,
    163, 166, 187
  pension funds, 39, 49, 137, 140–141
  private equity, 187
IFRS, 114
IMF, 1, 213
incumbents, *See* corporate insiders
index funds, 79
Index of Economic Freedom, 235
individual ownership company
    (Switzerland), 109
Industrivärden AB, 152, 167
Infocamere, 188
initial public offering (IPO), 48, 82, 89,
    190, 199, 226, 255
insider system, 101
insider trading, 60, 180
institutional change, 28, 99
institutional investors, 1–3, 6, 21–22,
    25, 36, 49, 88, 98, 104–105, 123,
    128, 136, 140–141, 143–144, 146,
    151–152, 155, 167, 169, 171, 176,
    191, 197, 201, 204, 236
institutional sclerosis, 12
interest groups, 12, 211, 220, 233
  and financial development, 7
  groups of special interests, 12

and political power, 13
Investor AB, 152
investors' protection, 6–7, 63, 77, 99,
    132, 180, 198, 203, 214, 224
Italy, 2, 22, 24, 80, 102, 175–205, 261

Japan, 14
Joint-Stock Companies Act (Austria),
    58, 62
joint-stock company (AD) (Bulgaria),
    210

Korea, 14
Kraakman, 4–5, 19, 23, 28, 56, 76, 83

La Porta, Rafael, 2, 7, 9, 17, 77, 152, 159
labour unions, 12, 99
largest shareholder, 16, 55, 65, 90, 128,
    132–134, 138, 159, 186, 200, 218,
    220, 222, 226, 251, 253, 255–256
largest shareholders, 20, 25, 28, 41, 43,
    51, 65, 93, 96, 108, 117, 133, 159,
    163, 167, 171, 249
law and finance, 1–2, 14, 26, 77, 98,
    224
Law on Commercial Registry
    (Bulgaria), 214
Law on Privatization and Post-
    Privatization Control (Bulgaria),
    213, 216
Law on Public Enterprises (Bulgaria), 234
Law on Public Offering of Securities
    (Bulgaria), 215
Law on Securities, Stock Exchanges and
    Investment Companies (Bulgaria),
    215
Law on the Corporate Governance of
    State Capital Investments
    (Slovenia), 247
Law on Transformation and
    Privatization of State and
    Municipal Owned Enterprises
    (Bulgaria), 211
Lehman Brothers, 105
liberal market economy, 80, 99
liberalization, 11–12, 152, 235, 237
liberalization of capital market. *See*
    financial liberalization
life cycle theory for family firms, 21,
    132, 145

limited liability company (OOD)
(Bulgaria), 210
limited liability company (Switzerland),
109
limited partnership (*Kommanditbolag,
KB*) (Sweden), 154
limited partnership
(*Kommanditgesellschaft*) with a
GmbH as general partner (GmbH
& Co. KG) (Germany), 86
listed companies, 19–21, 24–25, 38,
40–41, 43, 55, 57–59, 64, 68, 72,
81, 85, 88–90, 93, 96, 101–104,
108, 111, 113, 115–116,
122–123, 129, 134, 137–138,
146, 153, 156–157, 159, 171,
178, 185, 189–196, 200, 204,
217–218, 222, 224, 226, 235,
242, 256
Listing Rules (Switzerland), 114
Ljubljana Stock Exchange, 243,
245
Lloyds Banking Group, 50
London Share Price Database (LSPD),
40
London Stock Exchange, 34, 41, 48,
50, 177, 180
Lower Saxony, 102
LSPD, 16
Lundberg family, 167
Luxembourg, 79

managerial capitalism, 15
mandatory bid rule, 113, 116
market for corporate control, 1, 49, 56,
79, 81, 104–105, 132, 224
Market in Financial Instruments Act
(Slovenia), 243
Markets in Financial Instruments Act
(Bulgaria), 234
Mark J. Roe, 2, 8–9, 11, 21, 23, 98–99,
111, 143, 168, 230
Mayer, Colin, 1, 6, 14, 19, 56, 72, 76,
78, 83, 84, 90, 93, 151
Measures Against Money Laundering
Act (MAMLA) (Bulgaria), 215
Mediobanca, 182
Megginson, William and Jeffry Netter,
10, 80
Milan Stock Exchange, 179

Ministry of Economic Development and
Technology (Slovenia), 246
minority shareholders, 7, 63, 82, 93,
98, 102, 129, 157, 187, 236,
243–244
Morck, Randall, 11, 26, 132, 146, 169,
200, 228
MTA (Mercato Telematico Azionario),
177
Mueller, Dennis C., 10, 12, 212

Nasdaq, 180
Nasdaq Stockholm AB, 153. *See also*
Stockholm Stock Exchange
National Commission for Companies
and the Stock Exchange (Italy), 176
National Health Service (NHS), 51
national pension funds (AP1–4)
(Sweden), 152, 167
nationalization, 99
neoliberalism, 230
Netherlands, 78, 144
Neuer Markt, 89
NGM Main Regulated, 157
NKBM, 263
NLB, 263
non-domestic investors, 21, 108, 129,
140, 143, 145
non-domestic shareholders. *See* non-
domestic investors
non-listed companies, 111, 117, 242.
See also unlisted companies
non-Swiss shareholders. *See* non-
domestic investors
Northern Cyprus, 34
Nuovo Mercato, 180

OECD, 1, 77, 163, 238, 242–243
Olson, Mancur, 12, 14, 230, 232
Olsson family, 167
Orbis, 123
Ordinance against Excessive
Compensation (OaEC)
(Switzerland), 111
Österreichischer Kreditschutzverband
von 1870, 63
outsider system, 101
ownership disclosure, 38, 59, 87, 157
Ownership Transformation Act 1992
(Slovenia), 240

Partnership and Non-registered
  Partnership Act (Sweden), 154
partnership limited by shares
  (Germany), 86
passive investment strategy, 137
passive investors, 138, 146
path dependence, 2, 10, 20, 27, 99, 101,
  104, 170
personal capitalism, 14
Persson family, 167
Poland, 77, 247
political economy of corporate
  governance, 23
politics, 2, 26–27, 78, 83, 169–170
  Demos, 260
  French Socialist party, 13
  German left wing government, 15
  lobbying, 15, 103
  Minder Initiative, 111
  political class, 258
  political ideology, 230
  popular initiative (Switzerland), 110
  social democratic politics, 9, 169
  Swiss constitution, 110
  Swiss political system, 110
Portugal, 258
post-communist transition, 24,
  237–238
  driving forces, 230
Prime Standard, Deutsche Börse, 89, 98
Principles of Corporate Governance,
  214
private equity funds, 197
private limited company (Germany),
  86, 88
private limited company (UK), 33
privatization, 75, 80, 96, 102, 179, 187,
  203, 209, 226, 231, 233, 235, 239
  Capital Fund for Pension and Disability
    Insurance (KAD), 238, 240
  in developed, developing and
    transition countries, 10
  insiders privatization, 240
  management and employee buyout
    (MEBO), 212, 241
  partially privatized public utilities, 185
  post-communist, 1, 22, 209,
    211–214, 216, 220, 222, 228,
    231, 235–238, 240, 252–254,
    259, 262

privatization funds, 212, 218, 222,
  235
  Restitution Fund (SOD), 238, 240
  in the United Kingdom, 49, 51
  voucher privatization, 212, 222, 231,
    240
public companies, 6, 220
Public Enterprise and Control Agency
  (Bulgaria), 216
public limited company (Germany),
  86–87
public limited company (Switzerland),
  109
public limited company (UK), 33
Public Takeover Act (Austria), 61
pyramidal structures, 12, 21, 72, 75,
  81–82, 99, 117, 151–153, 176,
  179, 187–188, 190, 193, 198
pyramid-holding companies, 159, 167.
  See also closed-end investment
  funds

RAI, 183
remuneration, 62
rent-seeking, 101, 232
Review of Corporate Governance in
  Slovenia, 237, 242–243, 247
Ringe, Wolf-Georg, 1, 5, 9, 15, 23, 26,
  97, 104–105
risk aversion, 78
Roe, Mark J., 2, 8–9, 11, 21, 23, 98–99,
  111, 143, 168, 230
roving bandit, 232
Royal Bank of Scotland, 50
Russia, 228, 231

Sarbanes–Oxley Act, 38
say-on-pay, 114
Scandinavian model, 151
SE Regulation (Austria), 58
Securities Acquisition and Takeover Act
  (Germany), 87
Securities and Stock Exchange
  Commission (Bulgaria), 212
Securities Trading Act (Germany),
  87
Security and Stock Exchange
  Commission (Bulgaria), 217
Selin, Erik, 167
Serious Fraud Office (SFO), 34

shareholder capitalism, 5, 29, 78,
80–81, 169
Shareholder Rights Directive II (SRD
II), 88
shareholders agreement, 59, 188, 191,
193, 198
shareholders meeting, 170
shareholders protection, *See* investors
protection
shareholders protection index, 98
Shareholders' Rights Directive (EU)
2017/828, 62
single capital market, 1, 10, 75, 100,
105–106
SIX Swiss Exchange, 114, 123
Slovenia, 2, 24, 26–27, 237–263
Slovenian Directors Association,
245–246
Slovenian Privatization Law 1992, 240
Slovenian Sovereign Holding (SSH),
243, 247
social ownership, 238, 259
Socialist Federal Republic of
Yugoslavia, 238
Societas Europaea (SE), 57, 86
Societas Europaea Act (Austria), 58
SOFIX, 216, 229
Spain, 80, 258
Standard & Poor's Capital IQ, 16, 40
state, 2, 19, 22, 24, 29, 70, 72, 76,
79–80, 82, 96, 101, 220, 224, 226
public sector in the United Kingdom,
39, 50
state ownership, 187, 232
state ownership under communism,
209
state-controlled firms, 24, 166, 185,
196
state-controlled funds (KAD and
SOD) (Slovenia), 241–242, 244,
247, 260–261. *See also*
privatization
state-owned companies, 10, 163,
253, 257
state-owned enterprises (SOEs), 236,
242–243, 247
State Assets Management Strategy
(Slovenia), 247
state capture, 234
State Street Global Advisors, 138

stewardship, 88
Stinnes–Legien-Pact, 99
Stock Corporation Act ('Aktiengesetz',
'AktG') (Germany), 87
Stock Exchange Act (Austria), 58, 60,
62
Stock Exchange and the Financial
Market Authority (Austria), 59
Stockholm, 163
Stockholm Stock Exchange, 152–153,
155, 162
Strategy of the Republic of Slovenia for
the Accession to the European
Union: Economic and Social Part,
237
subscription rights, 113
subsidiaries, 46, 51, 68, 185, 204
wholly owned subsidiaries, 24, 41,
43, 48, 163
supervisory board, 61, 87, 99, 241,
248, 261
Sweden, 1, 14, 24–27, 151–171
Swedish Academy of Directors, 155
Swedish Annual Accounts Act, 156
Swedish Companies Act, 156
Swedish Companies Registration
Office, 157
Swedish Corporate Governance Board,
155
Swedish Financial Reporting Board,
156
Swedish Industry and Commerce Stock
Exchange Committee, 155
Swedish model, 27, 152–153, 156
Swedish Securities Council, 155
Swedish Shareholders Association, 155
SWIPRA Services, 124
Swiss Code of Obligations (CO), 111,
146
Swiss Federal Statistical Office, 109
Swiss GAAP, 114
Swiss investors, 129, 133
Swiss Leader Index, 136
Swiss Market Index. *See* Swiss
Performance Index Large
Swiss parliament, 111
Swiss Performance Index Large, 123
Swiss Performance Index M, 123
Swiss shareholders. *See* Swiss investors
Switzerland, 2, 24–25, 27, 68, 147

takeover, 100, 256
Takeover Act (Austria), 58, 77
tax reform, 26, 49–50, 78, 97, 99, 103,
    170
TB Express, 213
territorial insiders, 6. *See also* corporate
    insiders
theory of the firm, 26
Thomson Reuters Datastream, 123
trading partnership (*Handelsbolag,*
    HB) (Sweden), 154
tunnelling, 231
Turkey, 78

UBS, 138
UK (United Kingdom), 2, 12, 14, 21,
    24, 26, 33, 78, 80, 89, 100, 102,
    105, 128–129, 138, 140, 143–144,
    153, 231
UK Listing Authority (UKLA), 38
UK Stewardship Code, 36
ultimate ownership, 55, 60, 70, 72, 76,
    157, 166, 193, 217, 224
United Bulgarian Bank, 213
United Kingdom, *See* UK
United States, *See* USA
unlisted companies, 19, 38, 55, 58, 81,
    85, 104, 158, 171, 176, 186–189
US Fortune 500, 35
US government, 1, 153
USA, 6, 12, 14, 21, 26, 36, 78, 89, 100,
    128–129, 138, 140, 143–144, 153,
    180–181, 214
US-GAAP, 114

Vanguard, 138
varieties of capitalism, 7, 11, 80
Vienna Stock Exchange, 58, 77
voting rights, 39, 59, 87, 108, 112, 141,
    157, 203, 217
    'against votes', 144
    dual-class shares, 152, 158–159, 169
    golden shares, 158
    loyalty shares, 197, 199
    multiple voting shares, 98, 197
    non-voting shares, 199
    one-share one-vote, 49, 199
    superior voting shares, 132
    super-voting rights, 12

Walker Review, 36
Wallenberg family, 152, 162, 167–168
Washington Consensus policy, 10, 209,
    211, 235
widely held companies, 2, 8, 11, 13–14,
    20, 41, 48, 76, 78, 80–81, 85,
    98–99, 106, 129, 132, 196, 226
widely held corporations, 55, *See also*
    widely held companies
Wirtschafts-Trend
    Zeitschriftenverlagsgesellschaft m.
    b.H, 16, 63
Wolf-Georg Ringe, 1, 5, 9, 15, 23, 26,
    97, 104–105
World Bank, 1, 77, 213
World War II, 99, 179

Zingales, Luigi, 13, 21, 145, 175, 199,
    235

Printed in the United States
by Baker & Taylor Publisher Services